Founding Fathers Four Pack

Founding Fathers Four Pack

By

Various Artists

Enhanced Media
2017

The Autobiography of Benjamin Franklin by Benjamin Franklin. First published in 1793.

Autobiography of Thomas Jefferson by Thomas Jefferson. First published in 1821.

Alexander Hamilton by Charles A. Conant. First published in 1901.
John Jay by Elbert Hubbard. First published in *Little Journeys to the Homes of American Statesmen* by Elbert Hubbard, in 1916.

Founding Fathers Four Pack. Published by Enhanced Media Publishing, 2017.

Cover and interior design © 2017 Enhanced Media Publishing.

Enhanced Media Publishing
Los Angeles, CA.

First Printing: 2017.

ISBN-13: 978-1974536658.

ISBN-10: 1974536653.

Contents

The Autobiography of Benjamin Franklin by Benjamin Franklin 7

Autobiography of Thomas Jefferson by Thomas Jefferson . 123

Alexander Hamilton by Charles A. Conant 136

John Jay by Elbert Hubbard 182

The Autobiography of Benjamin Franklin by Benjamin Franklin

I: Ancestry and Early Youth in Boston

Twyford, at the Bishop of St. Asaph's, 1771.

DEAR SON: I have ever had pleasure in obtaining any little anecdotes of my ancestors. You may remember the inquiries I made among the remains of my relations when you were with me in England, and the journey I undertook for that purpose. Imagining it may be equally agreeable to you to know the circumstances of my life, many of which you are yet unacquainted with, and expecting the enjoyment of a week's uninterrupted leisure in my present country retirement, I sit down to write them for you. To which I have besides some other inducements. Having emerged from the poverty and obscurity in which I was born and bred, to a state of affluence and some degree of reputation in the world, and having gone so far through life with a considerable share of felicity, the conducing means I made use of, which with the blessing of God so well succeeded, my posterity may like to know, as they may find some of them suitable to their own situations, and therefore fit to be imitated.

That felicity, when I reflected on it, has induced me sometimes to say, that were it offered to my choice, I should have no objection to a repetition of the same life from its beginning, only asking the advantages authors have in a second edition to correct some faults of the first. So I might, besides correcting the faults, change some sinister accidents and events of it for others more favourable. But though this were denied, I should still accept the offer. Since such a repetition is not to be expected, the next thing most like living one's life over again seems to be a recollection of that life, and to make that recollection as durable as possible by putting it down in writing.

Hereby, too, I shall indulge the inclination so natural in old men, to be talking of themselves and their own past actions; and I shall indulge it without being tiresome to others, who, through respect to age, might conceive themselves obliged to give me a hearing, since this may be read or not as anyone pleases. And, lastly (I may as well confess it, since my denial of it will be believed by nobody), perhaps I shall a good deal gratify my own vanity. Indeed, I scarce ever heard or saw the introductory words, "Without vanity I may say," etc., but some vain thing immediately followed. Most people dislike vanity in others, whatever share they have of it themselves; but I give it fair quarter wherever I meet with it, being persuaded that it is often productive of good to the possessor, and to others that are within his sphere of action; and therefore, in many cases, it would not be altogether absurd if a man were to thank God for his vanity among the other comforts of life.

Gibbon and Hume, the great British historians, who were contemporaries of Franklin, express in their autobiographies the same feeling about the propriety of just self-praise.

And now I speak of thanking God, I desire with all humility to acknowledge that I owe the mentioned happiness of my past life to His kind providence, which lead me to the means I used and gave them success. My belief of this induces me to hope, though I must not presume, that the same goodness will still be exercised toward me, in continuing that happiness, or enabling me to bear a fatal reverse, which I may experience as others have done; the complexion of my future fortune being known to Him only in whose power it is to bless to us even our afflictions.

The notes one of my uncles (who had the same kind of curiosity in collecting family anecdotes) once put into my hands, furnished me with several particulars relating to our ancestors. From these notes I learned that the family had lived in the same village, Ecton, in Northamptonshire, for three hundred years, and how much longer he knew not (perhaps from the time when the name of Franklin, that before was the name of an order of people, was assumed by them as a surname when others took surnames all over the kingdom), on a freehold of about thirty acres, aided by the smith's business, which had continued in the family till his time, the eldest son being always bred to that business; a custom which he and my father followed as to their eldest sons. When I searched the registers at Ecton, I found an account of their births, marriages and burials from the year 1555 only, there being no registers kept in that parish at any time preceding. By that register I perceived that I was the youngest son of the youngest son for five generations back. My grandfather Thomas, who was born in 1598, lived at Ecton till he grew too old to follow business longer, when he went to live with his son John, a dyer at Banbury, in Oxfordshire, with whom my father served an apprenticeship. There my grandfather died and lies buried. We saw his gravestone in 1758. His eldest son Thomas lived in the house at Ecton, and left it with the land to his only child, a daughter, who, with her husband, one Fisher, of Wellingborough, sold it to Mr. Isted, now lord of the manor there. My grandfather had four sons that grew up, viz.: Thomas, John, Benjamin and Josiah. I will give you what account I can of them at this distance from my papers, and if these are not lost in my absence, you will among them find many more particulars.

Thomas was bred a smith under his father; but, being ingenious, and encouraged in learning (as all my brothers were) by an Esquire Palmer, then the principal gentleman in that parish, he qualified himself for the business of scrivener; became a considerable man in the county; was a chief mover of all public-spirited undertakings for the county or town of Northampton, and his own village, of which many instances were related of him; and much taken notice of and patronized by the then Lord Halifax. He died in 1702, January 6, old style, just four years to a day before I was born. The account we received of his life and character from some old people at Ecton, I remember, struck you as something extraordinary, from its similarity to what you knew of mine. "Had he died on the same day," you said, "one might have supposed a transmigration."

John was bred a dyer, I believe of woolens, Benjamin was bred a silk dyer, serving an apprenticeship at London. He was an ingenious man. I remember him well, for when I was a boy he came over to my father in Boston, and lived in the house with us some years. He lived to a great age. His grandson, Samuel Franklin, now lives in Boston. He left behind him two quarto volumes, MS., of his own poetry, consisting of little occasional pieces addressed to his friends and relations, of which the following, sent to me, is a specimen. He had formed a short-hand of his own, which he taught me, but, never practicing it, I have now forgot it. I was named after this uncle, there being a particular affection between him and my father. He was very pious, a great attender of sermons of the best preachers, which he took down in his short-hand, and had with him many volumes of them. He was also much of a politician; too much, perhaps, for his station. There fell lately into my hands, in London, a collection he had made of all the principal pamphlets relating to public affairs, from 1641 to 1717; many of the volumes are wanting as appears by the numbering, but there still remain eight volumes in folio, and twenty-four in quarto and in octavo. A dealer in old books met with them, and knowing me by my sometimes buying of him, he brought them to me. It seems my uncle must have left them here when he went to America, which was about fifty years since. There are many of his notes in the margins.

This obscure family of ours was early in the Reformation, and continued Protestants through the reign of Queen Mary, when they were sometimes in danger of trouble on account of their zeal against popery. They had got an English Bible, and to conceal and secure it, it was fastened open with tapes under and within the cover of a joint-stool. When my great-great-grandfather read it to his family, he turned up the joint-stool upon his knees, turning over the leaves then under the tapes. One of the children stood at the door to give notice if he saw the apparitor coming, who was an officer of the spiritual court. In that case the stool was turned down again upon its feet, when the Bible remained concealed under it as before. This anecdote I had from my uncle Benjamin. The family continued all of the Church of England till about the end of Charles the Second's reign, when some of the ministers that had been outed for nonconformity, holding conventicles in Northamptonshire, Benjamin and Josiah adhered to them, and so continued all their lives: the rest of the family remained with the Episcopal Church.

Josiah, my father, married young, and carried his wife with three children into New England, about 1682. The conventicles having been forbidden by law, and frequently disturbed, induced some considerable men of his acquaintance to remove to that country, and he was prevailed with to accompany them thither, where they expected to enjoy their mode of religion with freedom. By the same wife he had four children more born there, and by a second wife ten more, in all seventeen; of which I remember thirteen sitting at one time at his table, who all grew up to be men and women, and married; I was the youngest son, and the youngest child but two, and was born in Boston, New England. My mother, the second wife, was Abiah Folger, daughter of Peter Folger, one of the first settlers of New England, of whom honorable mention is made by Cotton Mather, in his church history of that country, entitled Magnalia Christi Americana, as "a godly, learned Englishman," if I remember the words rightly. I have heard that he wrote sundry small occasional pieces, but only one of them was printed, which I saw now many years since. It was written in 1675, in the home-spun verse of that time and people, and addressed to those then concerned in the government there. It was in favor of liberty of conscience, and in behalf of the Baptists, Quakers, and other sectaries that had been under persecution, ascribing the Indian wars, and other distresses that had befallen the country, to that persecution, as so many judgments of God to punish so heinous an offense, and exhorting a repeal of those uncharitable laws. The whole appeared to me as written with a good deal of decent plainness and manly freedom. The six concluding lines I remember, though I have forgotten the two first of the stanza; but the purport of them was, that his censures proceeded from good-will, and, therefore, he would be known to be the author.

"Because to be a libeler (says he)
I hate it with my heart;
From Sherburne town, where now I dwell
My name I do put here;
Without offense your real friend,
It is Peter Folgier."

My elder brothers were all put apprentices to different trades. I was put to the grammar-school at eight years of age, my father intending to devote me, as the tithe of his sons, to the service of the Church. My early readiness in learning to read (which must have been very early, as I do not remember when I could not read), and the opinion of all his friends, that I should certainly make a good scholar, encouraged him in this purpose of his. My uncle Benjamin, too, approved of it, and proposed to give me all his short-hand volumes of sermons, I suppose as a stock to set up with, if I would learn his character. I continued, however, at the grammar-school not quite one year, though in that time I had risen gradually from the middle of the class of that year to be the head of it, and farther was removed into the next class above it, in order to go with that into the third at the end of the year. But my father, in the meantime, from a view of the expense of a college education, which having so large a family he could not well afford, and the mean living many so educated were afterwards able to obtain—reasons that he gave to his friends in my hearing—altered his first intention, took me from the grammar-school, and sent me to a school for writing and arithmetic, kept by a then famous man, Mr. George Brownell, very successful in his profession generally, and that by mild, encouraging methods. Under him I acquired fair writing pretty soon, but I failed in the arithmetic, and made no progress in it. At ten years old I was taken home to assist my father in his business, which was that of a tallow-chandler and soap-boiler; a business he was not bred to, but had assumed on his arrival in New England, and on finding his dyeing trade would not maintain his family, being in little request. Accordingly, I was employed in cutting wick for the candles, filling the dipping mold and the mounds for cast candles, attending the shop, going of errands, etc.

I disliked the trade, and had a strong inclination for the sea, but my father declared against it; however, living near the water, I was much in and about it, learnt early to swim well, and to manage boats; and when in a boat or canoe with other boys, I was commonly allowed to govern, especially in any case of difficulty; and upon other occasions I was generally a leader among the boys, and sometimes led them into scrapes, of which I will mention one instance, as it shows an early projecting public spirit, tho' not then justly conducted.

There was a salt-marsh that bounded part of the mill-pond, on the edge of which, at high water, we used to stand to fish for minnows. By much trampling, we had made it a mere quagmire. My proposal was to build a wharf there fit for us to stand upon, and I showed my comrades a large heap of stones, which were intended for a new house near the marsh, and which would very well suit our purpose. Accordingly, in the evening, when the workmen were gone, I assembled a number of my playfellows, and working with them diligently like so many emmets, sometimes two or three to a stone, we brought them all away and built our little wharf. The next morning the workmen were surprised at missing the stones, which were found in our wharf. Inquiry was made after the removers; we were discovered and complained of; several of us were corrected by our fathers; and, though I pleaded the usefulness of the work, mine convinced me that nothing was useful which was not honest.

I think you may like to know something of his person and character. He had an excellent constitution of body, was of middle stature, but well set, and very strong; he was ingenious, could draw prettily, was skilled a little in music, and had a clear, pleasing voice, so that when he played psalm tunes on his violin and sung withal, as he sometimes did in an evening after the business of the day was over, it was extremely agreeable to hear. He had a mechanical genius too, and, on occasion, was very handy in the use of other tradesmen's tools; but his great excellence lay in a sound understanding and solid judgment in prudential matters, both in private and public affairs. In the latter, indeed, he was never employed, the numerous family he had to educate and the straitness of his circumstances keeping him close to his trade; but I remember well his being frequently visited by leading people, who consulted him for his opinion in affairs of the town or of the church he belonged to, and showed a good deal of respect for his judgment and advice: he was also much consulted by private persons about their affairs when any difficulty occurred, and frequently chosen an arbitrator between contending parties. At his table he liked to have, as often as he could, some sensible friend or neighbor to converse with, and always took care to start some ingenious or useful topic for discourse, which might tend to improve the minds of his children. By this means he turned our attention to what was good, just, and prudent in the conduct of life; and little or no notice was ever taken of what related to the victuals on the table, whether it was well or ill dressed, in or out of season, of good or bad flavor, preferable or inferior to this or that other thing of the kind, so that I was brought up in such a perfect inattention to those matters as to be quite indifferent what kind of food was set before me, and so unobservant of it, that to this day if I am asked I can scarce tell a few hours after dinner what I dined upon. This has been a convenience to me in traveling, where my companions have been sometimes very unhappy for want of a suitable gratification of their more delicate, because better instructed, tastes and appetites.

My mother had likewise an excellent constitution: she suckled all her ten children. I never knew either my father or mother to have any sickness but that of which they died, he at 89, and she at 85 years of age. They lie buried together at Boston, where I some years since placed a marble over their grave, with this inscription:

> Josiah Franklin and Abiah his wife lie here interred.
> They lived lovingly together in wedlock fifty-five years.
> Without an estate, or any gainful employment,
> By constant labor and industry,
> with God's blessing,
> They maintained a large family comfortably,
> and brought up thirteen children and seven grandchildren reputably.
> From this instance, reader,
> Be encouraged to diligence in thy calling,
> And distrust not Providence.
> He was a pious and prudent man;
> She, a discreet and virtuous woman.
> Their youngest son,
> In filial regard to their memory,
> Places this stone.
> J. F. born 1655, died 1744, Ætat 89.
> A. F. born 1667, died 1752, —— 85.

By my rambling digressions I perceive myself to be grown old. I used to write more methodically. But one does not dress for private company as for a public ball. 'Tis perhaps only negligence.

To return: I continued thus employed in my father's business for two years, that is, till I was twelve years old; and my brother John, who was bred to that business, having left my father, married, and set up for himself at Rhode Island, there was all appearance that I was destined to supply his place, and become a tallow-chandler. But my dislike to the trade continuing, my father was under apprehensions that if he did not find one for me more agreeable, I should break away and get to sea, as his son Josiah had done, to his great vexation. He therefore sometimes took me to walk with him, and see joiners, bricklayers, turners, braziers, etc., at their work, that he might observe my inclination, and endeavor to fix it on some trade or other on land. It has ever since been a pleasure to me to see good workmen handle their tools; and it has been useful to me, having learnt so much by it as to be able to do little jobs myself in my house when a workman could not readily be got, and to construct little machines for my experiments, while the intention of making the experiment was fresh and warm in my mind. My father at last fixed upon the cutler's trade, and my uncle Benjamin's son Samuel, who was bred to that business in London, being about that time established in Boston, I was sent to be with him some time on liking. But his expectations of a fee with me displeasing my father, I was taken home again.

II: Beginning Life as a Printer

FROM a child I was fond of reading, and all the little money that came into my hands was ever laid out in books. Pleased with the Pilgrim's Progress, my first collection was of John Bunyan's works in separate little volumes. I afterward sold them to enable me to buy R. Burton's Historical Collections; they were small chapmen's books, and cheap, 40 or 50 in all. My father's little library consisted chiefly of books in polemic divinity, most of which I read, and have since often regretted that, at a time when I had such a thirst for knowledge, more proper books had not fallen in my way, since it was now resolved I should not be a clergyman. Plutarch's Lives there was in which I read abundantly, and I still think that time spent to great advantage. There was also a book of Defoe's, called an Essay on Projects, and another of Dr. Mather's, called Essays to do Good, which perhaps gave me a turn of thinking that had an influence on some of the principal future events of my life.

This bookish inclination at length determined my father to make me a printer, though he had already one son (James) of that profession. In 1717 my brother James returned from England with a press and letters to set up his business in Boston. I liked it much better than that of my father, but still had a hankering for the sea. To prevent the apprehended effect of such an inclination, my father was impatient to have me bound to my brother. I stood out some time, but at last was persuaded, and signed the indentures when I was yet but twelve years old. I was to serve as an apprentice till I was twenty-one years of age, only

I was to be allowed journeyman's wages during the last year. In a little time I made great proficiency in the business, and became a useful hand to my brother. I now had access to better books. An acquaintance with the apprentices of booksellers enabled me sometimes to borrow a small one, which I was careful to return soon and clean. Often I sat up in my room reading the greatest part of the night, when the book was borrowed in the evening and to be returned early in the morning, lest it should be missed or wanted.

And after some time an ingenious tradesman, Mr. Matthew Adams, who had a pretty collection of books, and who frequented our printing-house, took notice of me, invited me to his library, and very kindly lent me such books as I chose to read. I now took a fancy to poetry, and made some little pieces; my brother, thinking it might turn to account, encouraged me, and put me on composing occasional ballads. One was called The Lighthouse Tragedy, and contained an account of the drowning of Captain Worthilake, with his two daughters: the other was a sailor's song, on the taking of Teach (or Blackbeard) the pirate. They were wretched stuff, in the Grub-street-ballad style; and when they were printed he sent me about the town to sell them. The first sold wonderfully, the event being recent, having made a great noise. This flattered my vanity; but my father discouraged me by ridiculing my performances, and telling me verse-makers were generally beggars. So I escaped being a poet, most probably a very bad one; but as prose writing has been of great use to me in the course of my life, and was a principal means of my advancement, I shall tell you how, in such a situation, I acquired what little ability I have in that way.

There was another bookish lad in the town, John Collins by name, with whom I was intimately acquainted. We sometimes disputed, and very fond we were of argument, and very desirous of confuting one another, which disputatious turn, by the way, is apt to become a very bad habit, making people often extremely disagreeable in company by the contradiction that is necessary to bring it into practice; and thence, besides souring and spoiling the conversation, is productive of disgusts and, perhaps enmities where you may have occasion for friendship. I had caught it by reading my father's books of dispute about religion. Persons of good sense, I have since observed, seldom fall into it, except lawyers, university men, and men of all sorts that have been bred at Edinburgh.

A question was once, somehow or other, started between Collins and me, of the propriety of educating the female sex in learning, and their abilities for study. He was of opinion that it was improper, and that they were naturally unequal to it. I took the contrary side, perhaps a little for dispute's sake. He was naturally more eloquent, had a ready plenty of words, and sometimes, as I thought, bore me down more by his fluency than by the strength of his reasons. As we parted without settling the point, and were not to see one another again for some time, I sat down to put my arguments in writing, which I copied fair and sent to him. He answered, and I replied. Three or four letters of a side had passed, when my father happened to find my papers and read them. Without entering into the discussion, he took occasion to talk to me about the manner of my writing; observed that, though I had the advantage of my antagonist in correct spelling and pointing (which I owed to the printing-house), I fell far short in elegance of expression, in method and in perspicuity, of which he convinced me by several instances. I saw the justice of his remarks, and thence grew more attentive to the manner in writing, and determined to endeavor at improvement.

About this time I met with an odd volume of the Spectator. It was the third. I had never before seen any of them. I bought it, read it over and over, and was much delighted with it. I thought the writing excellent, and wished, if possible, to imitate it. With this view I took some of the papers, and, making short hints of the sentiment in each sentence, laid them by a few days, and then, without looking at the book, tried to complete the papers again, by expressing each hinted sentiment at length, and as fully as it had been expressed before, in any suitable words that should come to hand. Then I compared my Spectator with the original, discovered some of my faults, and corrected them. But I found I wanted a stock of words, or a readiness in recollecting and using them, which I thought I should have acquired before that time if I had gone on making verses; since the continual occasion for words of the same import, but of different length, to suit the measure, or of different sound for the rhyme, would have laid me under a constant necessity of searching for variety, and also have tended to fix that variety in my mind, and make me master of it. Therefore I took some of the tales and turned them into verse; and, after a time, when I had pretty well forgotten the prose, turned them back again. I also sometimes jumbled my collections of hints into confusion, and after some weeks endeavored to reduce them into the best order, before I began to form the full sentences and complete the paper. This was to teach me method in the arrangement of thoughts. By comparing my work afterwards with the original, I discovered many faults and amended them; but I sometimes had the pleasure of fancying that, in certain particulars of small import, I had been lucky enough to improve the method of the language, and this encouraged me to think I might possibly in time come to be a tolerable English writer, of which I was extremely ambitious. My time for these exercises and for reading was at night, after work or before it began in the morning, or on Sundays, when I contrived to be in the printing-house alone, evading as much as I could the common attendance on public worship which my father used to exact of me when I was under his care, and which indeed I still thought a duty, thought I could not, as it seemed to me, afford time to practice it.

When about 16 years of age I happened to meet with a book, written by one Tryon, recommending a vegetable diet. I determined to go into it. My brother, being yet unmarried, did not keep house, but boarded himself and his apprentices in another family. My refusing to eat flesh occasioned an inconveniency, and I was frequently chided for my singularity. I made myself acquainted with Tryon's manner of preparing some of his dishes, such as boiling potatoes or rice, making hasty pudding, and a few others, and then proposed to my brother, that if he would give me, weekly, half the money he paid for my board, I would board myself. He instantly agreed to it, and I presently found that I could save half what he paid me. This was an additional fund for buying books. But I had another advantage in it. My brother and the rest going from the printing-house to their meals, I remained there alone, and, dispatching presently my light repast, which often was no more than a biscuit or a slice of bread, a handful of raisins or a tart from the pastry-cook's, and a glass of water, had the rest of the time till their return for study, in which I made the greater progress, from that greater clearness of head and quicker apprehension which usually attend temperance in eating and drinking.

And now it was that, being on some occasion made ashamed of my ignorance in figures, which I had twice failed in learning when at school, I took Cocker's book of Arithmetic, and went through the whole by myself with great ease. I also read Seller's and Shermy's books of Navigation, and became acquainted with the little geometry they contain; but never proceeded far in that science. And I read about this time Locke's On Human Understanding, and The Art of Thinking, by Messrs. du Port Royal.

While I was intent on improving my language, I met with an English grammar (I think it was Greenwood's), at the end of which there were two little sketches of the arts of rhetoric and logic, the latter finishing with a specimen of a dispute in the Socratic method; and soon after I procured Xenophon's Memorable Things of Socrates, wherein there are many instances of the same method. I was charmed with it, adopted it, dropt my abrupt contradiction and positive argumentation, and put on the humble inquirer and doubter. And being then, from reading Shaftesbury and Collins, become a real doubter in many points of our religious doctrine, I found this method safest for myself and very embarrassing to those against whom I used it; therefore I took a delight in it, practiced it continually, and grew very artful and expert in drawing people, even of superior knowledge, into concessions, the consequences of which they did not foresee, entangling them in difficulties out of which they could not extricate themselves, and so obtaining victories that neither myself nor my cause always deserved. I continued this method some few years, but gradually left it, retaining only the habit of expressing myself in terms of modest diffidence; never using, when I advanced anything that may possibly be disputed, the words certainly, undoubtedly, or any others that give the air of positiveness to an opinion; but rather say, I conceive or apprehend a thing to be so and so; it appears to me, or I should think it so or so, for such and such reasons; or I imagine it to be so; or it is so, if I am not mistaken. This habit, I believe, has been of great advantage to me when I have had occasion to inculcate my opinions, and persuade men into measures that I have been from time to time engaged in promoting; and, as the chief ends of conversation are to inform or to be informed, to please or to persuade, I wish well-meaning, sensible men would not lessen their power of doing good by a positive, assuming manner, that seldom fails to disgust, tends to create opposition, and to defeat every one of those purposes for which speech was given to us, to wit, giving or receiving information or pleasure. For, if you would inform, a positive and dogmatical manner in advancing your sentiments may provoke contradiction and prevent a candid attention. If you wish information and improvement from the knowledge of others, and yet at the same time express yourself as firmly fixed in your present opinions, modest, sensible men, who do not love disputation, will probably leave you undisturbed in the possession of your error. And by such a manner, you can seldom hope to recommend yourself in pleasing your hearers, or to persuade those whose concurrence you desire. Pope says, judiciously:

"Men should be taught as if you taught them not,
And things unknown proposed as things forgot;"

farther recommending to us

"To speak, tho' sure, with seeming diffidence."

And he might have coupled with this line that which he has coupled with another, I think, less properly,

"For want of modesty is want of sense."

If you ask, Why less properly? I must repeat the lines,

"Immodest words admit of no defense,
For want of modesty is want of sense."

Now, is not want of sense (where a man is so unfortunate as to want it) some apology for his want of modesty? and would not the lines stand more justly thus?

"Immodest words admit but this defense,
That want of modesty is want of sense."

This, however, I should submit to better judgments.

My brother had, in 1720 or 1721, begun to print a newspaper. It was the second that appeared in America, and was called the New England Courant. The only one before it was the Boston News-Letter. I remember his being dissuaded by some of his friends from the undertaking, as not likely to succeed, one newspaper being, in their judgment, enough for America. At this time (1771) there are not less than five-and-twenty. He went on, however, with the undertaking, and after having worked in composing the types and printing off the sheets, I was employed to carry the papers thro' the streets to the customers.

He had some ingenious men among his friends, who amused themselves by writing little pieces for this paper, which gained it credit and made it more in demand, and these gentlemen often visited us. Hearing their conversations, and their accounts of the approbation their papers were received with, I was excited to try my hand among them; but, being still a boy, and suspecting that my brother would object to printing anything of mine in his paper if he knew it to be mine, I contrived to disguise my hand, and, writing an anonymous paper, I put it in at night under the door of the printing-house. It was found in the morning, and communicated to his writing friends when they called in as usual. They read it, commented on it in my hearing, and I had the exquisite pleasure of finding it met with their approbation, and that, in their different guesses at the author, none were named but men of some character among us for learning and ingenuity. I suppose now that I was rather lucky in my judges, and that perhaps they were not really so very good ones as I then esteemed them.

Encouraged, however, by this, I wrote and conveyed in the same way to the press several more papers which were equally approved; and I kept my secret till my small fund of sense for such performances was pretty well exhausted, and then I discovered it, when I began to be considered a little more by my brother's acquaintance, and in a manner that did not quite please him, as he thought, probably with reason, that it tended to make me too vain. And, perhaps, this might be one occasion of the differences that we began to have about this time. Though a brother, he considered himself as my master, and me as his apprentice, and, accordingly, expected the same services from me as he would from another, while I thought he demeaned me too much in some he required of me, who from a brother expected more indulgence. Our disputes were often brought before our father, and I fancy I was either generally in the right, or else a better pleader, because the judgment was generally in my favor. But my brother was passionate, and had often beaten me, which I took extremely amiss; and, thinking my apprenticeship very tedious, I was continually wishing for some opportunity of shortening it, which at length offered in a manner unexpected.

One of the pieces in our newspaper on some political point, which I have now forgotten, gave offense to the Assembly. He was taken up, censured, and imprisoned for a month, by the speaker's warrant, I suppose, because he would not discover his author. I too was taken up and examined before the council; but, tho' I did not give them any satisfaction, they contented themselves with admonishing me, and dismissed me, considering me, perhaps, as an apprentice, who was bound to keep his master's secrets.

During my brother's confinement, which I resented a good deal, notwithstanding our private differences, I had the management of the paper; and I made bold to give our rulers some rubs in it, which my brother took very kindly, while others began to consider me in an unfavorable light, as a young genius that had a turn for libeling and satyr. My brother's discharge was accompanied with an order of the House (a very odd one), that "James Franklin should no longer print the paper called the New England Courant."

There was a consultation held in our printing-house among his friends, what he should do in this case. Some proposed to evade the order by changing the name of the paper; but my brother, seeing inconveniences in that, it was finally concluded on as a better way, to let it be printed for the future under the name of Benjamin Franklin; and to avoid the censure of the Assembly, that might fall on him as still printing it by his apprentice, the contrivance was that my old indenture should be returned to me, with a full discharge on the back of it, to be shown on occasion, but to secure to him the benefit of my service, I was to sign new indentures for the remainder of the term, which were to be kept private. A very flimsy scheme it was; however, it was immediately executed, and the paper went on accordingly, under my name for several months.

At length, a fresh difference arising between my brother and me, I took upon me to assert my freedom, presuming that he would not venture to produce the new indentures. It was not fair in me to take this advantage, and this I therefore reckon one of the first errata of my life; but the unfairness of it weighed little with me, when under the impressions of resentment for the blows his passion too often urged him to bestow upon me, though he was otherwise not an ill-natured man: perhaps I was too saucy and provoking.

When he found I would leave him, he took care to prevent my getting employment in any other printing-house of the town, by going round and speaking to every master, who accordingly refused to give me work. I then thought of going to New York, as the nearest place where there was a printer; and I was rather inclined to leave Boston when I reflected that I had already made myself a little obnoxious to the governing party, and, from the arbitrary proceedings of the Assembly in my brother's case, it was likely I might, if I stayed, soon bring myself into scrapes; and farther, that my indiscreet disputations about religion began to make me pointed at with horror by good people as an infidel or atheist. I determined on the point, but my father now siding with my brother, I was sensible that, if I attempted to go openly, means would be used to prevent me. My friend Collins, therefore, undertook to manage a little for me. He agreed with the captain of a New York sloop for my passage, under the notion of my being a young acquaintance of his. So I sold some of my books to raise a little money, was taken on board privately, and as we had a fair wind, in three days I found myself in New York, near 300 miles from home, a boy of but 17, without the least recommendation to, or knowledge of, any person in the place, and with very little money in my pocket.

III: Arrival in Philadelphia

MY inclinations for the sea were by this time worn out, or I might now have gratified them. But, having a trade, and supposing myself a pretty good workman, I offered my service to the printer in the place, old Mr. William Bradford, who had been the first printer in Pennsylvania, but removed from thence upon the quarrel of George Keith. He could give me no employment, having little to do, and help enough already; but says he, "My son at Philadelphia has lately lost his principal hand, Aquilla Rose, by death; if you go thither, I believe he may employ you." Philadelphia was a hundred miles further; I set out, however, in a boat for Amboy, leaving my chest and things to follow me round by sea.

In crossing the bay, we met with a squall that tore our rotten sails to pieces, prevented our getting into the Kill, and drove us upon Long Island. In our way, a drunken Dutchman, who was a passenger too, fell overboard; when he was sinking, I reached through the water to his shock pate, and drew him up, so that we got him in again. His ducking sobered him a little, and he went to sleep, taking first out of his pocket a book, which he desired I would dry for him. It proved to be my old favorite author, Bunyan's Pilgrim's Progress, in Dutch, finely printed on good paper, with copper cuts, a dress better than I had ever seen it wear in its own language. I have since found that it has been translated into most of the languages of Europe, and suppose it has been more generally read than any other book, except perhaps the Bible. Honest John was the first that I know of who mixed narration and dialogue; a method of writing very engaging to the reader, who in the most interesting parts finds himself, as it were, brought into the company and present at the discourse. Defoe in his Crusoe, his Moll Flanders, Religious Courtship, Family Instructor, and other pieces, has imitated it with success; and Richardson has done the same in his Pamela, etc.

When we drew near the island, we found it was at a place where there could be no landing, there being a great surf on the stony beach. So we dropped anchor, and swung round towards the shore. Some people came down to the water edge and hallowed to us, as we did to them; but the wind was so high, and the surf so loud, that we could not hear so as to understand each other. There were canoes on the shore, and we made signs, and hallowed that they should fetch us; but they either did not understand us, or thought it impracticable, so they went away, and night coming on, we had no remedy but to wait till the wind should abate; and, in the meantime, the boatman and I concluded to sleep, if we could; and so crowded into the scuttle, with the Dutchman, who was still wet, and the spray beating over the head of our boat, leaked thro' to us, so that we were soon almost as wet as he. In this manner we lay all night, with very little rest; but, the wind abating the next day, we made a shift to reach Amboy before night, having been thirty hours on the water, without victuals, or any drink but a bottle of filthy rum, and the water we sailed on being salt.

In the evening I found myself very feverish, and went in to bed; but, having read somewhere that cold water drank plentifully was good for a fever, I followed the prescription, sweat plentifully most of the night, my fever left me, and in the morning, crossing the ferry, I proceeded on my journey on foot, having fifty miles to Burlington, where I was told I should find boats that would carry me the rest of the way to Philadelphia.

It rained very hard all the day; I was thoroughly soaked, and by noon a good deal tired; so I stopped at a poor inn, where I staid all night, beginning now to wish that I had never left home. I cut so miserable a figure, too, that I found, by the questions asked me, I was suspected to be some runaway servant, and in danger of being taken up on that suspicion. However, I proceeded the next day, and got in the evening to an inn, within eight or ten miles of Burlington, kept by one Dr. Brown. He entered into conversation with me while I took some refreshment, and, finding I had read a little, became very sociable and friendly. Our acquaintance continued as long as he lived. He had been, I imagine, an itinerant doctor, for there was no town in England, or country in Europe, of which he could not give a very particular account. He had some letters, and was ingenious, but much of an unbeliever, and wickedly undertook, some years after, to travesty the Bible in doggerel verse, as Cotton had done Virgil. By this means he set many of the facts in a very ridiculous light, and might have hurt weak minds if his work had been published; but it never was.

At his house I lay that night, and the next morning reached Burlington, but had the mortification to find that the regular boats were gone a little before my coming, and no other expected to go before Tuesday, this being Saturday; wherefore I returned to an old woman in the town, of whom I had bought gingerbread to eat on the water, and asked her advice. She invited me to lodge at her house till a passage by water should offer; and being tired with my foot traveling, I accepted the invitation. She understanding I was a printer, would have had me stay at that town and follow my business, being ignorant of the stock necessary to begin with. She was very hospitable, gave me a dinner of ox-cheek with great good will, accepting only of a pot of ale in return; and I thought myself fixed till Tuesday should come. However, walking in the evening by the side of the river, a boat came by, which I found was going towards Philadelphia, with several people in her. They took me in, and, as there was no wind, we rowed all the way; and about midnight, not having yet seen the city, some of the company were confident we must have passed it, and would row no farther; the others knew not where we were; so we put toward the shore, got into a creek, landed near an old fence, with the rails of which we made a fire, the night being cold, in October, and there we remained till daylight. Then one of the company knew the place to be Cooper's Creek, a little above Philadelphia, which we saw as soon as we got out of the creek, and arrived there about eight or nine o'clock on the Sunday morning, and landed at the Market-street wharf.

I have been the more particular in this description of my journey, and shall be so of my first entry into that city, that you may in your mind compare such unlikely beginnings with the figure I have since made there. I was in my working dress, my best clothes being to come round by sea. I was dirty from my journey; my pockets were stuffed out with shirts and stockings, and I knew no soul nor where to look for lodging. I was fatigued with traveling, rowing, and want of rest, I was very hungry; and my whole stock of cash consisted of a Dutch dollar, and about a shilling in copper. The latter I gave the people of the boat for my passage, who at first refused it, on account of my rowing; but I insisted on their taking it. A man being sometimes more generous when he has but a little money than when he has plenty, perhaps thro' fear of being thought to have but little.

Then I walked up the street, gazing about till near the market-house I met a boy with bread. I had made many a meal on bread, and, inquiring where he got it, I went immediately to the baker's he directed me to, in Second-street, and asked for biscuit, intending such as we had in Boston; but they, it seems, were not made in Philadelphia. Then I asked for a three-penny loaf, and was told they had none such. So not considering or knowing the difference of money, and the greater cheapness nor the names of his bread, I bade him give me three-penny worth of any sort. He gave me, accordingly, three great puffy rolls. I was surprised at the quantity, but took it, and, having no room in my pockets, walked off with a roll under each arm, and eating the other. Thus I went up Market-street as far as Fourth-street, passing by the door of Mr. Read, my future wife's father; when she, standing at the door, saw me, and thought I made, as I certainly did, a most awkward, ridiculous appearance. Then I turned and went down Chestnut-street and part of Walnut-street, eating my roll all the way, and, coming round, found myself again at Market-street wharf, near the boat I came in, to which I went for a draught of the river water; and, being filled with one of my rolls, gave the other two to a woman and her child that came down the river in the boat with us, and were waiting to go farther.

She, standing at the door, saw me, and thought I made, as I certainly did, a most awkward, ridiculous appearance. Thus refreshed, I walked again up the street, which by this time had many clean-dressed people in it, who were all walking the same way. I joined them, and thereby was led into the great meeting-house of the Quakers near the market. I sat down among them, and, after looking round awhile and hearing nothing said, being very drowsy thro' labour and want of rest the preceding night, I fell fast asleep, and continued so till the meeting broke up, when one was kind enough to rouse me. This was, therefore, the first house I was in, or slept in, in Philadelphia.

Walking down again toward the river, and, looking in the faces of people, I met a young Quaker man, whose countenance I liked, and, accosting him, requested he would tell me where a stranger could get lodging. We were then near the sign of the Three Mariners. "Here," says he, "is one place that entertains strangers, but it is not a reputable house; if thee wilt walk with me, I'll show thee a better." He brought me to the Crooked Billet in Water-street. Here I got a dinner; and, while I was eating it, several sly questions were asked me, as it seemed to be suspected from my youth and appearance, that I might be some runaway.

After dinner, my sleepiness returned, and being shown to a bed, I lay down without undressing, and slept till six in the evening, was called to supper, went to bed again very early, and slept soundly till next morning. Then I made myself as tidy as I could, and went to Andrew Bradford the printer's. I found in the shop the old man his father, whom I had seen at New York, and who, traveling on horseback, had got to Philadelphia before me. He introduced me to his son, who received me civilly, gave me a breakfast, but told me he did not at present want a hand, being lately supplied with one; but there was another printer in town, lately set up, one Keimer, who, perhaps, might employ me; if not, I should be welcome to lodge at his house, and he would give me a little work to do now and then till fuller business should offer.

The old gentleman said he would go with me to the new printer; and when we found him, "Neighbour," says Bradford, "I have brought to see you a young man of your business; perhaps you may want such a one." He asked me a few questions, put a composing stick in my hand to see how I worked, and then said he would employ me soon, though he had just then nothing for me to do; and, taking old Bradford, whom he had never seen before, to be one of the town's people that had a good will for him, entered into a conversation on his present undertaking and prospects; while Bradford, not discovering that he was the other printer's father, on Keimer's saying he expected soon to get the greatest part of the business into his own hands, drew him on by artful questions, and starting little doubts, to explain all his views, what interest he relied on, and in what manner he intended to proceed. I, who stood by and heard all, saw immediately that one of them was a crafty old sophister, and the other a mere novice. Bradford left me with Keimer, who was greatly surprised when I told him who the old man was.

Keimer's printing-house, I found, consisted of an old shattered press, and one small, worn-out font of English, which he was then using himself, composing an Elegy on Aquilla Rose, before mentioned, an ingenious young man, of excellent character, much respected in the town, clerk of the Assembly, and a pretty poet. Keimer made verses too, but very indifferently. He could not be said to write them, for his manner was to compose them in the types directly out of his head. So there being no copy, but one pair of cases, and the Elegy likely to require all the letter, no one could help him. I endeavored to put his press (which he had not yet used, and of which he understood nothing) into order fit to be worked with; and, promising to come and print off his Elegy as soon as he should have got it ready, I returned to Bradford's, who gave me a little job to do for the present, and there I lodged and dieted. A few days after, Keimer sent for me to print off the Elegy. And now he had got another pair of cases, and a pamphlet to reprint, on which he set me to work.

These two printers I found poorly qualified for their business. Bradford had not been bred to it, and was very illiterate; and Keimer, tho' something of a scholar, was a mere compositor, knowing nothing of presswork. He had been one of the French prophets, and could act their enthusiastic agitations. At this time he did not profess any particular religion, but something of all on occasion; was very ignorant of the world, and had, as I afterward found, a good deal of the knave in his composition. He did not like my lodging at Bradford's while I worked with him. He had a house, indeed, but without furniture, so he could not lodge me; but he got me a lodging at Mr. Read's before mentioned, who was the owner of his house; and, my chest and clothes being come by this time, I made rather a more respectable appearance in the eyes of Miss Read than I had done when she first happened to see me eating my roll in the street.

I began now to have some acquaintance among the young people of the town, that were lovers of reading, with whom I spent my evenings very pleasantly; and gaining money by my industry and frugality, I lived very agreeably, forgetting Boston as much as I could, and not desiring that any there should know where I resided, except my friend Collins, who was in my secret, and kept it when I wrote to him. At length, an incident happened that sent me back again much sooner than I had intended. I had a brother-in-law, Robert Holmes, master of a sloop that traded between Boston and Delaware. He being at Newcastle, forty miles below Philadelphia, heard there of me, and wrote me a letter mentioning the concern of my friends in Boston at my abrupt departure, assuring me of their good will to me, and that everything would be accommodated to my mind if I would return, to which he exhorted me very earnestly. I wrote an answer to his letter, thanked him for his advice, but stated my reasons for quitting Boston fully and in such a light as to convince him I was not so wrong as he had apprehended.

IV: First Visit to Boston

SIR WILLIAM KEITH, governor of the province, was then at Newcastle, and Captain Holmes, happening to be in company with him when my letter came to hand, spoke to him of me, and showed him the letter. The governor read it, and seemed surprised when he was told my age. He said I appeared a young man of promising parts, and therefore should be encouraged; the printers at Philadelphia were wretched ones; and, if I would set up there, he made no doubt I should succeed; for his part, he would procure me the public business, and do me every other service in his power. This my brother-in-law afterwards told me in Boston, but I knew as yet nothing of it; when, one day, Keimer and I being at work together near the window, we saw the governor and another gentleman (which proved to be Colonel French, of Newcastle), finely dressed, come directly across the street to our house, and heard them at the door.

Keimer ran down immediately, thinking it a visit to him; but the governor inquired for me, came up, and with a condescension and politeness I had been quite unused to, made me many compliments, desired to be acquainted with me, blamed me kindly for not having made myself known to him when I first came to the place, and would have me away with him to the tavern, where he was going with Colonel French to taste, as he said, some excellent Madeira. I was not a little surprised, and Keimer stared like a pig poisoned. I went, however, with the governor and Colonel French to a tavern, at the corner of Third-street, and over the Madeira he proposed my setting up my business, laid before me the probabilities of success, and both he and Colonel French assured me I should have their interest and influence in procuring the public business of both governments. On my doubting whether my father would assist me in it, Sir William said he would give me a letter to him, in which he would state the advantages, and he did not doubt of prevailing with him. So it was concluded I should return to Boston in the first vessel, with the governor's letter recommending me to my father. In the meantime the intention was to be kept a secret, and I went on working with Keimer as usual, the governor sending for me now and then to dine with him, a very great honor I thought it, and conversing with me in the most affable, familiar, and friendly manner imaginable.

About the end of April, 1724, a little vessel offered for Boston. I took leave of Keimer as going to see my friends. The governor gave me an ample letter, saying many flattering things of me to my father, and strongly recommending the project of my setting up at Philadelphia as a thing that must make my fortune. We struck on a shoal in going down the bay, and sprung a leak; we had a blustering time at sea, and were obliged to pump almost continually, at which I took my turn. We arrived safe, however, at Boston in about a fortnight. I had been absent seven months, and my friends had heard nothing of me; for my br. Holmes was not yet returned, and had not written about me. My unexpected appearance surprised the family; all were, however, very glad to see me, and made me welcome, except my brother. I went to see him at his printing-house. I was better dressed than ever while in his service, having a genteel new suit from head to foot, a watch, and my pockets lined with near five pounds sterling in silver. He received me not very frankly, looked me all over, and turned to his work again.

The journeymen were inquisitive where I had been, what sort of a country it was, and how I liked it. I praised it much, and the happy life I led in it, expressing strongly my intention of returning to it; and, one of them asking what kind of money we had there, I produced a handful of silver, and spread it before them, which was a kind of rare-show they had not been used to, paper being the money of Boston. Then I took an opportunity of letting them see my watch; and, lastly (my brother still glum and sullen), I gave them a piece of eight to drink, and took my leave. This visit of mine offended him extremely; for, when my mother sometime after spoke to him of a reconciliation, and of her wishes to see us on good terms together, and that we might live for the future as brothers, he said I had insulted him in such a manner before his people that he could never forget or forgive it. In this, however, he was mistaken.

My father received the governor's letter with some apparent surprise, but said little of it to me for some days, when Capt. Holmes returning he showed it to him, asked him if he knew Keith, and what kind of man he was; adding his opinion that he must be of small discretion to think of setting a boy up in business who wanted yet three years of being at man's estate. Holmes said what he could in favor of the project, but my father was clear in the impropriety of it, and at last, gave a flat denial to it. Then he wrote a civil letter to Sir William, thanking him for the patronage he had so kindly offered me, but declining to assist me as yet in setting up, I being, in his opinion, too young to be trusted with the management of a business so important, and for which the preparation must be so expensive.

My friend and companion Collins, who was a clerk in the post-office, pleased with the account I gave him of my new country, determined to go thither also; and, while I waited for my father's determination, he set out before me by land to Rhode Island, leaving his books, which were a pretty collection of mathematics and natural philosophy, to come with mine and me to New York, where he proposed to wait for me.

My father, tho' he did not approve Sir William's proposition, was yet pleased that I had been able to obtain so advantageous a character from a person of such note where I had resided, and that I had been so industrious and careful as to equip myself so handsomely in so short a time; therefore, seeing no prospect of an accommodation between my brother and me, he gave his consent to my returning again to Philadelphia, advised me to behave respectfully to the people there, endeavor to obtain the general esteem, and avoid lampooning and libeling, to which he thought I had too much inclination; telling me, that by steady industry and a prudent parsimony I might save enough by the time I was one-and-twenty to set me up; and that, if I came near the matter, he would help me out with the rest. This was all I could obtain, except some small gifts as tokens of his and my mother's love, when I embarked again for New York, now with their approbation and their blessing.

The sloop putting in at Newport, Rhode Island, I visited my brother John, who had been married and settled there some years. He received me very affectionately, for he always loved me. A friend of his, one Vernon, having some money due to him in Pennsylvania, about thirty-five pounds currency, desired I would receive it for him, and keep it till I had his directions what to remit it in. Accordingly, he gave me an order. This afterwards occasion's me a good deal of uneasiness.

At Newport we took in a number of passengers for New York, among which were two young women, companions, and a grave, sensible, matron like Quaker woman, with her attendants. I had shown an obliging readiness to do her some little services, which impressed her I suppose with a degree of good will toward me; therefore, when she saw a daily growing familiarity between me and the two young women, which they appeared to encourage, she took me aside, and said, "Young man, I am concerned for thee, as thou hast no friend with thee, and seems not to know much of the world, or of the snares youth is exposed to; depend upon it, those are very bad women; I can see it in all their actions; and if thee art not upon thy guard, they will draw thee into some danger; they are strangers to thee, and I advise thee, in a friendly concern for thy welfare, to have no acquaintance with them." As I seemed at first not to think so ill of them as she did, she mentioned some things she had observed and heard that had escaped my notice, but now convinced me she was right. I thanked her for her kind advice, and promised to follow it. When we arrived at New York, they told me where they lived, and invited me to come and see them; but I avoided it, and it was well I did; for the next day the captain missed a silver spoon and some other things, that had been taken out of his cabin, and, knowing that these were a couple of strumpets, he got a warrant to search their lodgings, found the stolen goods, and had the thieves punished. So, tho' we had escaped a sunken rock, which we scraped upon in the passage, I thought this escape of rather more importance to me.

At New York I found my friend Collins, who had arrived there some time before me. We had been intimate from children, and had read the same books together; but he had the advantage of more time for reading and studying, and a wonderful genius for mathematical learning, in which he far outstripped me. While I lived in Boston, most of my hours of leisure for conversation were spent with him, and he continued a sober as well as an industrious lad; was much respected for his learning by several of the clergy and other gentlemen, and seemed to promise making a good figure in life. But, during my absence, he had acquired a habit of sotting with brandy; and I found by his own account, and what I heard from others, that he had been drunk every day since his arrival at New York, and behaved very oddly. He had gamed, too, and lost his money, so that I was obliged to discharge his lodgings, and defray his expenses to and at Philadelphia, which proved extremely inconvenient to me.

The then governor of New York, Burnet (son of Bishop Burnet), hearing from the captain that a young man, one of his passengers, had a great many books, desired he would bring me to see him. I waited upon him accordingly, and should have taken Collins with me but that he was not sober. The gov'r. treated me with great civility, showed me his library, which was a very large one, and we had a good deal of conversation about books and authors. This was the second governor who had done me the honor to take notice of me; which, to a poor boy like me, was very pleasing.

We proceeded to Philadelphia. I received on the way Vernon's money, without which we could hardly have finished our journey. Collins wished to be employed in some counting-house; but, whether they discovered his dramming by his breath, or by his behavior, tho' he had some recommendations, he met with no success in any application, and continued lodging and boarding at the same house with me, and at my expense. Knowing I had that money of Vernon's, he was continually borrowing of me, still promising repayment as soon as he should be in business. At length he had got so much of it that I was distressed to think what I should do in case of being called on to remit it.

His drinking continued, about which we sometimes quarreled; for, when a little intoxicated, he was very fractious. Once, in a boat on the Delaware with some other young men, he refused to row in his turn. "I will be rowed home," says he. "We will not row you," says I. "You must, or stay all night on the water," says he, "just as you please." The others said, "Let us row; what signifies it?" But, my mind being soured with his other conduct, I continued to refuse. So he swore he would make me row, or throw me overboard; and coming along, stepping on the thwarts, toward me, when he came up and struck at me, I clapped my hand under his crutch, and, rising, pitched him head-foremost into the river. I knew he was a good swimmer, and so was under little concern about him; but before he could get round to lay hold of the boat, we had with a few strokes pulled her out of his reach; and ever when he drew near the boat, we asked if he would row, striking a few strokes to slide her away from him. He was ready to die with vexation, and obstinately would not promise to row. However, seeing him at last beginning to tire, we lifted him in and brought him home dripping wet in the evening. We hardly exchanged a civil word afterwards, and a West India captain, who had a commission to procure a tutor for the sons of a gentleman at Barbados, happening to meet with him, agreed to carry him thither. He left me then, promising to remit me the first money he should receive in order to discharge the debt; but I never heard of him after.

The breaking into this money of Vernon's was one of the first great errata of my life; and this affair showed that my father was not much out in his judgment when he supposed me too young to manage business of importance. But Sir William, on reading his letter, said he was too prudent. There was great difference in persons; and discretion did not always accompany years, nor was youth always without it. "And since he will not set you up," says he, "I will do it myself. Give me an inventory of the things necessary to be had from England, and I will send for them. You shall repay me when you are able; I am resolved to have a good printer here, and I am sure you must succeed." This was spoken with such an appearance of cordiality, that I had not the least doubt of his meaning what he said. I had hitherto kept the proposition of my setting up, a secret in Philadelphia, and I still kept it. Had it been known that I depended on the governor, probably some friend, that knew him better, would have advised me not to rely on him, as I afterwards heard it as his known character to be liberal of promises which he never meant to keep. Yet, unsolicited as he was by me, how could I think his generous offers insincere? I believed him one of the best men in the world.

I presented him an inventory of a little print-house, amounting by my computation to about one hundred pounds sterling. He liked it, but asked me if my being on the spot in England to chuse the types, and see that everything was good of the kind, might not be of some advantage. "Then," says he, "when there, you may make acquaintances, and establish correspondences in the bookselling and stationery way." I agreed that this might be advantageous. "Then," says he, "get yourself ready to go with Annis;" which was the annual ship, and the only one at that time usually passing between London and Philadelphia. But it would be some months before Annis sailed, so I continued working with Keimer, fretting about the money Collins had got from me, and in daily apprehensions of being called upon by Vernon, which, however, did not happen for some years after.

I believe I have omitted mentioning that, in my first voyage from Boston, being becalmed off Block Island, our people set about catching cod, and hauled up a great many. Hitherto I had stuck to my resolution of not eating animal food, and on this occasion I considered, with my master Tryon, the taking every fish as a kind of unprovoked murder, since none of them had, or ever could do us any injury that might justify the slaughter. All this seemed very reasonable. But I had formerly been a great lover of fish, and, when this came hot out of the frying-pan, it smelt admirably well. I balanced sometime between principle and inclination, till I recollected that, when the fish were opened, I saw smaller fish taken out of their stomachs; then thought I, "If you eat one another, I don't see why we mayn't eat you." So I dined upon cod very heartily, and continued to eat with other people, returning only now and then occasionally to a vegetable diet. So convenient a thing is it to be a reasonable creature, since it enables one to find or make a reason for everything one has a mind to do.

V: Early Friends in Philadelphia

KEIMER and I lived on a pretty good familiar footing, and agreed tolerably well, for he suspected nothing of my setting up. He retained a great deal of his old enthusiasms and loved argumentation. We therefore had many disputations. I used to work him so with my Socratic method, and had trepanned him so often by questions apparently so distant from any point we had in hand, and yet by degrees led to the point, and brought him into difficulties and contradictions, that at last he grew ridiculously cautious, and would hardly answer me the most common question, without asking first, "What do you intend to infer from that?" However, it gave him so high an opinion of my abilities in the confuting way, that he seriously proposed my being his colleague in a project he had of setting up a new sect. He was to preach the doctrines, and I was to confound all opponents. When he came to explain with me upon the doctrines, I found several conundrums which I objected to, unless I might have my way a little too, and introduce some of mine.

Keimer wore his beard at full length, because somewhere in the Mosaic law it is said, "Thou shalt not mar the corners of thy beard." He likewise kept the Seventh day, Sabbath; and these two points were essentials with him. I disliked both; but agreed to admit them upon condition of his adopting the doctrine of using no animal food. "I doubt," said he, "my constitution will not bear that." I assured him it would, and that he would be the better for it. He was usually a great glutton, and I promised myself some diversion in half starving him. He agreed to try the practice, if I would keep him company. I did so, and we held it for three months. We had our victuals dressed, and brought to us regularly by a woman in the neighborhood, who had from me a list of forty dishes, to be prepared for us at different times, in all which there was neither fish, flesh, nor fowl, and the whim suited me the better at this time from the cheapness of it, not costing us above eighteen pence sterling each per week. I have since kept several Lents most strictly, leaving the common diet for that, and that for the common, abruptly, without the least inconvenience, so that I think there is little in the advice of making those changes by easy gradations. I went on pleasantly, but poor Keimer suffered grievously, tired of the project, longed for the flesh-pots of Egypt, and ordered a roast pig. He invited me and two women friends to dine with him; but, it being brought too soon upon table, he could not resist the temptation, and ate the whole before we came.

    I had made some courtship during this time to Miss Read. I had a great respect and affection for her, and had some reason to believe she had the same for me; but, as I was about to take a long voyage, and we were both very young, only a little above eighteen, it was thought most prudent by her mother to prevent our going too far at present, as a marriage, if it was to take place, would be more convenient after my return, when I should be, as I expected, set up in my business. Perhaps, too, she thought my expectations not so well founded as I imagined them to be.

    My chief acquaintances at this time were Charles Osborne, Joseph Watson, and James Ralph, all lovers of reading. The two first were clerks to an eminent scrivener or conveyancer in the town, Charles Brockden; the other was clerk to a merchant. Watson was a pious, sensible young man, of great integrity; the others rather more lax in their principles of religion, particularly Ralph, who, as well as Collins, had been unsettled by me, for which they both made me suffer. Osborne was sensible, candid, frank; sincere and affectionate to his friends; but, in literary matters, too fond of criticizing. Ralph was ingenious, genteel in his manners, and extremely eloquent; I think I never knew a prettier talker. Both of them were great admirers of poetry, and began to try their hands in little pieces. Many pleasant walks we four had together on Sundays into the woods, near Schuylkill, where we read to one another, and conferred on what we read.

    Ralph was inclined to pursue the study of poetry, not doubting but he might become eminent in it, and make his fortune by it, alleging that the best poets must, when they first began to write, make as many faults as he did. Osborne dissuaded him, assured him he had no genius for poetry, and advised him to think of nothing beyond the business he was bred to; that, in the mercantile way, tho' he had no stock, he might, by his diligence and punctuality, recommend himself to employment as a factor, and in time acquire wherewith to trade on his own account. I approved the amusing one's self with poetry now and then, so far as to improve one's language, but no farther.

On this it was proposed that we should each of us, at our next meeting, produce a piece of our own composing, in order to improve by our mutual observations, criticisms, and corrections. As language and expression were what we had in view, we excluded all considerations of invention by agreeing that the task should be a version of the eighteenth Psalm, which describes the descent of a Deity. When the time of our meeting drew nigh, Ralph called on me first, and let me know his piece was ready. I told him I had been busy, and, having little inclination, had done nothing. He then showed me his piece for my opinion, and I much approved it, as it appeared to me to have great merit. "Now," says he, "Osborne never will allow the least merit in anything of mine, but makes 1000 criticisms out of mere envy. He is not so jealous of you; I wish, therefore, you would take this piece, and produce it as yours; I will pretend not to have had time, and so produce nothing. We shall then see what he will say to it." It was agreed, and I immediately transcribed it, that it might appear in my own hand.

We met; Watson's performance was read; there were some beauties in it, but many defects. Osborne's was read; it was much better; Ralph did it justice; remarked some faults, but applauded the beauties. He himself had nothing to produce. I was backward; seemed desirous of being excused; had not had sufficient time to correct, etc.; but no excuse could be admitted; produce I must. It was read and repeated; Watson and Osborne gave up the contest, and joined in applauding it. Ralph only made some criticisms, and proposed some amendments; but I defended my text. Osborne was against Ralph, and told him he was no better a critic than poet, so he dropped the argument. As they two went home together, Osborne expressed himself still more strongly in favor of what he thought my production; having restrained himself before, as he said, lest I should think it flattery. "But who would have imagined," said he, "that Franklin had been capable of such a performance; such painting, such force, such fire! He has even improved the original. In his common conversation he seems to have no choice of words; he hesitates and blunders; and yet, good God! how he writes!" When we next met, Ralph discovered the trick we had plaid him, and Osborne was a little laughed at.

This transaction fixed Ralph in his resolution of becoming a poet. I did all I could to dissuade him from it, but he continued scribbling verses till Pope cured him. He became, however, a pretty good prose writer. More of him hereafter. But, as I may not have occasion again to mention the other two, I shall just remark here, that Watson died in my arms a few years after, much lamented, being the best of our set. Osborne went to the West Indies, where he became an eminent lawyer and made money, but died young. He and I had made a serious agreement, that the one who happened first to die should, if possible, make a friendly visit to the other, and acquaint him how he found things in that separate state. But he never fulfilled his promise.

VI: First Visit to London

THE governor, seeming to like my company, had me frequently to his house, and his setting me up was always mentioned as a fixed thing. I was to take with me letters recommendatory to a number of his friends, besides the letter of credit to furnish me with the necessary money for purchasing the press and types, paper, etc. For these letters I was appointed to call at different times, when they were to be ready; but a future time was still named. Thus he went on till the ship, whose departure too had been several times postponed, was on the point of sailing. Then, when I called to take my leave and receive the letters, his secretary, Dr. Bard, came out to me and said the governor was extremely busy in writing, but would be down at Newcastle, before the ship, and there the letters would be delivered to me.

Ralph, though married, and having one child, had determined to accompany me in this voyage. It was thought he intended to establish a correspondence, and obtain goods to sell on commission; but I found afterwards, that, thro' some discontent with his wife's relations, he purposed to leave her on their hands, and never return again. Having taken leave of my friends, and interchanged some promises with Miss Read, I left Philadelphia in the ship, which anchor's at Newcastle. The governor was there; but when I went to his lodging, the secretary came to me from him with the civillest message in the world, that he could not then see me, being engaged in business of the utmost importance, but should send the letters to me on board, wished me heartily a good voyage and a speedy return, etc. I returned on board a little puzzled, but still not doubting.

Mr. Andrew Hamilton, a famous lawyer of Philadelphia, had taken passage in the same ship for himself and son, and with Mr. Denham, a Quaker merchant, and Messrs. Onion and Russel, masters of an iron work in Maryland, had engaged the great cabin; so that Ralph and I were forced to take up with a berth in the steerage, and none on board knowing us, were considered as ordinary persons. But Mr. Hamilton and his son (it was James, since governor) returned from Newcastle to Philadelphia, the father being recalled by a great fee to plead for a seized ship; and, just before we sailed, Colonel French coming on board, and showing me great respect, I was more taken notice of, and, with my friend Ralph, invited by the other gentlemen to come into the cabin, there being now room. Accordingly, we removed thither.

Understanding that Colonel French had brought on board the governor's dispatches, I asked the captain for those letters that were to be under my care. He said all were put into the bag together and he could not then come at them; but, before we landed in England, I should have an opportunity of picking them out; so I was satisfied for the present, and we proceeded on our voyage. We had a sociable company in the cabin, and lived uncommonly well, having the addition of all Mr. Hamilton's stores, who had laid in plentifully. In this passage Mr.

Denham contracted a friendship for me that continued during his life. The voyage was otherwise not a pleasant one, as we had a great deal of bad weather.

When we came into the Channel, the captain kept his word with me, and gave me an opportunity of examining the bag for the governor's letters. I found none upon which my name was put as under my care. I picked out six or seven, that, by the handwriting, I thought might be the promised letters, especially as one of them was directed to Basket, the king's printer, and another to some stationer. We arrived in London the 24th of December, 1724. I waited upon the stationer, who came first in my way, delivering the letter as from Governor Keith. "I don't know such a person," says he; but, opening the letter, "O! this is from Riddlesden. I have lately found him to be a complete rascal, and I will have nothing to do with him, nor receive any letters from him." So, putting the letter into my hand, he turned on his heel and left me to serve some customer. I was surprised to find these were not the governor's letters; and, after recollecting and comparing circumstances, I began to doubt his sincerity. I found my friend Denham, and opened the whole affair to him. He let me into Keith's character; told me there was not the least probability that he had written any letters for me; that no one, who knew him, had the smallest dependence on him; and he laughed at the notion of the governor's giving me a letter of credit, having, as he said, no credit to give. On my expressing some concern about what I should do, he advised me to endeavor getting some employment in the way of my business. "Among the printers here," said he, "you will improve yourself, and when you return to America, you will set up to greater advantage."

We both of us happened to know, as well as the stationer, that Riddlesden, the attorney, was a very knave. He had half-ruined Miss Read's father by persuading him to be bound for him. By this letter it appeared there was a secret scheme on foot to the prejudice of Hamilton (supposed to be then coming over with us); and that Keith was concerned in it with Riddlesden. Denham, who was a friend of Hamilton's, thought he ought to be acquainted with it; so, when he arrived in England, which was soon after, partly from resentment and ill-will to Keith and Riddlesden, and partly from good-will to him, I waited on him, and gave him the letter. He thanked me cordially, the information being of importance to him; and from that time he became my friend, greatly to my advantage afterwards on many occasions.

But what shall we think of a governor's playing such pitiful tricks, and imposing so grossly on a poor ignorant boy! It was a habit he had acquired. He wished to please everybody; and, having little to give, he gave expectations. He was otherwise an ingenious, sensible man, a pretty good writer, and a good governor for the people, tho' not for his constituents, the proprietaries, whose instructions he sometimes disregarded. Several of our best laws were of his planning and passed during his administration.

Ralph and I were inseparable companions. We took lodgings together in Little Britain at three shillings and sixpence a week—as much as we could then afford. He found some relations, but they were poor, and unable to assist him. He now let me know his intentions of remaining in London, and that he never meant to return to Philadelphia. He had brought no money with him, the whole he could muster having been expended in paying his passage. I had fifteen pistoles; so he borrowed occasionally of me to subsist, while he was looking out for business. He first endeavored to get into the play-house, believing himself qualified for an actor; but Wilkes, to whom he applied, advised him candidly not to think of that employment, as it was impossible he should succeed in it. Then he proposed to Roberts, a publisher in Paternoster Row, to write for him a weekly paper like the Spectator, on certain conditions, which Roberts did not approve. Then he endeavored to get employment as a hackney writer, to copy for the stationers and lawyers about the Temple, but could find no vacancy.

I immediately got into work at Palmer's, then a famous printing-house in Bartholomew Close, and here I continued near a year. I was pretty diligent, but spent with Ralph a good deal of my earnings in going to plays and other places of amusement. We had together consumed all my pistoles, and now just rubbed on from hand to mouth. He seemed quite to forget his wife and child, and I, by degrees, my engagements with Miss Read, to whom I never wrote more than one letter, and that was to let her know I was not likely soon to return. This was another of the great errata of my life, which I should wish to correct if I were to live it over again. In fact, by our expenses, I was constantly kept unable to pay my passage.

At Palmer's I was employed in composing for the second edition of Wollaston's "Religion of Nature." Some of his reasonings not appearing to me well founded, I wrote a little metaphysical piece in which I made remarks on them. It was entitled "A Dissertation on Liberty and Necessity, Pleasure and Pain." I inscribed it to my friend Ralph; I printed a small number. It occasioned my being more considered by Mr. Palmer as a young man of some ingenuity, tho' he seriously expostulated with me upon the principles of my pamphlet, which to him appeared abominable. My printing this pamphlet was another erratum.

While I lodged in Little Britain, I made an acquaintance with one Wilcox, a bookseller, whose shop was at the next door. He had an immense collection of second-hand books. Circulating libraries were not then in use; but we agreed that, on certain reasonable terms, which I have now forgotten, I might take, read, and return any of his books. This I esteemed a great advantage, and I made as much use of it as I could.

My pamphlet by some means falling into the hands of one Lyons, a surgeon, author of a book entitled "The Infallibility of Human Judgment," it occasioned an acquaintance between us. He took great notice of me, called on me often to converse on those subjects, carried me to the Horns, a pale alehouse in—— Lane, Cheapside, and introduced me to Dr. Mandeville, author of the "Fable of the Bees," who had a club there, of which he was the soul, being a most facetious, entertaining companion. Lyons, too, introduced me to Dr. Pemberton, at Batson's Coffee-house, who promised to give me an opportunity, sometime or other, of seeing Sir Isaac Newton, of which I was extremely desirous; but this never happened.

I had brought over a few curiosities, among which the principal was a purse made of the asbestos, which purifies by fire. Sir Hans Sloane heard of it, came to see me, and invited me to his house in Bloomsbury Square, where he showed me all his curiosities, and persuaded me to let him add that to the number, for which he paid me handsomely.

In our house there lodged a young woman, a milliner, who, I think, had a shop in the Cloisters. She had been genteelly bred, was sensible and lively, and of most pleasing conversation. Ralph read plays to her in the evenings, they grew intimate, she took another lodging, and he followed her. They lived together some time; but, he being still out of business, and her income not sufficient to maintain them with her child, he took a resolution of going from London, to try for a country school, which he thought himself well qualified to undertake, as he wrote an excellent hand, and was a master of arithmetic and accounts. This, however, he deemed a business below him, and confident of future better fortune, when he should be unwilling to have it known that he once was so meanly employed, he changed his name, and did me the honor to assume mine; for I soon after had a letter from him, acquainting me that he was settled in a small village (in Berkshire, I think it was, where he taught reading and writing to ten or a dozen boys, at sixpence each per week), recommending Mrs. T—— to my care, and desiring me to write to him, directing for Mr. Franklin, schoolmaster, at such a place.

He continued to write frequently, sending me large specimens of an epic poem which he was then composing, and desiring my remarks and corrections. These I gave him from time to time, but endeavored rather to discourage his proceeding. One of Young's Satires was then just published. I copied and sent him a great part of it, which set in a strong light the folly of pursuing the Muses with any hope of advancement by them. All was in vain; sheets of the poem continued to come by every post. In the meantime, Mrs. T——, having on his account lost her friends and business, was often in distresses, and used to send for me and borrow what I could spare to help her out of them. I grew fond of her company, and, being at that time under no religious restraint, and presuming upon my importance to her, I attempted familiarities (another erratum) which she repulsed with a proper resentment, and acquainted him with my behavior. This made a breach between us; and, when he returned again to London, he let me know he thought I had cancelled all the obligations he had been under to me. So I found I was never to expect his repaying me what I lent to him or advanced for him. This, however, was not then of much consequence, as he was totally unable; and in the loss of his friendship I found myself relieved from a burthen. I now began to think of getting a little money beforehand, and, expecting better work, I left Palmer's to work at Watts's, near Lincoln's Inn Fields, a still greater printing-house. Here I continued all the rest of my stay in London.

At my first admission into this printing-house I took to working at press, imagining I felt a want of the bodily exercise I had been used to in America, where presswork is mixed with composing. I drank only water; the other workmen, near fifty in number, were great guzzlers of beer. On occasion, I carried up and down stairs a large form of types in each hand, when others carried but one in both hands. They wondered to see, from this and several instances, that the Water-American, as they called me, was stronger than themselves, who drank strong beer! We had an alehouse boy who attended always in the house to supply the workmen. My companion at the press drank every day a pint before breakfast, a pint at breakfast with his bread and cheese, a pint between breakfast and dinner, a pint at dinner, a pint in the afternoon about six o'clock, and another when he had done his day's work. I thought it a detestable custom; but it was necessary, he supposed, to drink strong beer, that he might be strong to labour. I endeavored to convince him that the bodily strength afforded by beer could only be in proportion to the grain or flour of the barley dissolved in the water of which it was made; that there was more flour in a pennyworth of bread; and therefore, if he would eat that with a pint of water, it would give him more strength than a quart of beer. He drank on, however, and had four or five shillings to pay out of his wages every Saturday night for that muddling liquor; an expense I was free from. And thus these poor devils keep themselves always under.

Watts, after some weeks, desiring to have me in the composing-room, I left the pressmen; a new *bien venu* or sum for drink, being five shillings, was demanded of me by the compositors. I thought it an imposition, as I had paid below; the master thought so too, and forbade my paying it. I stood out two or three weeks, was accordingly considered as an excommunicate, and had so many little pieces of private mischief done me, by mixing my sorts, transposing my pages, breaking my matter, etc., etc., if I were ever so little out of the room, and all ascribed to the chapel ghost, which they said ever haunted those not regularly admitted, that, notwithstanding the master's protection, I found myself obliged to comply and pay the money, convinced of the folly of being on ill terms with those one is to live with continually.

I was now on a fair footing with them, and soon acquired considerable influence. I proposed some reasonable alterations in their chapel laws, and carried them against all opposition. From my example, a great part of them left their muddling breakfast of beer, and bread, and cheese, finding they could with me be supplied from a neighboring house with a large porringer of hot water-gruel, sprinkled with pepper, crumbed with bread, and a bit of butter in it, for the price of a pint of beer, viz., three half-pence. This was a more comfortable as well as cheaper breakfast, and keep their heads clearer. Those who continued sotting with beer all day, were often, by not paying, out of credit at the alehouse, and used to make interest with me to get beer; their light, as they phrased it, being out. I watched the pay-table on Saturday night, and collected what I stood engaged for them, having to pay sometimes near thirty shillings a week on their accounts. This, and my being esteemed a pretty good riggite, that is, a jocular verbal satirist, supported my consequence in the society. My constant attendance (I never making a St. Monday) recommended me to the master; and my uncommon quickness at composing occasioned my being put upon all work of dispatch, which was generally better paid. So I went on now very agreeably.

My lodging in Little Britain being too remote, I found another in Duke-street, opposite to the Rome-ish Chapel. It was two pair of stairs backwards, at an Italian warehouse. A widow lady kept the house; she had a daughter, and a maid servant, and a journeyman who attended the warehouse, but lodged abroad. After sending to inquire my character at the house where I last lodged she agreed to take me in at the same rate, 3s. 6d. per week; cheaper, as she said, from the protection she expected in having a man lodge in the house. She was a widow, an elderly woman; had been bred a Protestant, being a clergyman's daughter, but was converted to the Catholic religion by her husband, whose memory she much revered; had lived much among people of distinction, and knew a thousand anecdotes of them as far back as the times of Charles the Second. She was lame in her knees with the gout, and, therefore, seldom stirred out of her room, so sometimes wanted company; and hers was so highly amusing to me, that I was sure to spend an evening with her whenever she desired it. Our supper was only half an anchovy each, on a very little strip of bread and butter, and half a pint of ale between us; but the entertainment was in her conversation. My always keeping good hours, and giving little trouble in the family, made her unwilling to part with me, so that, when I talked of a lodging I had heard of, nearer my business, for two shillings a week, which, intent as I now was on saving money, made some difference, she bid me not think of it, for she would abate me two shillings a week for the future; so I remained with her at one shilling and sixpence as long as I stayed in London.

In a garret of her house there lived a maiden lady of seventy, in the most retired manner, of whom my landlady gave me this account: that she was a Roman Catholic, had been sent abroad when young, and lodged in a nunnery with an intent of becoming a nun; but, the country not agreeing with her, she returned to England, where, there being no nunnery, she had vowed to lead the life of a nun, as near as might be done in those circumstances. Accordingly, she had given all her estate to charitable uses, reserving only twelve pounds a year to live on, and out of this sum she still gave a great deal in charity, living herself on water-gruel only, and using no fire but to boil it. She had lived many years in that garret, being permitted to remain there gratis by successive Catholic tenants of the house below, as they deemed it a blessing to have her there. A priest visited her to confess her every day. "I have asked her," says my landlady, "how she, as she lived, could possibly find so much employment for a confessor?"

"Oh," said she, "it is impossible to avoid vain thoughts." I was permitted once to visit her. She was cheerful and polite, and conversed pleasantly. The room was clean, but had no other furniture than a mattress, a table with a crucifix and book, a stool which she gave me to sit on, and a picture over the chimney of Saint Veronica displaying her handkerchief, with the miraculous figure of Christ's bleeding face on it, which she explained to me with great seriousness. She looked pale, but was never sick; and I give it as another instance on how small an income, life and health may be supported.

At Watts's printing-house I contracted an acquaintance with an ingenious young man, one Wygate, who, having wealthy relations, had been better educated than most printers; was a tolerable Latinist, spoke French, and loved reading. I taught him and a friend of his to swim at twice going into the river, and they soon became good swimmers. They introduced me to some gentlemen from the country, who went to Chelsea by water to see the College and Don Saltero's curiosities. In our return, at the request of the company, whose curiosity Wygate had excited, I stripped and leaped into the river, and swam from near Chelsea to Blackfriar's, performing on the way many feats of activity, both upon and under water, that surprised and pleased those to whom they were novelties.

I had from a child been ever delighted with this exercise, had studied and practiced all Thevenot's motions and positions, added some of my own, aiming at the graceful and easy as well as the useful. All these I took this occasion of exhibiting to the company, and was much flattered by their admiration; and Wygate, who was desirous of becoming a master, grew more and more attached to me on that account, as well as from the similarity of our studies. He at length proposed to me traveling all over Europe together, supporting ourselves everywhere by working at our business. I was once inclined to it; but, mentioning it to my good friend Mr. Denham, with whom I often spent an hour when I had leisure, he dissuaded me from it, advising me to think only of returning to Pennsylvania, which he was now about to do.

I must record one trait of this good man's character. He had formerly been in business at Bristol, but failed in debt to a number of people, compounded and went to America. There, by a close application to business as a merchant, he acquired a plentiful fortune in a few years. Returning to England in the ship with me, he invited his old creditors to an entertainment, at which he thanked them for the easy composition they had favoured him with, and, when they expected nothing but the treat, every man at the first remove found under his plate an order on a banker for the full amount of the unpaid remainder with interest.

He now told me he was about to return to Philadelphia, and should carry over a great quantity of goods in order to open a store there. He proposed to take me over as his clerk, to keep his books, in which he would instruct me, copy his letters, and attend the store. He added, that, as soon as I should be acquainted with mercantile business, he would promote me by sending me with a cargo of flour and bread, etc., to the West Indies, and procure me commissions from others which would be profitable; and, if I managed well, would establish me handsomely. The thing pleased me; for I was grown tired of London, remembered with pleasure the happy months I had spent in Pennsylvania, and wished again to see it; therefore I immediately agreed on the terms of fifty pounds a year, Pennsylvania money; less, indeed, than my present gettings as a compositor, but affording a better prospect.

I now took leave of printing, as I thought, forever, and was daily employed in my new business, going about with Mr. Denham among the tradesmen to purchase various articles, and seeing them packed up, doing errands, calling upon workmen to dispatch, etc.; and, when all was on board, I had a few days' leisure. On one of these days, I was, to my surprise, sent for by a great man I knew only by name, a Sir William Wyndham, and I waited upon him. He had heard by some means or other of my swimming from Chelsea to Blackfriars, and of my teaching Wygate and another young man to swim in a few hours. He had two sons, about to set out on their travels; he wished to have them first taught swimming, and proposed to gratify me handsomely if I would teach them. They were not yet come to town, and my stay was uncertain, so I could not undertake it; but, from this incident, I thought it likely that, if I were to remain in England and open a swimming-school, I might get a good deal of money; and it struck me so strongly, that, had the overture been sooner made me, probably I should not so soon have returned to America. After many years, you and I had something of more importance to do with one of these sons of Sir William Wyndham, become Earl of Egremont, which I shall mention in its place.

Thus I spent about eighteen months in London; most part of the time I worked hard at my business, and spent but little upon myself except in seeing plays and in books. My friend Ralph had kept me poor; he owed me about twenty-seven pounds, which I was now never likely to receive; a great sum out of my small earnings! I loved him, notwithstanding, for he had many amiable qualities. I had by no means improved my fortune; but I had picked up some very ingenious acquaintance, whose conversation was of great advantage to me; and I had read considerably.

VII: Beginning Business in Philadelphia

WE sailed from Gravesend on the 23rd of July, 1726. For the incidents of the voyage, I refer you to my Journal, where you will find them all minutely related. Perhaps the most important part of that journal is the plan to be found in it, which I formed at sea, for regulating my future conduct in life. It is the more remarkable, as being formed when I was so young, and yet being pretty faithfully adhered to quite thro' to old age.

We landed in Philadelphia on the 11th of October, where I found sundry alterations. Keith was no longer governor, being superseded by Major Gordon. I met him walking the streets as a common citizen. He seemed a little ashamed at seeing me, but passed without saying anything. I should have been as much ashamed at seeing Miss Read, had not her friends, despairing with reason of my return after the receipt of my letter, persuaded her to marry another, one Rogers, a potter, which was done in my absence. With him, however, she was never happy, and soon parted from him, refusing to cohabit with him or bear his name, it being now said that he had another wife. He was a worthless fellow, tho' an excellent workman, which was the temptation to her friends. He got into debt, ran away in 1727 or 1728, went to the West Indies, and died there. Keimer had got a better house, a shop well supplied with stationery, plenty of new types, a number of hands, tho' none good, and seemed to have a great deal of business.

Mr. Denham took a store in Water-street, where we opened our goods; I attended the business diligently, studied accounts, and grew, in a little time, expert at selling. We lodged and boarded together; he counselled me as a father, having a sincere regard for me. I respected and loved him, and we might have gone on together very happy; but, in the beginning of February, 1726/7, when I had just passed my twenty-first year, we both were taken ill. My distemper was a pleurisy, which very nearly carried me off. I suffered a good deal, gave up the point in my own mind, and was rather disappointed when I found myself recovering, regretting, in some degree, that I must now, some time or other, have all that disagreeable work to do over again. I forget what his distemper was; it held him a long time, and at length carried him off. He left me a small legacy in a nuncupative will, as a token of his kindness for me, and he left me once more to the wide world; for the store was taken into the care of his executors, and my employment under him ended.

Mr. Denham took a store in Water-street

My brother-in-law, Holmes, being now at Philadelphia, advised my return to my business; and Keimer tempted me, with an offer of large wages by the year, to come and take the management of his printing-house, that he might better attend his stationer's shop. I had heard a bad character of him in London from his wife and her friends, and was not fond of having any more to do with him. I tried for farther employment as a merchant's clerk; but, not readily meeting with any, I closed again with Keimer. I found in his house these hands: Hugh Meredith, a Welsh Pennsylvanian, thirty years of age, bred to country work; honest, sensible, had a great deal of solid observation, was something of a reader, but given to drink. Stephen Potts, a young countryman of full age, bred to the same, of uncommon natural parts, and great wit and humor, but a little idle. These he had agreed with at extreme low wages per week to be raised a shilling every three months, as they would deserve by improving in their business; and the expectation of these high wages, to come on hereafter, was what he had drawn them in with. Meredith was to work at press, Potts at bookbinding, which he, by agreement, was to teach them, though he knew neither one nor t'other. John——, a wild Irishman, brought up to no business, whose service, for four years, Keimer had purchased from the captain of a ship; he, too, was to be made a pressman. George Webb, an Oxford scholar, whose time for four years he had likewise bought, intending him for a compositor, of whom more presently; and David Harry, a country boy, whom he had taken apprentice.

I soon perceived that the intention of engaging me at wages so much higher than he had been used to give, was, to have these raw, cheap hands formed through me; and, as soon as I had instructed them, then they being all articled to him, he should be able to do without me. I went on, however, very cheerfully, put his printing-house in order, which had been in great confusion, and brought his hands by degrees to mind their business and to do it better.

It was an odd thing to find an Oxford scholar in the situation of a bought servant. He was not more than eighteen years of age, and gave me this account of himself; that he was born in Gloucester, educated at a grammar-school there, had been distinguished among the scholars for some apparent superiority in performing his part, when they exhibited plays; belonged to the Witty Club there, and had written some pieces in prose and verse, which were printed in the Gloucester newspapers; thence he was sent to Oxford; where he continued about a year, but not well satisfied, wishing of all things to see London, and become a player. At length, receiving his quarterly allowance of fifteen guineas, instead of discharging his debts he walked out of town, hid his gown in a furze bush, and footed it to London, where, having no friend to advise him, he fell into bad company, soon spent his guineas, found no means of being introduced among the players, grew necessitous, pawned his clothes, and wanted bread. Walking the street very hungry, and not knowing what to do with himself, a crimp's bill was put into his hand, offering immediate entertainment and encouragement to such as would bind themselves to serve in America. He went directly, signed the indentures, was put into the ship, and came over, never writing a line to acquaint his friends what was become of him. He was lively, witty, good-natured, and a pleasant companion, but idle, thoughtless, and imprudent to the last degree.

John, the Irishman, soon ran away; with the rest I began to live very agreeably, for they all respected me the more, as they found Keimer incapable of instructing them, and that from me they learned something daily. We never worked on Saturday, that being Keimer's Sabbath, so I had two days for reading. My acquaintance with ingenious people in the town increased. Keimer himself treated me with great civility and apparent regard, and nothing now made me uneasy but my debt to Vernon, which I was yet unable to pay, being hitherto but a poor economist. He, however, kindly made no demand of it.

Our printing-house often wanted sorts, and there was no letter-founder in America; I had seen types cast at James's in London, but without much attention to the manner; however, I now contrived a mold, made use of the letters we had as puncheons, struck the mattrices in lead, and thus supplied in a pretty tolerable way all deficiencies. I also engraved several things on occasion; I made the ink; I was warehouseman, and everything, and, in short, quite a factotum.

But, however serviceable I might be, I found that my services became every day of less importance, as the other hands improved in the business; and, when Keimer paid my second quarter's wages, he let me know that he felt them too heavy, and thought I should make an abatement. He grew by degrees less civil, put on more of the master, frequently found fault, was captious, and seemed ready for an outbreaking. I went on, nevertheless, with a good deal of patience, thinking that his encumbered circumstances were partly the cause. At length a trifle snapped our connections; for, a great noise happening near the court-house, I put my head out of the window to see what was the matter. Keimer, being in the street, looked up and saw me, called out to me in a loud voice and angry tone to mind my business, adding some reproachful words, that nettled me the more for their publicity, all the neighbors who were looking out on the same occasion being witnesses how I was treated. He came up immediately into the printing-house, continued the quarrel, high words passed on both sides, he gave me the quarter's warning we had stipulated, expressing a wish that he had not been obliged to so long a warning. I told him his wish was unnecessary, for I would leave him that instant; and so, taking my hat, walked out of doors, desiring Meredith, whom I saw below, to take care of some things I left, and bring them to my lodgings.

Meredith came accordingly in the evening, when we talked my affair over. He had conceived a great regard for me, and was very unwilling that I should leave the house while he remained in it. He dissuaded me from returning to my native country, which I began to think of; he reminded me that Keimer was in debt for all he possessed; that his creditors began to be uneasy; that he kept his shop miserably, sold often without profit for ready money, and often trusted without keeping accounts; that he must therefore fail, which would make a vacancy I might profit of. I objected my want of money. He then let me know that his father had a high opinion of me, and, from some discourse that had passed between them, he was sure would advance money to set us up, if I would enter into partnership with him. "My time," says he, "will be out with Keimer in the spring; by that time we may have our press and types in from London. I am sensible I am no workman; if you like it, your skill in the business shall be set against the stock I furnish, and we will share the profits equally."

The proposal was agreeable, and I consented; his father was in town and approved of it; the more as he saw I had great influence with his son, had prevailed on him to abstain long from dram-drinking, and he hoped might break him of that wretched habit entirely, when we came to be so closely connected. I gave an inventory to the father, who carried it to a merchant; the things were sent for, the secret was to be kept till they should arrive, and in the meantime I was to get work, if I could, at the other printing-house. But I found no vacancy there, and so remained idle a few days, when Keimer, on a prospect of being employed to print some paper money in New Jersey, which would require cuts and various types that I only could supply, and apprehending Bradford might engage me and get the job from him, sent me a very civil message, that old friends should not part for a few words, the effect of sudden passion, and wishing me to return. Meredith persuaded me to comply, as it would give more opportunity for his improvement under my daily instructions; so I returned, and we went on more smoothly than for some time before. The New Jersey job was obtained, I contrived a copperplate press for it, the first that had been seen in the country; I cut several ornaments and checks for the bills. We went together to Burlington, where I executed the whole to satisfaction; and he received so large a sum for the work as to be enabled thereby to keep his head much longer above water.

At Burlington I made an acquaintance with many principal people of the province. Several of them had been appointed by the Assembly a committee to attend the press, and take care that no more bills were printed than the law directed. They were therefore, by turns, constantly with us, and generally he who attended, brought with him a friend or two for company. My mind having been much more improved by reading than Keimer's, I suppose it was for that reason my conversation seemed to be more valued. They had me to their houses, introduced me to their friends, and showed me much civility; while he, tho' the master, was a little neglected. In truth, he was an odd fish; ignorant of common life, fond of rudely opposing received opinions, slovenly to extreme dirtiness, enthusiastic in some points of religion, and a little knavish withal.

We continued there near three months; and by that time I could reckon among my acquired friends, Judge Allen, Samuel Bustill, the secretary of the Province, Isaac Pearson, Joseph Cooper, and several of the Smiths, members of Assembly, and Isaac Decow, the surveyor-general. The latter was a shrewd, sagacious old man, who told me that he began for himself, when young, by wheeling clay for brick-makers, learned to write after he was of age, carried the chain for surveyors, who taught him surveying, and he had now by his industry, acquired a good estate; and says he, "I foresee that you will soon work this man out of his business, and make a fortune in it at Philadelphia." He had not then the least intimation of my intention to set up there or anywhere. These friends were afterwards of great use to me, as I occasionally was to some of them. They all continued their regard for me as long as they lived.

Before I enter upon my public appearance in business, it may be well to let you know the then state of my mind with regard to my principles and morals, that you may see how far those influenced the future events of my life. My parents had early given me religious impressions, and brought me through my childhood piously in the Dissenting way. But I was scarce fifteen, when, after doubting by turns of several points, as I found them disputed in the different books I read, I began to doubt of Revelation itself. Some books against Deism fell into my hands; they were said to be the substance of sermons preached at Boyle's Lectures. It happened that they wrought an effect on me quite contrary to what was intended by them; for the arguments of the Deists, which were quoted to be refuted, appeared to me much stronger than the refutations; in short, I soon became a thorough Deist. My arguments perverted some others, particularly Collins and Ralph; but, each of them having afterwards wronged me greatly without the least compunction, and recollecting Keith's conduct towards me (who was another free-thinker), and my own towards Vernon and Miss Read, which at times gave me great trouble, I began to suspect that this doctrine, tho' it might be true, was not very useful. My London pamphlet, which had for its motto these lines of Dryden:

"Whatever is, is right. Though purblind man
Sees but a part o' the chain, the nearest link:
His eyes not carrying to the equal beam,
That poises all above;"

and from the attributes of God, his infinite wisdom, goodness and power, concluded that nothing could possibly be wrong in the world, and that vice and virtue were empty distinctions, no such things existing, appeared now not so clever a performance as I once thought it; and I doubted whether some error had not insinuated itself unperceived into my argument, so as to infect all that followed, as is common in metaphysical reasonings.

I grew convinced that truth, sincerity and integrity in dealings between man and man were of the utmost importance to the felicity of life; and I formed written resolutions, which still remain in my journal book, to practice them ever while I lived. Revelation had indeed no weight with me, as such; but I entertained an opinion that, though certain actions might not be bad because they were forbidden by it, or good because it commanded them, yet probably these actions might be forbidden because they were bad for us, or commanded because they were beneficial to us, in their own natures, all the circumstances of things considered. And this persuasion, with the kind hand of Providence, or some guardian angel, or accidental favourable circumstances and situations, or all together, preserved me, thro' this dangerous time of youth, and the hazardous situations I was sometimes in among strangers, remote from the eye and advice of my father, without any willful gross immorality or injustice, that might have been expected from my want of religion. I say willful, because the instances I have mentioned had something of necessity in them, from my youth, inexperience, and the knavery of others. I had therefore a tolerable character to begin the world with; I valued it properly, and determined to preserve it.

We had not been long returned to Philadelphia before the new types arrived from London. We settled with Keimer, and left him by his consent before he heard of it. We found a house to hire near the market, and took it. To lessen the rent, which was then but twenty-four pounds a year, tho' I have since known it to let for seventy, we took in Thomas Godfrey, a glazier, and his family, who were to pay a considerable part of it to us, and we to board with them. We had scarce opened our letters and put our press in order, before George House, an acquaintance of mine, brought a countryman to us, whom he had met in the street inquiring for a printer. All our cash was now expended in the variety of particulars we had been obliged to procure, and this countryman's five shillings, being our first-fruits, and coming so seasonably, gave me more pleasure than any crown I have since earned; and the gratitude I felt toward House has made me often more ready than perhaps I should otherwise have been to assist young beginners.

There are croakers in every country, always boding its ruin. Such a one then lived in Philadelphia; a person of note, an elderly man, with a wise look and a very grave manner of speaking; his name was Samuel Mickle. This gentleman, a stranger to me, stopped one day at my door, and asked me if I was the young man who had lately opened a new printing-house. Being answered in the affirmative, he said he was sorry for me, because it was an expensive undertaking, and the expense would be lost; for Philadelphia was a sinking place, the people already half-bankrupts, or near being so; all appearances to the contrary, such as new buildings and the rise of rents, being to his certain knowledge fallacious; for they were, in fact, among the things that would soon ruin us. And he gave me such a detail of misfortunes now existing, or that were soon to exist, that he left me half melancholy. Had I known him before I engaged in this business, probably I never should have done it. This man continued to live in this decaying place, and to declaim in the same strain, refusing for many years to buy a house there, because all was going to destruction; and at last I had the pleasure of seeing him give five times as much for one as he might have bought it for when he first began his croaking.

I should have mentioned before, that, in the autumn of the preceding year, I had formed most of my ingenious acquaintance into a club of mutual improvement, which was called the Junto; we met on Friday evenings. The rules that I drew up required that every member, in his turn, should produce one or more queries on any point of Morals, Politics, or Natural Philosophy, to be discussed by the company; and once in three months produce and read an essay of his own writing, on any subject he pleased. Our debates were to be under the direction of a president, and to be conducted in the sincere spirit of inquiry after truth, without fondness for dispute, or desire of victory; and, to prevent warmth, all expressions of positiveness in opinions, or direct contradiction, were after some time made contraband, and prohibited under small pecuniary penalties.

The first members were Joseph Breintnal, a copier of deeds for the scriveners, a good-natured, friendly middle-aged man, a great lover of poetry, reading all he could meet with, and writing some that was tolerable; very ingenious in many little Nicknackeries, and of sensible conversation.

Thomas Godfrey, a self-taught mathematician, great in his way, and afterward inventor of what is now called Hadley's Quadrant. But he knew little out of his way, and was not a pleasing companion; as, like most great mathematicians I have met with, he expected universal precision in everything said, or was forever denying or distinguishing upon trifles, to the disturbance of all conversation. He soon left us.

Nicholas Scull, a surveyor, afterwards surveyor-general, who loved books, and sometimes made a few verses.

William Parsons, bred a shoemaker, but, loving reading, had acquired a considerable share of mathematics, which he first studied with a view to astrology, that he afterwards laughed at it. He also became surveyor-general.

William Maugridge, a joiner, a most exquisite mechanic, and a solid, sensible man.

Hugh Meredith, Stephen Potts, and George Webb I have characterized before.

Robert Grace, a young gentleman of some fortune, generous, lively, and witty; a lover of punning and of his friends.

And William Coleman, then a merchant's clerk, about my age, who had the coolest, clearest head, the best heart, and the exactest morals of almost any man I ever met with. He became afterwards a merchant of great note, and one of our provincial judges. Our friendship continued without interruption to his death, upwards of forty years; and the club continued almost as long, and was the best school of philosophy, morality, and politics that then existed in the province; for our queries, which were read the week preceding their discussion, put us upon reading with attention upon the several subjects, that we might speak more to the purpose; and here, too, we acquired better habits of conversation, everything being studied in our rules which might prevent our disgusting each other. From hence the long continuance of the club, which I shall have frequent occasion to speak further of hereafter.

But my giving this account of it here is to show something of the interest I had, every one of these exerting themselves in recommending business to us. Breintnal particularly procured us from the Quakers the printing forty sheets of their history, the rest being to be done by Keimer; and upon this we worked exceedingly hard, for the price was low. It was a folio, pro patria size, in pica, with long primer notes. I composed of it a sheet a day, and Meredith worked it off at press; it was often eleven at night, and sometimes later, before I had finished my distribution for the next day's work, for the little jobs sent in by our other friends now and then put us back. But so determined I was to continue doing a sheet a day of the folio, that one night, when, having imposed my forms, I thought my day's work over, one of them by accident was broken, and two pages reduced to pi, I immediately distributed and composed it over again before I went to bed; and this industry, visible to our neighbors, began to give us character and credit; particularly, I was told, that mention being made of the new printing-office at the merchants' Every-night club, the general opinion was that it must fail, there being already two printers in the place, Keimer and Bradford; but Dr. Baird (whom you and I saw many years after at his native place, St. Andrew's in Scotland) gave a contrary opinion: "For the industry of that Franklin," says he, "is superior to anything I ever saw of the kind; I see him still at work when I go home from club, and he is at work again before his neighbors are out of bed." This struck the rest, and we soon after had offers from one of them to supply us with stationery; but as yet we did not chuse to engage in shop business.

I mention this industry the more particularly and the more freely, tho' it seems to be talking in my own praise, that those of my posterity, who shall read it, may know the use of that virtue, when they see its effects in my favor throughout this relation.

George Webb, who had found a female friend that lent him wherewith to purchase his time of Keimer, now came to offer himself as a journeyman to us. We could not then employ him; but I foolishly let him know as a secret that I soon intended to begin a newspaper, and might then have work for him. My hopes of success, as I told him, were founded on this, that the then only newspaper, printed by Bradford, was a paltry thing, wretchedly managed, no way entertaining, and yet was profitable to him; I therefore thought a good paper would scarcely fail of good encouragement. I requested Webb not to mention it; but he told it to Keimer, who immediately, to be beforehand with me, published proposals for printing one himself, on which Webb was to be employed. I resented this; and, to counteract them, as I could not yet begin our paper, I wrote several pieces of entertainment for Bradford's paper, under the title of the Busy Body, which Breintnal continued some months. By this means the attention of the public was fixed on that paper, and Keimer's proposals, which we burlesqued and ridiculed, were disregarded. He began his paper, however, and, after carrying it on three quarters of a year, with at most only ninety subscribers, he offered it to me for a trifle; and I, having been ready some time to go on with it, took it in hand directly; and it proved in a few years extremely profitable to me.

I perceive that I am apt to speak in the singular number, though our partnership still continued; the reason may be that, in fact, the whole management of the business lay upon me. Meredith was no compositor, a poor pressman, and seldom sober. My friends lamented my connection with him, but I was to make the best of it.

Our first papers made a quite different appearance from any before in the province; a better type, and better printed; but some spirited remarks of my writing, on the dispute then going on between Governor Burnet and the Massachusetts Assembly, struck the principal people, occasioned the paper and the manager of it to be much talked of, and in a few weeks brought them all to be our subscribers.

Their example was followed by many, and our number went on growing continually. This was one of the first good effects of my having learnt a little to scribble; another was, that the leading men, seeing a newspaper now in the hands of one who could also handle a pen, thought it convenient to oblige and encourage me. Bradford still printed the votes, and laws, and other public business. He had printed an address of the House to the governor, in a coarse, blundering manner; we reprinted it elegantly and correctly, and sent one to every member. They were sensible of the difference: it strengthened the hands of our friends in the House, and they voted us their printers for the year ensuing.

Among my friends in the House I must not forget Mr. Hamilton, before mentioned, who was then returned from England, and had a seat in it. He interested himself for me strongly in that instance, as he did in many others afterward, continuing his patronage till his death.

Mr. Vernon, about this time, put me in mind of the debt I owed him, but did not press me. I wrote him an ingenuous letter of acknowledgment, craved his forbearance a little longer, which he allowed me, and as soon as I was able, I paid the principal with interest, and many thanks; so that erratum was in some degree corrected.

But now another difficulty came upon me which I had never the least reason to expect. Mr. Meredith's father, who was to have paid for our printing-house, according to the expectations given me, was able to advance only one hundred pounds currency, which had been paid; and a hundred more was due to the merchant, who grew impatient, and sued us all. We gave bail, but saw that, if the money could not be raised in time, the suit must soon come to a judgment and execution, and our hopeful prospects must, with us, be ruined, as the press and letters must be sold for payment, perhaps at half price.

In this distress two true friends, whose kindness I have never forgotten, nor ever shall forget while I can remember anything, came to me separately, unknown to each other, and, without any application from me, offering each of them to advance me all the money that should be necessary to enable me to take the whole business upon myself, if that should be practicable; but they did not like my continuing the partnership with Meredith, who, as they said, was often seen drunk in the streets, and playing at low games in alehouses, much to our discredit. These two friends were William Coleman and Robert Grace. I told them I could not propose a separation while any prospect remained of the Meredith's fulfilling their part of our agreement, because I thought myself under great obligations to them for what they had done, and would do if they could; but, if they finally failed in their performance, and our partnership must be dissolved, I should then think myself at liberty to accept the assistance of my friends.

Thus the matter rested for some time, when I said to my partner, "Perhaps your father is dissatisfied at the part you have undertaken in this affair of ours, and is unwilling to advance for you and me what he would for you alone. If that is the case, tell me, and I will resign the whole to you, and go about my business." "No," said he, "my father has really been disappointed, and is really unable; and I am unwilling to distress him farther. I see this is a business I am not fit for. I was bred a farmer, and it was a folly in me to come to town, and put myself, at thirty years of age, an apprentice to learn a new trade. Many of our Welsh people are going to settle in North Carolina, where land is cheap. I am inclined to go with them, and follow my old employment. You may find friends to assist you. If you will take the debts of the company upon you; return to my father the hundred pounds he has advanced; pay my little personal debts, and give me thirty pounds and a new saddle, I will relinquish the partnership, and leave the whole in your hands." I agreed to this proposal: it was drawn up in writing, signed, and seal's immediately. I gave him what he demanded, and he went soon after to Carolina, from whence he sent me next year two long letters, containing the best account that had been given of that country, the climate, the soil, husbandry, etc., for in those matters he was very judicious. I printed them in the papers, and they gave great satisfaction to the public.

As soon as he was gone, I recurred to my two friends; and because I would not give an unkind preference to either, I took half of what each had offered and I wanted of one, and half of the other; paid off the company's debts, and went on with the business in my own name, advertising that the partnership was dissolved. I think this was in or about the year 1729.

VIII: Business Success and First Public Service

ABOUT this time there was a cry among the people for more paper money, only fifteen thousand pounds being extant in the province, and that soon to be sunk. The wealthy inhabitants opposed any addition, being against all paper currency, from an apprehension that it would depreciate, as it had done in New England, to the prejudice of all creditors. We had discussed this point in our Junto, where I was on the side of an addition, being persuaded that the first small sum struck in 1723 had done much good by increasing the trade, employment, and number of inhabitants in the province, since I now saw all the old houses inhabited, and many new ones building: whereas I remembered well, that when I first walked about the streets of Philadelphia, eating my roll, I saw most of the houses in Walnut Street, between Second and Front streets, with bills on their doors, "To be let"; and many likewise in Chestnut-street and other streets, which made me then think the inhabitants of the city were deserting it one after another.

Our debates possessed me so fully of the subject, that I wrote and printed an anonymous pamphlet on it, entitled "The Nature and Necessity of a Paper Currency." It was well received by the common people in general; but the rich men disliked it, for it increased and strengthened the clamor for more money, and they happening to have no writers among them that were able to answer it, their opposition slackened, and the point was carried by a majority in the House. My friends there, who conceived I had been of some service, thought fit to reward me by employing me in printing the money; a very profitable job and a great help to me. This was another advantage gained by my being able to write.

The utility of this currency became by time and experience so evident as never afterwards to be much disputed; so that it grew soon to fifty-five thousand pounds, and in 1739 to eighty thousand pounds, since which it arose during war to upwards of three hundred and fifty thousand pounds, trade, building, and inhabitants all the while increasing, tho' I now think there are limits beyond which the quantity may be hurtful.

I soon after obtained, thro' my friend Hamilton, the printing of the Newcastle paper money, another profitable job as I then thought it; small things appearing great to those in small circumstances; and these, to me, were really great advantages, as they were great encouragements. He procured for me, also, the printing of the laws and votes of that government, which continued in my hands as long as I followed the business.

I now opened a little stationer's shop. I had in it blanks of all sorts, the correctest that ever appeared among us, being assisted in that by my friend Breintnal. I had also paper, parchment, chapmen's books, etc. One Whitemash, a compositor I had known in London, an excellent workman, now came to me, and worked with me constantly and diligently; and I took an apprentice, the son of Aquilla Rose.

I was under for the printing-house. In order to secure my credit and character as a tradesman, I took care not only to be in reality industrious and frugal, but to avoid all appearances to the contrary. I dressed plainly; I was seen at no places of idle diversion. I never went out a fishing or shooting; a book, indeed, sometimes debauched me from my work, but that was seldom, snug, and gave no scandal; and, to show that I was not above my business, I sometimes brought home the paper I purchased at the stores thro' the streets on a wheelbarrow. Thus being esteemed an industrious, thriving young man, and paying duly for what I bought, the merchants who imported stationery solicited my custom; others proposed supplying me with books, and I went on swimmingly. In the meantime, Keimer's credit and business declining daily, he was at last forced to sell his printing-house to satisfy his creditors. He went to Barbados, and there lived some years in very poor circumstances.

His apprentice, David Harry, whom I had instructed while I worked with him, set up in his place at Philadelphia, having bought his materials. I was at first apprehensive of a powerful rival in Harry, as his friends were very able, and had a good deal of interest. I therefore proposed a partnership to him, which he, fortunately for me, rejected with scorn. He was very proud, dressed like a gentleman, lived expensively, took much diversion and pleasure abroad, ran in debt, and neglected his business; upon which, all business left him; and, finding nothing to do, he followed Keimer to Barbados, taking the printing-house with him. There this apprentice employed his former master as a journeyman; they quarreled often; Harry went continually behindhand, and at length was forced to sell his types and return to his country work in Pennsylvania. The person that bought them employed Keimer to use them, but in a few years he died.

There remained now no competitor with me at Philadelphia but the old one, Bradford; who was rich and easy, did a little printing now and then by straggling hands, but was not very anxious about the business. However, as he kept the post-office, it was imagined he had better opportunities of obtaining news; his paper was thought a better distributer of advertisements than mine, and therefore had many more, which was a profitable thing to him, and a disadvantage to me; for, tho' I did indeed receive and send papers by the post, yet the public opinion was otherwise, for what I did send was by bribing the riders, who took them privately, Bradford being unkind enough to forbid it, which occasioned some resentment on my part; and I thought so meanly of him for it, that, when I afterward came into his situation, I took care never to imitate it.

I had hitherto continued to board with Godfrey, who lived in part of my house with his wife and children, and had one side of the shop for his glazier's business, tho' he worked little, being always absorbed in his mathematics. Mrs. Godfrey projected a match for me with a relation's daughter, took opportunities of bringing us often together, till a serious courtship on my part ensued, the girl being in herself very deserving. The old folks encouraged me by continual invitations to supper, and by leaving us together, till at length it was time to explain. Mrs. Godfrey managed our little treaty. I let her know that I expected as much money with their daughter as would pay off my remaining debt for the printing-house, which I believe was not then above a hundred pounds. She brought me word they had no such sum to spare; I said they might mortgage their house in the loan-office. The answer to this, after some days, was, that they did not approve the match; that, on inquiry of Bradford, they had been informed the printing business was not a profitable one; the types would soon be worn out, and more wanted; that S. Keimer and D. Harry had failed one after the other, and I should probably soon follow them; and, therefore, I was forbidden the house, and the daughter shut up.

Whether this was a real change of sentiment or only artifice, on a supposition of our being too far engaged in affection to retract, and therefore that we should steal a marriage, which would leave them at liberty to give or withhold what they pleased, I know not; but I suspected the latter, resented it, and went no more. Mrs. Godfrey brought me afterward some more favorable accounts of their disposition, and would have drawn me on again; but I declared absolutely my resolution to have nothing more to do with that family. This was resented by the Godfreys; we differed, and they removed, leaving me the whole house, and I resolved to take no more inmates.

But this affair having turned my thoughts to marriage, I looked round me and made overtures of acquaintance in other places; but soon found that, the business of a printer being generally thought a poor one, I was not to expect money with a wife, unless with such a one as I should not otherwise think agreeable. A friendly correspondence as neighbors and old acquaintances had continued between me and Mrs. Read's family, who all had a regard for me from the time of my first lodging in their house. I was often invited there and consulted in their affairs, wherein I sometimes was of service. I pitied poor Miss Read's unfortunate situation, who was generally dejected, seldom cheerful, and avoided company. I considered my giddiness and inconstancy when in London as in a great degree the cause of her unhappiness, tho' the mother was good enough to think the fault more her own than mine, as she had prevented our marrying before I went thither, and persuaded the other match in my absence. Our mutual affection was revived, but there were now great objections to our union. The match was indeed looked upon as invalid, a preceding wife being said to be living in England; but this could not easily be proved, because of the distance; and, tho' there was a report of his death, it was not certain. Then, tho' it should be true, he had left many debts, which his successor might be called upon to pay. We ventured, however, over all these difficulties, and I took her to wife, September 1st, 1730. None of the inconveniences happened that we had apprehended; she proved a good and faithful helpmate, assisted me much by attending the shop; we throve together, and have ever mutually endeavored to make each other happy. Thus I corrected that great erratum as well as I could.

About this time, our club meeting, not at a tavern, but in a little room of Mr. Grace's, set apart for that purpose, a proposition was made by me, that, since our books were often referred to in our disquisitions upon the queries, it might be convenient to us to have them altogether where we met, that upon occasion they might be consulted; and by thus clubbing our books to a common library, we should, while we liked to keep them together, have each of us the advantage of using the books of all the other members, which would be nearly as beneficial as if each owned the whole. It was liked and agreed to, and we filled one end of the room with such books as we could best spare. The number was not so great as we expected; and tho' they had been of great use, yet some inconveniences occurring for want of due care of them, the collection, after about a year, was separated, and each took his books home again.

And now I set on foot my first project of a public nature, that for a subscription library. I drew up the proposals, got them put into form by our great scrivener, Brockden, and, by the help of my friends in the Junto, procured fifty subscribers of forty shillings each to begin with, and ten shillings a year for fifty years, the term our company was to continue. We afterwards obtained a charter, the company being increased to one hundred: this was the mother of all the North American subscription libraries, now so numerous. It is become a great thing itself, and continually increasing. These libraries have improved the general conversation of the Americans, made the common tradesmen and farmers as intelligent as most gentlemen from other countries, and perhaps have contributed in some degree to the stand so generally made throughout the colonies in defense of their privileges.

Mem°. Thus far was written with the intention expressed in the beginning and therefore contains several little family anecdotes of no importance to others. What follows was written many years after in compliance with the advice contained in these letters, and accordingly intended for the public. The affairs of the Revolution occasioned the interruption.

[Continuation of the Account of my Life, begun at Passy, near Paris, 1784.]

It is some time since I received the above letters, but I have been too busy till now to think of complying with the request they contain. It might, too, be much better done if I were at home among my papers, which would aid my memory, and help to ascertain dates; but my return being uncertain, and having just now a little leisure, I will endeavor to recollect and write what I can; if I live to get home, it may there be corrected and improved.

Not having any copy here of what is already written, I know not whether an account is given of the means I used to establish the Philadelphia public library, which, from a small beginning, is now become so considerable, though I remember to have come down to near the time of that transaction (1730). I will therefore begin here with an account of it, which may be struck out if found to have been already given.

At the time I established myself in Pennsylvania, there was not a good bookseller's shop in any of the colonies to the southward of Boston. In New York and Philad'a the printers were indeed stationers; they sold only paper, etc., almanacs, ballads, and a few common school-books. Those who loved reading were obliged to send for their books from England; the members of the Junto had each a few. We had left the alehouse, where we first met, and hired a room to hold our club in. I proposed that we should all of us bring our books to that room, where they would not only be ready to consult in our conferences, but become a common benefit, each of us being at liberty to borrow such as he wished to read at home. This was accordingly done, and for some time contented us.

Finding the advantage of this little collection, I proposed to render the benefit from books more common, by commencing a public subscription library. I drew a sketch of the plan and rules that would be necessary, and got a skillful conveyancer, Mr. Charles Brockden, to put the whole in form of articles of agreement to be subscribed, by which each subscriber engaged to pay a certain sum down for the first purchase of books, and an annual contribution for increasing them. So few were the readers at that time in Philadelphia, and the majority of us so poor, that I was not able, with great industry, to find more than fifty persons, mostly young tradesmen, willing to pay down for this purpose forty shillings each, and ten shillings per annum. On this little fund we began. The books were imported; the library was opened one day in the week for lending to the subscribers, on their promissory notes to pay double the value if not duly returned. The institution soon manifested its utility, was imitated by other towns, and in other provinces. The libraries were augmented by donations; reading became fashionable; and our people, having no public amusements to divert their attention from study, became better acquainted with books, and in a few years were observed by strangers to be better instructed and more intelligent than people of the same rank generally are in other countries.

When we were about to sign the above mentioned articles, which were to be binding on us, our heirs, etc., for fifty years, Mr. Brockden, the scrivener, said to us, "You are young men, but it is scarcely probable that any of you will live to see the expiration of the term fixed in the instrument." A number of us, however, are yet living; but the instrument was after a few years rendered null by a charter that incorporated and gave perpetuity to the company.

The objections and reluctances I met with in soliciting the subscriptions, made me soon feel the impropriety of presenting one's self as the proposer of any useful project, that might be supposed to raise one's reputation in the smallest degree above that of one's neighbors, when one has need of their assistance to accomplish that project. I therefore put myself as much as I could out of sight, and stated it as a scheme of a number of friends, who had requested me to go about and propose it to such as they thought lovers of reading. In this way my affair went on more smoothly, and I ever after practiced it on such occasions; and, from my frequent successes, can heartily recommend it. The present little sacrifice of your vanity will afterwards be amply repaid. If it remains a while uncertain to whom the merit belongs, someone more vain than yourself will be encouraged to claim it, and then even envy will be disposed to do you justice by plucking those assumed feathers, and restoring them to their right owner.

This library afforded me the means of improvement by constant study, for which I set apart an hour or two each day, and thus repaired in some degree the loss of the learned education my father once intended for me. Reading was the only amusement I allowed myself. I spent no time in taverns, games, or frolics of any kind; and my industry in my business continued as indefatigable as it was necessary. I was indebted for my printing-house; I had a young family coming on to be educated, and I had to contend with for business two printers, who were established in the place before me. My circumstances, however, grew daily easier. My original habits of frugality continuing, and my father having, among his instructions to me when a boy, frequently repeated a proverb of Solomon, "Seest thou a man diligent in his calling, he shall stand before kings, he shall not stand before mean men," I from thence considered industry as a means of obtaining wealth and distinction, which encouraged me, tho' I did not think that I should ever literally stand before kings, which, however, has since happened; for I have stood before five, and even had the honor of sitting down with one, the King of Denmark, to dinner.

We have an English proverb that says, "He that would thrive, must ask his wife." It was lucky for me that I had one as much disposed to industry and frugality as myself. She assisted me cheerfully in my business, folding and stitching pamphlets, tending shop, purchasing old linen rags for the papermakers, etc., etc. We kept no idle servants, our table was plain and simple, our furniture of the cheapest. For instance, my breakfast was a long time break and milk (no tea), and I ate it out of a two penny earthen porringer, with a pewter spoon. But mark how luxury will enter families, and make a progress, in spite of principle: being called one morning to breakfast, I found it in a China bowl, with a spoon of silver! They had been bought for me without my knowledge by my wife, and had cost her the enormous sum of three-and-twenty shillings, for which she had no other excuse or apology to make, but that she thought her husband deserved a silver spoon and China bowl as well as any of his neighbors. This was the first appearance of plate and China in our house, which afterward, in a course of years, as our wealth increased, augmented gradually to several hundred pounds in value.

I had been religiously educated as a Presbyterian; and though some of the dogmas of that persuasion, such as the eternal decrees of God, election, reprobation, etc., appeared to me unintelligible, others doubtful, and I early absented myself from the public assemblies of the sect, Sunday being my studying day, I never was without some religious principles. I never doubted, for instance, the existence of the Deity; that he made the world, and governed it by his Providence; that the most acceptable service of God was the doing good to man; that our souls are immortal; and that all crime will be punished, and virtue rewarded, either here or hereafter. These I esteemed the essentials of every religion; and, being to be found in all the religions we had in our country, I respected them all, tho' with different degrees of respect, as I found them more or less mixed with other articles, which, without any tendency to inspire, promote, or confirm morality, served principally to divide us, and make us unfriendly to one another. This respect to all, with an opinion that the worst had some good effects, induced me to avoid all discourse that might tend to lessen the good opinion another might have of his own religion; and as our province increased in people, and new places of worship were continually wanted, and generally erected by voluntary contribution, my mite for such purpose, whatever might be the sect, was never refused.

Tho' I seldom attended any public worship, I had still an opinion of its propriety, and of its utility when rightly conducted, and I regularly paid my annual subscription for the support of the only Presbyterian minister or meeting we had in Philadelphia. He used to visit me sometimes as a friend, and admonished me to attend his administrations, and I was now and then prevailed on to do so, once for five Sundays successively. Had he been in my opinion a good preacher, perhaps I might have continued, notwithstanding the occasion I had for the Sunday's leisure in my course of study; but his discourses were chiefly either polemic arguments, or explications of the peculiar doctrines of our sect, and were all to me very dry, uninteresting, and unedifying, since not a single moral principle was inculcated or enforced, their aim seeming to be rather to make us Presbyterians than good citizens.

At length he took for his text that verse of the fourth chapter of Philippians, "Finally, brethren, whatsoever things are true, honest, just, pure, lovely, or of good report, if there be any virtue, or any praise, think on these things." And I imagined, in a sermon on such a text, we could not miss of having some morality. But he confined himself to five points only, as meant by the apostle, viz.: 1. Keeping holy the Sabbath day. 2. Being diligent in reading the holy Scriptures. 3. Attending duly the public worship. 4. Partaking of the Sacrament. 5. Paying a due respect to God's ministers. These might be all good things; but, as they were not the kind of good things that I expected from that text, I despaired of ever meeting with them from any other, was disgusted, and attended his preaching no more. I had some years before composed a little Liturgy, or form of prayer, for my own private use (viz., in 1728), entitled, Articles of Belief and Acts of Religion. I returned to the use of this, and went no more to the public assemblies. My conduct might be blamable, but I leave it, without attempting further to excuse it; my present purpose being to relate facts, and not to make apologies for them.

IX: Plan For Attaining Moral Perfection

IT was about this time I conceived the bold and arduous project of arriving at moral perfection. I wished to live without committing any fault at any time; I would conquer all that either natural inclination, custom, or company might lead me into. As I knew, or thought I knew, what was right and wrong, I did not see why I might not always do the one and avoid the other. But I soon found I had undertaken a task of more difficulty than I had imagined. While my care was employed in guarding against one fault, I was often surprised by another; habit took the advantage of inattention; inclination was sometimes too strong for reason. I concluded, at length, that the mere speculative conviction that it was our interest to be completely virtuous, was not sufficient to prevent our slipping; and that the contrary habits must be broken, and good ones acquired and established, before we can have any dependence on a steady, uniform rectitude of conduct. For this purpose I therefore contrived the following method.

In the various enumerations of the moral virtues I had met with in my reading, I found the catalogue more or less numerous, as different writers included more or fewer ideas under the same name. Temperance, for example, was by some confined to eating and drinking, while by others it was extended to mean the moderating every other pleasure, appetite, inclination, or passion, bodily or mental, even to our avarice and ambition. I proposed to myself, for the sake of clearness, to use rather more names, with fewer ideas annexed to each, than a few names with more ideas; and I included under thirteen names of virtues all that at that time occurred to me as necessary or desirable, and annexed to each a short precept, which fully expressed the extent I gave to its meaning.

These names of virtues, with their precepts, were:

1. Temperance.
Eat not to dullness; drink not to elevation.
2. Silence.
Speak not but what may benefit others or yourself; avoid trifling conversation.
3. Order.
Let all your things have their places; let each part of your business have its time.
4. Resolution.
Resolve to perform what you ought; perform without fail what you resolve.
5. Frugality.
Make no expense but to do good to others or yourself; i.e., waste nothing.
6. Industry.
Lose no time; be always employed in something useful; cut off all unnecessary actions.
7. Sincerity.
Use no hurtful deceit; think innocently and justly; and, if you speak, speak accordingly.
8. Justice.
Wrong none by doing injuries, or omitting the benefits that are your duty.
9. Moderation.
Avoid extremes; forbear resenting injuries so much as you think they deserve.
10. Cleanliness.
Tolerate no uncleanliness in body, clothes, or habitation.
11. Tranquility.
Be not disturbed at trifles, or at accidents common or unavoidable.
12. Chastity.
13. Humility.
Imitate Jesus and Socrates.

My intention being to acquire the habitude of all these virtues, I judged it would be well not to distract my attention by attempting the whole at once, but to fix it on one of them at a time; and, when I should be master of that, then to proceed to another, and so on, till I should have gone through the thirteen; and, as the previous acquisition of some might facilitate the acquisition of certain others, I arranged them with that view, as they stand above. Temperance first, as it tends to procure that coolness and clearness of head, which is so necessary where constant vigilance was to be kept up, and guard maintained against the unremitting attraction of ancient habits, and the force of perpetual temptations. This being acquired and established, Silence would be more easy; and my desire being to gain knowledge at the same time that I improved in virtue, and considering that in conversation it was obtained rather by the use of the ears than of the tongue, and therefore wishing to break a habit I was getting into of prattling, punning, and joking, which only made me acceptable to trifling company, I gave Silence the second place. This and the next, Order, I expected would allow me more time for attending to my project and my studies. Resolution, once become habitual, would keep me firm in my endeavors to obtain all the subsequent virtues; Frugality and Industry freeing me from my remaining debt, and producing affluence and independence, would make more easy the practice of Sincerity and Justice, etc., etc. Conceiving then, that, agreeably to the advice of Pythagoras in his Golden Verses, daily examination would be necessary, I contrived the following method for conducting that examination.

I made a little book, in which I allotted a page for each of the virtues. I ruled each page with red ink, so as to have seven columns, one for each day of the week, marking each column with a letter for the day. I crossed these columns with thirteen red lines, marking the beginning of each line with the first letter of one of the virtues, on which line, and in its proper column, I might mark, by a little black spot, every fault I found upon examination to have been committed respecting that virtue upon that day.

TEMPERANCE.
EAT NOT TO DULLNESS
DRINK NOT TO ELEVATION.

I determined to give a week's strict attention to each of the virtues successively. Thus, in the first week, my great guard was to avoid every the least offense against Temperance, leaving the other virtues to their ordinary chance, only marking every evening the faults of the day. Thus, if in the first week I could keep my first line, marked T, clear of spots, I supposed the habit of that virtue so much strengthened, and its opposite weakened, that I might venture extending my attention to include the next, and for the following week keep both lines clear of spots. Proceeding thus to the last, I could go through a course complete in thirteen weeks, and four courses in a year. And like him who, having a garden to weed, does not attempt to eradicate all the bad herbs at once, which would exceed his reach and his strength, but works on one of the beds at a time, and, having accomplished the first, proceeds to a second, so I should have, I hoped, the encouraging pleasure of seeing on my pages the progress I made in virtue, by clearing successively my lines of their spots, till in the end, by a number of courses, I should be happy in viewing a clean book, after a thirteen weeks' daily examination.

This my little book had for its motto these lines from Addison's Cato:
"Here will I hold. If there's a power above us
(And that there is, all nature cries aloud
Thro' all her works), He must delight in virtue;
And that which he delights in must be happy."
Another from Cicero,
"O vitae Philosophia dux! O virtutum indagatrix expultrixque vitiorum! Unus dies, bene et ex præceptis tuis actus, peccanti immortalitati est anteponendus."
Another from the Proverbs of Solomon, speaking of wisdom or virtue:
"Length of days is in her right hand, and in her left hand riches and honor. Her ways are ways of pleasantness, and all her paths are peace." iii. 16, 17.

And conceiving God to be the fountain of wisdom, I thought it right and necessary to solicit his assistance for obtaining it; to this end I formed the following little prayer, which was prefixed to my tables of examination, for daily use.

"O powerful Goodness! bountiful Father! merciful Guide! Increase in me that wisdom which discovers my truest interest. Strengthen my resolutions to perform what that wisdom dictates. Accept my kind offices to thy other children as the only return in my power for thy continual favors to me."

I used also sometimes a little prayer which I took from Thomson's Poems, viz.:
"Father of light and life, thou Good Supreme!
O teach me what is good; teach me Thyself!
Save me from folly, vanity, and vice,
From every low pursuit; and fill my soul
With knowledge, conscious peace, and virtue pure;
Sacred, substantial, never-fading bliss!"

The precept of Order requiring that every part of my business should have its allotted time, one page in my little book contained the following scheme of employment for the twenty-four hours of a natural day. The Morning. Question: What good shall I do this day? Rise, wash, and address day's business, and take the resolution of the day: prosecute the present study, and breakfast. Noon. Read, or overlook my accounts, and dine. Work. Evening. Put things in their places. Supper. Music or diversion, or conversation. Examination of the day. What good have I done today?

    I entered upon the execution of this plan for self-examination, and continued it with occasional intermissions for some time. I was surprised to find myself so much fuller of faults than I had imagined; but I had the satisfaction of seeing them diminish. To avoid the trouble of renewing now and then my little book, which, by scraping out the marks on the paper of old faults to make room for new ones in a new course, became full of holes, I transferred my tables and precepts to the ivory leaves of a memorandum book, on which the lines were drawn with red ink, that made a durable stain, and on those lines I marked my faults with a black-lead pencil, which marks I could easily wipe out with a wet sponge. After a while I went through one course only in a year, and afterward only one in several years, till at length I omitted them entirely, being employed in voyages and business abroad, with a multiplicity of affairs that interfered; but I always carried my little book with me.

    My scheme of Order gave me the most trouble; and I found that, tho' it might be practicable where a man's business was such as to leave him the disposition of his time, that of a journeyman printer, for instance, it was not possible to be exactly observed by a master, who must mix with the world, and often receive people of business at their own hours. Order, too, with regard to places for things, papers, etc., I found extremely difficult to acquire. I had not been early accustomed to it, and, having an exceeding good memory, I was not so sensible of the inconvenience attending want of method. This article, therefore, cost me so much painful attention, and my faults in it vexed me so much, and I made so little progress in amendment, and had such frequent relapses, that I was almost ready to give up the attempt, and content myself with a faulty character in that respect, like the man who, in buying an ax of a smith, my neighbour, desired to have the whole of its surface as bright as the edge. The smith consented to grind it bright for him if he would turn the wheel; he turned, while the smith pressed the broad face of the ax hard and heavily on the stone, which made the turning of it very fatiguing. The man came every now and then from the wheel to see how the work went on, and at length would take his ax as it was, without farther grinding. "No," said the smith, "turn on, turn on; we shall have it bright by-and-by; as yet, it is only speckled." "Yes," says the man, "but I think I like a speckled ax best." And I believe this may have been the case with many, who, having, for want of some such means as I employed, found the difficulty of obtaining good and breaking bad habits in other points of vice and virtue, have given up the struggle, and concluded that "a speckled ax was best"; for something, that pretended to be reason, was every now and then suggesting to me that such extreme nicety as I exacted of myself might be a kind of foppery in morals, which, if it were known, would make me ridiculous; that a perfect character might be attended with the inconvenience of being envied and hated;

and that a benevolent man should allow a few faults in himself, to keep his friends in countenance.

In truth, I found myself incorrigible with respect to Order; and now I am grown old, and my memory bad, I feel very sensibly the want of it. But, on the whole, tho' I never arrived at the perfection I had been so ambitious of obtaining, but fell far short of it, yet I was, by the endeavor, a better and a happier man than I otherwise should have been if I had not attempted it; as those who aim at perfect writing by imitating the engraved copies, tho' they never reach the wished-for excellence of those copies, their hand is mended by the endeavor, and is tolerable while it continues fair and legible.

It may be well my posterity should be informed that to this little artifice, with the blessing of God, their ancestor owed the constant felicity of his life, down to his 79th year, in which this is written. What reverses may attend the remainder is in the hand of Providence; but, if they arrive, the reflection on past happiness enjoyed ought to help his bearing them with more resignation. To Temperance he ascribes his long-continued health, and what is still left to him of a good constitution; to Industry and Frugality, the early easiness of his circumstances and acquisition of his fortune, with all that knowledge that enabled him to be a useful citizen, and obtained for him some degree of reputation among the learned; to Sincerity and Justice, the confidence of his country, and the honorable employs it conferred upon him; and to the joint influence of the whole mass of the virtues, even in the imperfect state he was able to acquire them, all that evenness of temper, and that cheerfulness in conversation, which makes his company still sought for, and agreeable even to his younger acquaintance. I hope, therefore, that some of my descendants may follow the example and reap the benefit.

It will be remarked that, tho' my scheme was not wholly without religion, there was in it no mark of any of the distinguishing tenets of any particular sect. I had purposely avoided them; for, being fully persuaded of the utility and excellency of my method, and that it might be serviceable to people in all religions, and intending some time or other to publish it, I would not have anything in it that should prejudice anyone, of any sect, against it. I purposed writing a little comment on each virtue, in which I would have shown the advantages of possessing it, and the mischiefs attending its opposite vice; and I should have called my book The Art of Virtue, because it would have shown the means and manner of obtaining virtue, which would have distinguished it from the mere exhortation to be good, that does not instruct and indicate the means, but is like the apostle's man of verbal charity, who only without showing to the naked and hungry how or where they might get clothes or victuals, exhorted them to be fed and clothed.—James ii. 15, 16.

But it so happened that my intention of writing and publishing this comment was never fulfilled. I did, indeed, from time to time, put down short hints of the sentiments, reasonings, etc., to be made use of in it, some of which I have still by me; but the necessary close attention to private business in the earlier part of my life, and public business since, have occasioned my postponing it; for, it being connected in my mind with a great and extensive project, that required the whole man to execute, and which an unforeseen succession of em-employs prevented my attending to, it has hitherto remained unfinished.

In this piece it was my design to explain and enforce this doctrine, that vicious actions are not hurtful because they are forbidden, but forbidden because they are hurtful, the nature of man alone considered; that it was, therefore, everyone's interest to be virtuous who wished to be happy even in this world; and I should, from this circumstance (there being always in the world a number of rich merchants, nobility, states, and princes, who have need of honest instruments for the management of their affairs, and such being so rare), have endeavored to convince young persons that no qualities were so likely to make a poor man's fortune as those of probity and integrity.

My list of virtues contained at first but twelve; but a Quaker friend having kindly informed me that I was generally thought proud; that my pride showed itself frequently in conversation; that I was not content with being in the right when discussing any point, but was overbearing, and rather insolent, of which he convinced me by mentioning several instances; I determined endeavoring to cure myself, if I could, of this vice or folly among the rest, and I added Humility to my list, giving an extensive meaning to the word.

I cannot boast of much success in acquiring the reality of this virtue, but I had a good deal with regard to the appearance of it. I made it a rule to forbear all direct contradiction to the sentiments of others, and all positive assertion of my own. I even forbid myself, agreeably to the old laws of our Junto, the use of every word or expression in the language that imported a fixed opinion, such as certainly, undoubtedly, etc., and I adopted, instead of them, I conceive, I apprehend, or I imagine a thing to be so or so; or it so appears to me at present. When another asserted something that I thought an error, I denied myself the pleasure of contradicting him abruptly, and of showing immediately some absurdity in his proposition; and in answering I began by observing that in certain cases or circumstances his opinion would be right, but in the present case there appeared or seemed to me some difference, etc. I soon found the advantage of this change in my manner; the conversations I engaged in went on more pleasantly. The modest way in which I proposed my opinions procured them a readier reception and less contradiction; I had less mortification when I was found to be in the wrong, and I more easily prevailed with others to give up their mistakes and join with me when I happened to be in the right.

And this mode, which I at first put on with some violence to natural inclination, became at length so easy, and so habitual to me, that perhaps for these fifty years past no one has ever heard a dogmatical expression escape me. And to this habit (after my character of integrity) I think it principally owing that I had early so much weight with my fellow-citizens when I proposed new institutions, or alterations in the old, and so much influence in public councils when I became a member; for I was but a bad speaker, never eloquent, subject to much hesitation in my choice of words, hardly correct in language, and yet I generally carried my points.

In reality, there is, perhaps, no one of our natural passions so hard to subdue as pride. Disguise it, struggle with it, beat it down, stifle it, mortify it as much as one pleases, it is still alive, and will every now and then peep out and show itself; you will see it, perhaps, often in this history; for, even if I could conceive that I had completely overcome it, I should probably be proud of my humility.

[Thus far written at Passy, 1784.]

["I am now about to write at home, August, 1788, but cannot have the help expected from my papers, many of them being lost in the war. I have, however, found the following."]

Having mentioned a great and extensive project which I had conceived, it seems proper that some account should be here given of that project and its object. Its first rise in my mind appears in the following little paper, accidentally preserved, viz.:

Observations on my reading history, in Library, May 19th, 1731.

"That the great affairs of the world, the wars, revolutions, etc., are carried on and effected by parties.

"That the view of these parties is their present general interest, or what they take to be such.

"That the different views of these different parties occasion all confusion.

"That while a party is carrying on a general design, each man has his particular private interest in view.

"That as soon as a party has gained its general point, each member becomes intent upon his particular interest; which, thwarting others, breaks that party into divisions, and occasions more confusion.

"That few in public affairs act from a mere view of the good of their country, whatever they may pretend; and, tho' their actings bring real good to their country, yet men primarily considered that their own and their country's interest was united, and did not act from a principle of benevolence.

"That fewer still, in public affairs, act with a view to the good of mankind.

"There seems to me at present to be great occasion for raising a United Party for Virtue, by forming the virtuous and good men of all nations into a regular body, to be governed by suitable good and wise rules, which good and wise men may probably be more unanimous in their obedience to, than common people are to common laws.

"I at present think that whoever attempts this aright, and is well qualified, cannot fail of pleasing God, and of meeting with success.

B. F."

Revolving this project in my mind, as to be undertaken hereafter, when my circumstances should afford me the necessary leisure, I put down from time to time, on pieces of paper, such thoughts as occurred to me respecting it. Most of these are lost; but I find one purporting to be the substance of an intended creed, containing, as I thought, the essentials of every known religion, and being free of everything that might shock the professors of any religion. It is expressed in these words, viz.:

"That there is one God, who made all things.

"That he governs the world by his providence.

"That he ought to be worshiped by adoration, prayer, and thanksgiving.

"But that the most acceptable service of God is doing good to man.

"That the soul is immortal.

"And that God will certainly reward virtue and punish vice, either here or hereafter."

My ideas at that time were, that the sect should be begun and spread at first among young and single men only; that each person to be initiated should not only declare his assent to such creed, but should have exercised himself with the thirteen weeks' examination and practice of the virtues, as in the before mentioned model; that the existence of such a society should be kept a secret, till it was become considerable, to prevent solicitations for the admission of improper persons, but that the members should each of them search among his acquaintance for ingenuous, well-disposed youths, to whom, with prudent caution, the scheme should be gradually communicated; that the members should engage to afford their advice, assistance, and support to each other in promoting one another's interests, business, and advancement in life; that, for distinction, we should be called The Society of the Free and Easy: free, as being, by the general practice and habit of the virtues, free from the dominion of vice; and particularly by the practice of industry and frugality, free from debt, which exposes a man to confinement, and a species of slavery to his creditors.

This is as much as I can now recollect of the project, except that I communicated it in part to two young men, who adopted it with some enthusiasm; but my then narrow circumstances, and the necessity I was under of sticking close to my business, occasioned my postponing the further prosecution of it at that time; and my multifarious occupations, public and private, induced me to continue postponing, so that it has been omitted till I have no longer strength or activity left sufficient for such an enterprise; though I am still of opinion that it was a practicable scheme, and might have been very useful, by forming a great number of good citizens; and I was not discouraged by the seeming magnitude of the undertaking, as I have always thought that one man of tolerable abilities may work great changes, and accomplish great affairs among mankind, if he first forms a good plan, and, cutting off all amusements or other employments that would divert his attention, makes the execution of that same plan his sole study and business.

X: Poor Richard's Almanac and Other Activities

IN 1732 I first published my Almanack, under the name of Richard Saunders; it was continued by me about twenty-five years, commonly called Poor Richard's Almanac. I endeavored to make it both entertaining and useful, and it accordingly came to be in such demand, that I reaped considerable profit from it, vending annually near ten thousand. And observing that it was generally read, scarce any neighborhood in the province being without it, I considered it as a proper vehicle for conveying instruction among the common people, who bought scarcely any other books; I therefore filled all the little spaces that occurred between the remarkable days in the calendar with proverbial sentences, chiefly such as inculcated industry and frugality, as the means of procuring wealth, and thereby securing virtue; it being more difficult for a man in want, to act always honestly, as, to use here one of those proverbs, it is hard for an empty sack to stand upright.

These proverbs, which contained the wisdom of many ages and nations, I assembled and formed into a connected discourse prefixed to the Almanack of 1757, as the harangue of a wise old man to the people attending an auction. The bringing all these scattered councils thus into a focus enabled them to make greater impression. The piece, being universally approved, was copied in all the newspapers of the Continent; reprinted in Britain on a broadside, to be stuck up in houses; two translations were made of it in French, and great numbers bought by the clergy and gentry, to distribute gratis among their poor parishioners and tenants. In Pennsylvania, as it discouraged useless expense in foreign superfluities, some thought it had its share of influence in producing that growing plenty of money which was observable for several years after its publication.

I considered my newspaper, also, as another means of communicating instruction, and in that view frequently reprinted in it extracts from the Spectator, and other moral writers; and sometimes published little pieces of my own, which had been first composed for reading in our Junto. Of these are a Socratic dialogue, tending to prove that, whatever might be his parts and abilities, a vicious man could not properly be called a man of sense; and a discourse on self-denial, showing that virtue was not secure till its practice became a habitude, and was free from the opposition of contrary inclinations. These may be found in the papers about the beginning of 1735.

In the conduct of my newspaper, I carefully excluded all libeling and personal abuse, which is of late years become so disgraceful to our country. Whenever I was solicited to insert anything of that kind, and the writers pleaded, as they generally did, the liberty of the press, and that a newspaper was like a stage-coach, in which anyone who would pay had a right to a place, my answer was, that I would print the piece separately if desired, and the author might have as many copies as he pleased to distribute himself, but that I would not take upon me to spread his detraction; and that, having contracted with my subscribers to furnish them with what might be either useful or entertaining, I could not fill their papers with private altercation, in which they had no concern, without doing them manifest injustice. Now, many of our printers make no scruple of gratifying the malice of individuals by false accusations of the fairest characters among ourselves, augmenting animosity even to the producing of duels; and are, moreover, so indiscreet as to print scurrilous reflections on the government of neighboring states, and even on the conduct of our best national allies, which may be attended with the most pernicious consequences. These things I mention as a caution to young printers, and that they may be encouraged not to pollute their presses and disgrace their profession by such infamous practices, but refuse steadily, as they may see by my example that such a course of conduct will not, on the whole, be injurious to their interests.

In 1733 I sent one of my journeymen to Charleston, South Carolina, where a printer was wanting. I furnished him with a press and letters, on an agreement of partnership, by which I was to receive one-third of the profits of the business, paying one-third of the expense. He was a man of learning, and honest but ignorant in matters of account; and, tho' he sometimes made me remittances, I could get no account from him, nor any satisfactory state of our partnership while he lived. On his decease, the business was continued by his widow, who, being born and bred in Holland, where, as I have been informed, the knowledge of accounts makes a part of female education, she not only sent me as clear a state as she could find of the transactions past, but continued to account with the greatest regularity and exactness every quarter afterwards, and managed the business with such success, that she not only brought up reputably a family of children, but, at the expiration of the term, was able to purchase of me the printing-house, and establish her son in it.

I mention this affair chiefly for the sake of recommending that branch of education for our young females, as likely to be of more use to them and their children, in case of widowhood, than either music or dancing, by preserving them from losses by imposition of crafty men, and enabling them to continue, perhaps, a profitable mercantile house, with established correspondence, till a son is grown up fit to undertake and go on with it, to the lasting advantage and enriching of the family.

About the year 1734 there arrived among us from Ireland a young Presbyterian preacher, named Hemphill, who delivered with a good voice, and apparently extempore, most excellent discourses, which drew together considerable numbers of different persuasions, who joined in admiring them. Among the rest, I became one of his constant hearers, his sermons pleasing me, as they had little of the dogmatical kind, but inculcated strongly the practice of virtue, or what in the religious stile are called good works. Those, however, of our congregation, who considered themselves as orthodox Presbyterians, disapproved his doctrine, and were joined by most of the old clergy, who arraigned him of heterodoxy before the synod, in order to have him silenced. I became his zealous partisan, and contributed all I could to raise a party in his favor, and we combated for him awhile with some hopes of success. There was much scribbling pro and con upon the occasion; and finding that, tho' an elegant preacher, he was but a poor writer, I lent him my pen and wrote for him two or three pamphlets, and one piece in the Gazette of April, 1735. Those pamphlets, as is generally the case with controversial writings, tho' eagerly read at the time, were soon out of vogue, and I question whether a single copy of them now exists.

During the contest an unlucky occurrence hurt his cause exceedingly. One of our adversaries having heard him preach a sermon that was much admired, thought he had somewhere read the sermon before, or at least a part of it. On search, he found that part quoted at length, in one of the British Reviews, from a discourse of Dr. Foster's. This detection gave many of our party disgust, who accordingly abandoned his cause, and occasioned our more speedy discomfiture in the synod. I stuck by him, however, as I rather approved his giving us good sermons composed by others, than bad ones of his own manufacture, tho' the latter was the practice of our common teachers. He afterward acknowledged to me that none of those he preached were his own; adding, that his memory was such as enabled him to retain and repeat any sermon after one reading only. On our defeat, he left us in search elsewhere of better fortune, and I quitted the congregation, never joining it after, tho' I continued many years my subscription for the support of its ministers.

I had begun in 1733 to study languages; I soon made myself so much a master of the French as to be able to read the books with ease. I then undertook the Italian. An acquaintance, who was also learning it, used often to tempt me to play chess with him. Finding this took up too much of the time I had to spare for study, I at length refused to play anymore, unless on this condition, that the victor in every game should have a right to impose a task, either in parts of the grammar to be got by heart, or in translations, etc., which tasks the vanquished was to perform upon honor, before our next meeting. As we played pretty equally, we thus beat one another into that language. I afterwards with a little painstaking, acquired as much of the Spanish as to read their books also.

I have already mentioned that I had only one year's instruction in a Latin school, and that when very young, after which I neglected that language entirely. But, when I had attained an acquaintance with the French, Italian, and Spanish, I was surprised to find, on looking over a Latin Testament, that I understood so much more of that language than I had imagined, which encouraged me to apply myself again to the study of it, and I met with more success, as those preceding languages had greatly smoothed my way.

From these circumstances, I have thought that there is some inconsistency in our common mode of teaching languages. We are told that it is proper to begin first with the Latin, and, having acquired that, it will be more easy to attain those modern languages which are derived from it; and yet we do not begin with the Greek, in order more easily to acquire the Latin. It is true that, if you can clamber and get to the top of a staircase without using the steps, you will more easily gain them in descending; but certainly, if you begin with the lowest you will with more ease ascend to the top; and I would therefore offer it to the consideration of those who superintend the education of our youth, whether, since many of those who begin with the Latin quit the same after spending some years without having made any great proficiency, and what they have learnt becomes almost useless, so that their time has been lost, it would not have been better to have begun with the French, proceeding to the Italian, etc.; for, tho', after spending the same time, they should quit the study of languages and never arrive at the Latin, they would, however, have acquired another tongue or two, that, being in modern use, might be serviceable to them in common life.

After ten years' absence from Boston, and having become easy in my circumstances, I made a journey thither to visit my relations, which I could not sooner well afford. In returning, I called at Newport to see my brother, then settled there with his printing-house. Our former differences were forgotten, and our meeting was very cordial and affectionate. He was fast declining in his health, and requested of me that, in case of his death, which he apprehended not far distant, I would take home his son, then but ten years of age, and bring him up to the printing business. This I accordingly performed, sending him a few years to school before I took him into the office. His mother carried on the business till he was grown up, when I assisted him with an assortment of new types, those of his father being in a manner worn out. Thus it was that I made my brother ample amends for the service I had deprived him of by leaving him so early.

Our former differences were forgotten, and our meeting was very cordial and affectionate

In 1736 I lost one of my sons, a fine boy of four years old, by the small-pox, taken in the common way. I long regretted bitterly, and still regret that I had not given it to him by inoculation. This I mention for the sake of parents who omit that operation, on the supposition that they should never forgive themselves if a child died under it; my example showing that the regret may be the same either way, and that, therefore, the safer should be chosen.

Our club, the Junto, was found so useful, and afforded such satisfaction to the members, that several were desirous of introducing their friends, which could not well be done without exceeding what we had settled as a convenient number, viz., twelve. We had from the beginning made it a rule to keep our institution a secret, which was pretty well observed; the intention was to avoid applications of improper persons for admittance, some of whom, perhaps, we might find it difficult to refuse. I was one of those who were against any addition to our number, but, instead of it, made in writing a proposal, that every member separately should endeavor to form a subordinate club, with the same rules respecting queries, etc., and without informing them of the connection with the Junto. The advantages proposed were, the improvement of so many more young citizens by the use of our institutions; our better acquaintance with the general sentiments of the inhabitants on any occasion, as the Junto member might propose what queries we should desire, and was to report to the Junto what passed in his separate club; the promotion of our particular interests in business by more extensive recommendation, and the increase of our influence in public affairs, and our power of doing good by spreading through the several clubs the sentiments of the Junto.

The project was approved, and every member undertook to form his club, but they did not all succeed. Five or six only were completed, which were called by different names, as the Vine, the Union, the Band, etc. They were useful to themselves, and afforded us a good deal of amusement, information, and instruction, besides answering, in some considerable degree, our views of influencing the public opinion on particular occasions, of which I shall give some instances in course of time as they happened.

My first promotion was my being chosen, in 1736, clerk of the General Assembly. The choice was made that year without opposition; but the year following, when I was again proposed (the choice, like that of the members, being annual), a new member made a long speech against me, in order to favor some other candidate. I was, however, chosen, which was the more agreeable to me, as, besides the pay for the immediate service as clerk, the place gave me a better opportunity of keeping up an interest among the members, which secured to me the business of printing the votes, laws, paper money, and other occasional jobs for the public, that, on the whole, were very profitable.

I therefore did not like the opposition of this new member, who was a gentleman of fortune and education, with talents that were likely to give him, in time, great influence in the House, which, indeed, afterwards happened. I did not, however, aim at gaining his favor by paying any servile respect to him, but, after some time, took this other method. Having heard that he had in his library a certain very scarce and curious book, I wrote a note to him, expressing my desire of perusing that book, and requesting he would do me the favor of lending it to me for a few days. He sent it immediately, and I returned it in about a week with another note, expressing strongly my sense of the favor. When we next met in the House, he spoke to me (which he had never done before), and with great civility; and he ever after manifested a readiness to serve me on all occasions, so that we became great friends, and our friendship continued to his death. This is another instance of the truth of an old maxim I had learned, which says, "He that has once done you a kindness will be more ready to do you another, than he whom you yourself have obliged." And it shows how much more profitable it is prudently to remove, than to resent, return, and continue inimical proceedings.

In 1737, Colonel Spotswood, late governor of Virginia, and then postmaster-general, being dissatisfied with the conduct of his deputy at Philadelphia, respecting some negligence in rendering, and inexactitude of his accounts, took from him the commission and offered it to me. I accepted it readily, and found it of great advantage; for, tho' the salary was small, it facilitated the correspondence that improved my newspaper, increased the number demanded, as well as the advertisements to be inserted, so that it came to afford me a considerable income. My old competitor's newspaper declined proportionately, and I was satisfied without retaliating his refusal, while postmaster, to permit my papers being carried by the riders. Thus he suffered greatly from his neglect in due accounting; and I mention it as a lesson to those young men who may be employed in managing affairs for others, that they should always render accounts, and make remittances, with great clearness and punctuality. The character of observing such a conduct is the most powerful of all recommendations to new employments and increase of business.

XI: Interest in Public Affairs

I BEGAN now to turn my thoughts a little to public affairs, beginning, however, with small matters. The city watch was one of the first things that I conceived to want regulation. It was managed by the constables of the respective wards in turn; the constable warned a number of housekeepers to attend him for the night. Those who chose never to attend, paid him six shillings a year to be excused, which was supposed to be for hiring substitutes, but was, in reality, much more than was necessary for that purpose, and made the constableship a place of profit; and the constable, for a little drink, often got such ragamuffins about him as a watch, that respectable housekeepers did not choose to mix with. Walking the rounds, too, was often neglected, and most of the nights spent in tippling. I thereupon wrote a paper to be read in Junto, representing these irregularities, but insisting more particularly on the inequality of this six-shilling tax of the constables, respecting the circumstances of those who paid it, since a poor widow housekeeper, all whose property to be guarded by the watch did not perhaps exceed the value of fifty pounds, paid as much as the wealthiest merchant, who had thousands of pounds' worth of goods in his stores.

On the whole, I proposed as a more effectual watch, the hiring of proper men to serve constantly in that business; and as a more equitable way of supporting the charge, the levying a tax that should be proportioned to the property. This idea, being approved by the Junto, was communicated to the other clubs, but as arising in each of them; and though the plan was not immediately carried into execution, yet, by preparing the minds of people for the change, it paved the way for the law obtained a few years after, when the members of our clubs were grown into more influence.

About this time I wrote a paper (first to be read in Junto, but it was afterward published) on the different accidents and carelessnesses by which houses were set on fire, with cautions against them, and means proposed of avoiding them. This was much spoken of as a useful piece, and gave rise to a project, which soon followed it, of forming a company for the more ready extinguishing of fires, and mutual assistance in removing and securing of goods when in danger. Associates in this scheme were presently found, amounting to thirty. Our articles of agreement obliged every member to keep always in good order, and fit for use, a certain number of leather buckets, with strong bags and baskets (for packing and transporting of goods), which were to be brought to every fire; and we agreed to meet once a month and spend a social evening together, in discoursing and communicating such ideas as occurred to us upon the subjects of fires, as might be useful in our conduct on such occasions.

The utility of this institution soon appeared, and many more desiring to be admitted than we thought convenient for one company, they were advised to form another, which was accordingly done; and this went on, one new company being formed after another, till they became so numerous as to include most of the inhabitants who were men of property; and now, at the time of my writing this, tho' upward of fifty years since its establishment, that which I first formed, called the Union Fire Company, still subsists and flourishes, tho' the first members are all deceased but myself and one, who is older by a year than I am. The small fines that have been paid by members for absence at the monthly meetings have been applied to the purchase of fire-engines, ladders, fire-hooks, and other useful implements for each company, so that I question whether there is a city in the world better provided with the means of putting a stop to beginning conflagrations; and, in fact, since these institutions, the city has never lost by fire more than one or two houses at a time, and the flames have often been extinguished before the house in which they began has been half consumed.

In 1739 arrived among us from Ireland the Reverend Mr. Whitefield, who had made himself remarkable there as an itinerant preacher. He was at first permitted to preach in some of our churches; but the clergy, taking a dislike to him, soon refused him their pulpits, and he was obliged to preach in the fields. The multitudes of all sects and denominations that attended his sermons were enormous, and it was matter of speculation to me, who was one of the number, to observe the extraordinary influence of his oratory on his hearers, and how much they admired and respected him, notwithstanding his common abuse of them, by assuring them they were naturally half beasts and half devils. It was wonderful to see the change soon made in the manners of our inhabitants. From being thoughtless or indifferent about religion, it seemed as if all the world were growing religious, so that one could not walk through the town in an evening without hearing psalms sung in different families of every street.

And it being found inconvenient to assemble in the open air, subject to its inclemencies, the building of a house to meet in was no sooner proposed, and persons appointed to receive contributions, but sufficient sums were soon received to procure the ground and erect the building, which was one hundred feet long and seventy broad, about the size of Westminster Hall; and the work was carried on with such spirit as to be finished in a much shorter time than could have been expected. Both house and ground were vested in trustees, expressly for the use of any preacher of any religious persuasion who might desire to say something to the people at Philadelphia; the design in building not being to accommodate any particular sect, but the inhabitants in general; so that even if the Mufti of Constantinople were to send a missionary to preach Mohammedanism to us, he would find a pulpit at his service.

Mr. Whitefield, in leaving us, went preaching all the way through the colonies to Georgia. The settlement of that province had lately been begun, but, instead of being made with hardy, industrious husbandmen, accustomed to labour, the only people fit for such an enterprise, it was with families of broken shop-keepers and other insolvent debtors, many of indolent and idle habits, taken out of the jails, who, being set down in the woods, unqualified for clearing land, and unable to endure the hardships of a new settlement, perished in numbers, leaving many helpless children unprovided for. The sight of their miserable situation inspired the benevolent heart of Mr. Whitefield with the idea of building an Orphan House there, in which they might be supported and educated. Returning northward, he preached up this charity, and made large collections, for his eloquence had a wonderful power over the hearts and purses of his hearers, of which I myself was an instance.

I did not disapprove of the design, but, as Georgia was then destitute of materials and workmen, and it was proposed to send them from Philadelphia at a great expense, I thought it would have been better to have built the house here, and brought the children to it. This I advised; but he was resolute in his first project, rejected my counsel, and I therefore refused to contribute. I happened soon after to attend one of his sermons, in the course of which I perceived he intended to finish with a collection, and I silently resolved he should get nothing from me. I had in my pocket a handful of copper money, three or four silver dollars, and five pistoles in gold. As he proceeded I began to soften, and concluded to give the coppers. Another stroke of his oratory made me ashamed of that, and determined me to give the silver; and he finished so admirably, that I emptied my pocket wholly into the collector's dish, gold and all. At this sermon there was also one of our club, who, being of my sentiments respecting the building in Georgia, and suspecting a collection might be intended, had, by precaution, emptied his pockets before he came from home. Towards the conclusion of the discourse, however, he felt a strong desire to give, and applied to a neighbour who stood near him, to borrow some money for the purpose. The application was unfortunately [made] to perhaps the only man in the company who had the firmness not to be affected by the preacher. His answer was, "At any other time, Friend Hopkinson, I would lend to thee freely; but not now, for thee seems to be out of thy right senses."

Some of Mr. Whitefield's enemies affected to suppose that he would apply these collections to his own private emolument; but I, who was intimately acquainted with him (being employed in printing his Sermons and Journals, etc.), never had the least suspicion of his integrity, but am to this day decidedly of opinion that he was in all his conduct a perfectly honest man; and methinks my testimony in his favor ought to have the more weight, as we had no religious connection. He used, indeed, sometimes to pray for my conversion, but never had the satisfaction of believing that his prayers were heard. Ours was a mere civil friendship, sincere on both sides, and lasted to his death.

The following instance will show something of the terms on which we stood. Upon one of his arrivals from England at Boston, he wrote to me that he should come soon to Philadelphia, but knew not where he could lodge when there, as he understood his old friend and host, Mr. Benezet was removed to Germantown. My answer was, "You know my house; if you can make shift with its scanty accommodations, you will be most heartily welcome." He replied, that if I made that kind offer for Christ's sake, I should not miss of a reward. And I returned, "Don't let me be mistaken; it was not for Christ's sake, but for your sake." One of our common acquaintance jocosely remarked, that, knowing it to be the custom of the saints, when they received any favor, to shift the burden of the obligation from off their own shoulders, and place it in heaven, I had contrived to fix it on earth.

The last time I saw Mr. Whitefield was in London, when he consulted me about his Orphan House concern, and his purpose of appropriating it to the establishment of a college.

He had a loud and clear voice, and articulated his words and sentences so perfectly, that he might be heard and understood at a great distance, especially as his auditories, however numerous, observed the most exact silence. He preached one evening from the top of the Courthouse steps, which are in the middle of Market-street, and on the west side of Second-street, which crosses it at right angles. Both streets were filled with his hearers to a considerable distance. Being among the hindmost in Market-street, I had the curiosity to learn how far he could be heard, by retiring backwards down the street towards the river; and I found his voice distinct till I came near Front-street, when some noise in that street obscured it. Imagining then a semicircle, of which my distance should be the radius, and that it were filled with auditors, to each of whom I allowed two square feet, I computed that he might well be heard by more than thirty thousand. This reconciled me to the newspaper accounts of his having preached to twenty-five thousand people in the fields, and to the ancient histories of generals haranguing whole armies, of which I had sometimes doubted.

By hearing him often, I came to distinguish easily between sermons newly composed, and those which he had often preached in the course of his travels. His delivery of the latter was so improved by frequent repetitions that every accent, every emphasis, every modulation of voice, was so perfectly well turned and well placed, that, without being interested in the subject, one could not help being pleased with the discourse; a pleasure of much the same kind with that received from an excellent piece of music. This is an advantage itinerant preachers have over those who are stationary, as the latter cannot well improve their delivery of a sermon by so many rehearsals.

His writing and printing from time to time gave great advantage to his enemies; unguarded expressions, and even erroneous opinions, delivered in preaching, might have been afterwards explained or qualified by supposing others that might have accompanied them, or they might have been denied; but litera scripta manet. Critics attacked his writings violently, and with so much appearance of reason as to diminish the number of his votaries and prevent their increase; so that I am of opinion if he had never written anything, he would have left behind him a much more numerous and important sect, and his reputation might in that case have been still growing, even after his death, as there being nothing of his writing on which to found a censure and give him a lower character, his proselytes would be left at liberty to feign for him as great a variety of excellences as their enthusiastic admiration might wish him to have possessed.

My business was now continually augmenting, and my circumstances growing daily easier, my newspaper having become very profitable, as being for a time almost the only one in this and the neighboring provinces. I experienced, too, the truth of the observation, "that after getting the first hundred pound, it is more easy to get the second," money itself being of a prolific nature.

The partnership at Carolina having succeeded, I was encouraged to engage in others, and to promote several of my workmen, who had behaved well, by establishing them with printing-houses in different colonies, on the same terms with that in Carolina. Most of them did well, being enabled at the end of our term, six years, to purchase the types of me and go on working for themselves, by which means several families were raised. Partnerships often finish in quarrels; but I was happy in this, that mine were all carried on and ended amicably, owing, I think, a good deal to the precaution of having very explicitly settled, in our articles, everything to be done by or expected from each partner, so that there was nothing to dispute, which precaution I would therefore recommend to all who enter into partnerships; for, whatever esteem partners may have for, and confidence in each other at the time of the contract, little jealousies and disgusts may arise, with ideas of inequality in the care and burden of the business, etc., which are attended often with breach of friendship and of the connection, perhaps with lawsuits and other disagreeable consequences.

XII: Defense of the Province

I HAD, on the whole, abundant reason to be satisfied with my being established in Pennsylvania. There were, however, two, things that I regretted, there being no provision for defense, nor for a complete education of youth; no militia, nor any college. I therefore, in 1743, drew up a proposal for establishing an academy; and at that time, thinking the Reverend Mr. Peters, who was out of employ, a fit person to superintend such an institution, I communicated the project to him; but he, having more profitable views in the service of the proprietaries, which succeeded, declined the undertaking; and, not knowing another at that time suitable for such a trust, I let the scheme lie awhile dormant. I succeeded better the next year, 1744, in proposing and establishing a Philosophical Society. The paper I wrote for that purpose will be found among my writings, when collected.

With respect to defense, Spain having been several years at war against Great Britain, and being at length joined by France, which brought us into great danger; and the labored and long-continued endeavor of our governor, Thomas, to prevail with our Quaker Assembly to pass a militia law, and make other provisions for the security of the province, having proved abortive, I determined to try what might be done by a voluntary association of the people. To promote this, I first wrote and published a pamphlet, entitled Plain Truth, in which I stated our defenseless situation in strong lights, with the necessity of union and discipline for our defense, and promised to propose in a few days an association, to be generally signed for that purpose. The pamphlet had a sudden and surprising effect. I was called upon for the instrument of association, and having settled the draft of it with a few friends, I appointed a meeting of the citizens in the large building before mentioned. The house was pretty full; I had prepared a number of printed copies, and provided pens and ink dispersed all over the room. I harangued them a little on the subject, read the paper, and explained it, and then distributed the copies, which were eagerly signed, not the least objection being made.

When the company separated, and the papers were collected, we found above twelve hundred hands; and, other copies being dispersed in the country, the subscribers amounted at length to upward of ten thousand. These all furnished themselves as soon as they could with arms, formed themselves into companies and regiments, chose their own officers, and met every week to be instructed in the manual exercise, and other parts of military discipline. The women, by subscriptions among themselves, provided silk colors, which they presented to the companies, painted with different devices and mottos, which I supplied.

The officers of the companies composing the Philadelphia regiment, being met, chose me for their colonel; but, conceiving myself unfit, I declined that station, and recommended Mr. Lawrence, a fine person, and man of influence, who was accordingly appointed. I then proposed a lottery to defray the expense of building a battery below the town, and furnishing it with cannon. It filled expeditiously, and the battery was soon erected, the merlons being framed of logs and filled with earth. We bought some old cannon from Boston, but, these not being sufficient, we wrote to England for more, soliciting, at the same time, our proprietaries for some assistance, tho' without much expectation of obtaining it.

Meanwhile, Colonel Lawrence, William Allen, Abram Taylor, Esqr., and myself were sent to New York by the associators, commission's to borrow some cannon of Governor Clinton. He at first refused us peremptorily; but at dinner with his council, where there was great drinking of Madeira wine, as the custom of that place then was, he softened by degrees, and said he would lend us six. After a few more bumpers he advanced to ten; and at length he very good-naturedly conceded eighteen. They were fine cannon, eighteen-pounders, with their carriages, which we soon transported and mounted on our battery, where the associators kept a nightly guard while the war lasted, and among the rest I regularly took my turn of duty there as a common soldier.

My activity in these operations was agreeable to the governor and council; they took me into confidence, and I was consulted by them in every measure wherein their concurrence was thought useful to the association. Calling in the aid of religion, I proposed to them the proclaiming a fast, to promote reformation, and implore the blessing of Heaven on our undertaking. They embraced the motion; but, as it was the first fast ever thought of in the province, the secretary had no precedent from which to draw the proclamation. My education in New England, where a fast is proclaimed every year, was here of some advantage: I drew it in the accustomed stile, it was translated into German, printed in both languages, and divulged through the province. This gave the clergy of the different sects an opportunity of influencing their congregations to join in the association, and it would probably have been general among all but Quakers if the peace had not soon intervened.

It was thought by some of my friends that, by my activity in these affairs, I should offend that sect, and thereby lose my interest in the Assembly of the province, where they formed a great majority. A young gentleman who had likewise some friends in the House, and wished to succeed me as their clerk, acquainted me that it was decided to displace me at the next election; and he, therefore, in good will, advised me to resign, as more consistent with my honor than being turned out. My answer to him was, that I had read or heard of some public man who made it a rule never to ask for an office, and never to refuse one when offered to him. "I approve," says I, "of his rule, and will practice it with a small addition; I shall never ask, never refuse, nor ever resign an office. If they will have my office of clerk to dispose of to another, they shall take it from me. I will not, by giving it up, lose my right of sometime or other making reprisals on my adversaries." I heard, however, no more of this; I was chosen again unanimously as usual at the next election. Possibly, as they disliked my late intimacy with the members of council, who had joined the governors in all the disputes about military preparations, with which the House had long been harassed, they might have been pleased if I would voluntarily have left them;

but they did not care to displace me on account merely of my zeal for the association, and they could not well give another reason.

Indeed I had some cause to believe that the defense of the country was not disagreeable to any of them, provided they were not required to assist in it. And I found that a much greater number of them than I could have imagined, tho' against offensive war, were clearly for the defensive. Many pamphlets pro and con were published on the subject, and some by good Quakers, in favor of defense, which I believe convinced most of their younger people.

A transaction in our fire company gave me some insight into their prevailing sentiments. It had been proposed that we should encourage the scheme for building a battery by laying out the present stock, then about sixty pounds, in tickets of the lottery. By our rules, no money could be disposed of till the next meeting after the proposal. The company consisted of thirty members, of which twenty-two were Quakers, and eight only of other persuasions. We eight punctually attended the meeting; but, tho' we thought that some of the Quakers would join us, we were by no means sure of a majority. Only one Quaker, Mr. James Morris, appeared to oppose the measure. He expressed much sorrow that it had ever been proposed, as he said Friends were all against it, and it would create such discord as might break up the company. We told him that we saw no reason for that; we were the minority, and if Friends were against the measure, and outvoted us, we must and should, agreeably to the usage of all societies, submit. When the hour for business arrived it was moved to put the vote; he allowed we might then do it by the rules, but, as he could assure us that a number of members intended to be present for the purpose of opposing it, it would be but candid to allow a little time for their appearing.

While we were disputing this, a waiter came to tell me two gentlemen below desired to speak with me. I went down, and found they were two of our Quaker members. They told me there were eight of them assembled at a tavern just by; that they were determined to come and vote with us if there should be occasion, which they hoped would not be the case, and desired we would not call for their assistance if we could do without it, as their voting for such a measure might embroil them with their elders and friends. Being thus secure of a majority, I went up, and after a little seeming hesitation, agreed to a delay of another hour. This Mr. Morris allowed to be extremely fair. Not one of his opposing friends appeared, at which he expressed great surprise; and, at the expiration of the hour, we carried the resolution eight to one; and as, of the twenty-two Quakers, eight were ready to vote with us, and thirteen, by their absence, manifested that they were not inclined to oppose the measure, I afterward estimated the proportion of Quakers sincerely against defense as one to twenty-one only; for these were all regular members of that society, and in good reputation among them, and had due notice of what was proposed at that meeting.

The honorable and learned Mr. Logan, who had always been of that sect, was one who wrote an address to them, declaring his approbation of defensive war, and supporting his opinion by many strong arguments. He put into my hands sixty pounds to be laid out in lottery tickets for the battery, with directions to apply what prizes might be drawn wholly to that service. He told me the following anecdote of his old master, William Penn, respecting defense. He came over from England, when a young man, with that proprietary, and as his secretary. It was war-time, and their ship was chased by an armed vessel, supposed to be an enemy. Their captain prepared for defense; but told William Penn, and his company of Quakers, that he did not expect their assistance, and they might retire into the cabin, which they did, except James Logan, who chose to stay upon deck, and was quartered to a gun. The supposed enemy proved a friend, so there was no fighting; but when the secretary went down to communicate the intelligence, William Penn rebuked him severely for staying upon deck, and undertaking to assist in defending the vessel, contrary to the principles of Friends, especially as it had not been required by the captain. This reproof, being before all the company, piqued the secretary, who answered, "I being thy servant, why did thee not order me to come down? But thee was willing enough that I should stay and help to fight the ship when thee thought there was danger."

My being many years in the Assembly, the majority of which were constantly Quakers, gave me frequent opportunities of seeing the embarrassment given them by their principle against war, whenever application was made to them, by order of the crown, to grant aids for military purposes. They were unwilling to offend government, on the one hand, by a direct refusal; and their friends, the body of the Quakers, on the other, by compliance contrary to their principles; hence a variety of evasions to avoid complying, and modes of disguising the compliance when it became unavoidable. The common mode at last was, to grant money under the phrase of its being "for the king's use," and never to inquire how it was applied.

But, if the demand was not directly from the crown, that phrase was found not so proper, and some other was to be invented. As, when powder was wanting (I think it was for the garrison at Louisburg), and the government of New England solicited a grant of some from Pennsylvania, which was much urged on the House by Governor Thomas, they could not grant money to buy powder, because that was an ingredient of war; but they voted an aid to New England of three thousand pounds, to be put into the hands of the governor, and appropriated it for the purchasing of bread, flour, wheat or other grain. Some of the council, desirous of giving the House still further embarrassment, advised the governor not to accept provision, as not being the thing he had demanded; but he replied, "I shall take the money, for I understand very well their meaning; other grain is gunpowder," which he accordingly bought, and they never objected to it.

It was in allusion to this fact that, when in our fire company we feared the success of our proposal in favor of the lottery, and I had said to my friend Mr. Sing, one of our members, "If we fail, let us move the purchase of a fire-engine with the money; the Quakers can have no objection to that; and then, if you nominate me and I you as a committee for that purpose, we will buy a great gun, which is certainly a fire-engine." "I see," says he, "you have improved by being so long in the Assembly; your equivocal project would be just a match for their wheat or other grain."

These embarrassments that the Quakers suffered from having established and published it as one of their principles that no kind of war was lawful, and which, being once published, they could not afterwards, however they might change their minds, easily get rid of, reminds me of what I think a more prudent conduct in another sect among us, that of the Dunkers. I was acquainted with one of its founders, Michael Welfare, soon after it appeared. He complained to me that they were grievously calumniated by the zealots of other persuasions, and charged with abominable principles and practices to which they were utter strangers. I told him this had always been the case with new sects, and that, to put a stop to such abuse, I imagined it might be well to publish the articles of their belief, and the rules of their discipline. He said that it had been proposed among them, but not agreed to, for this reason: "When we were first drawn together as a society," says he, "it had pleased God to enlighten our minds so far as to see that some doctrines, which we once esteemed truths, were errors; and that others, which we had esteemed errors, were real truths. From time to time He has been pleased to afford us farther light, and our principles have been improving, and our errors diminishing. Now we are not sure that we are arrived at the end of this progression, and at the perfection of spiritual or theological knowledge; and we fear that, if we should once print our confession of faith, we should feel ourselves as if bound and confined by it, and perhaps be unwilling to receive further improvement, and our successors still more so, as conceiving what we their elders and founders had done, to be something sacred, never to be departed from."

This modesty in a sect is perhaps a singular instance in the history of mankind, every other sect supposing itself in possession of all truth, and that those who differ are so far in the wrong; like a man traveling in foggy weather, those at some distance before him on the road he sees wrapped up in the fog, as well as those behind him, and also the people in the fields on each side, but near him all appears clear, tho' in truth he is as much in the fog as any of them. To avoid this kind of embarrassment, the Quakers have of late years been gradually declining the public service in the Assembly and in the magistracy, choosing rather to quit their power than their principle.

In order of time, I should have mentioned before, that having, in 1742, invented an open stove for the better warming of rooms, and at the same time saving fuel, as the fresh air admitted was warmed in entering, I made a present of the model to Mr. Robert Grace, one of my early friends, who, having an iron-furnace, found the casting of the plates for these stoves a profitable thing, as they were growing in demand. To promote that demand, I wrote and published a pamphlet, entitled "An Account of the new-invented Pennsylvania Fireplaces; wherein their Construction and Manner of Operation is particularly explained; their Advantages above every other Method of warming Rooms demonstrated; and all Objections that have been raised against the Use of them answered and obviated," etc. This pamphlet had a good effect. Gov'r. Thomas was so pleased with the construction of this stove, as described in it, that he offered to give me a patent for the sole vending of them for a term of years; but I declined it from a principle which has ever weighed with me on such occasions, viz., That, as we enjoy great advantages from the inventions of others, we should be glad of an opportunity to serve others by any invention of ours; and this we should do freely and generously.

An ironmonger in London however, assuming a good deal of my pamphlet, and working it up into his own, and making some small changes in the machine, which rather hurt its operation, got a patent for it there, and made, as I was told, a little fortune by it. And this is not the only instance of patents taken out for my inventions by others, tho' not always with the same success, which I never contested, as having no desire of profiting by patents myself, and hating disputes. The use of these fireplaces in very many houses, both of this and the neighboring colonies, has been, and is, a great saving of wood to the inhabitants.

XIII: Public Services and Duties (1749-1753)

PEACE being concluded, and the association business therefore at an end, I turned my thoughts again to the affair of establishing an academy. The first step I took was to associate in the design a number of active friends, of whom the Junto furnished a good part; the next was to write and publish a pamphlet, entitled Proposals Relating to the Education of Youth in Pennsylvania. This I distributed among the principal inhabitants gratis; and as soon as I could suppose their minds a little prepared by the perusal of it, I set on foot a subscription for opening and supporting an academy; it was to be paid in quotas yearly for five years; by so dividing it, I judged the subscription might be larger, and I believe it was so, amounting to no less, if I remember right, than five thousand pounds.

In the introduction to these proposals, I stated their publication, not as an act of mine, but of some public-spirited gentlemen, avoiding as much as I could, according to my usual rule, the presenting myself to the public as the author of any scheme for their benefit.

The subscribers, to carry the project into immediate execution, chose out of their number twenty-four trustees, and appointed Mr. Francis, then attorney-general, and myself to draw up constitutions for the government of the academy; which being done and signed, a house was hired, masters engaged, and the schools opened, I think, in the same year, 1749.

The scholars increasing fast, the house was soon found too small, and we were looking out for a piece of ground, properly situated, with intention to build, when Providence threw into our way a large house ready built, which, with a few alterations, might well serve our purpose. This was the building before mentioned, erected by the hearers of Mr. Whitefield, and was obtained for us in the following manner.

It is to be noted that the contributions to this building being made by people of different sects, care was taken in the nomination of trustees, in whom the building and ground was to be vested, that a predominancy should not be given to any sect, lest in time that predominancy might be a means of appropriating the whole to the use of such sect, contrary to the original intention. It was therefore that one of each sect was appointed, viz., one Church-of-England man, one Presbyterian, one Baptist, one Moravian, etc., those, in case of vacancy by death, were to fill it by election from among the contributors. The Moravian happened not to please his colleagues, and on his death they resolved to have no other of that sect. The difficulty then was, how to avoid having two of some other sect, by means of the new choice.

Several persons were named, and for that reason not agreed to. At length one mentioned me, with the observation that I was merely an honest man, and of no sect at all, which prevailed with them to chuse me. The enthusiasm which existed when the house was built had long since abated, and its trustees had not been able to procure fresh contributions for paying the ground-rent, and discharging some other debts the building had occasioned, which embarrassed them greatly. Being now a member of both sets of trustees, that for the building and that for the academy, I had a good opportunity of negotiating with both, and brought them finally to an agreement, by which the trustees for the building were to cede it to those of the academy, the latter undertaking to discharge the debt, to keep forever open in the building a large hall for occasional preachers, according to the original intention, and maintain a free-school for the instruction of poor children. Writings were accordingly drawn, and on paying the debts the trustees of the academy were put in possession of the premises; and by dividing the great and lofty hall into stories, and different rooms above and below for the several schools, and purchasing some additional ground, the whole was soon made fit for our purpose, and the scholars removed into the building. The care and trouble of agreeing with the workmen, purchasing materials, and superintending the work, fell upon me; and I went through it the more cheerfully, as it did not then interfere with my private business, having the year before taken a very able, industrious, and honest partner, Mr. David Hall, with whose character

I was well acquainted, as he had worked for me four years. He took off my hands all care of the printing-office, paying me punctually my share of the profits. The partnership continued eighteen years, successfully for us both.

The trustees of the academy, after a while, were incorporated by a charter from the governor; their funds were increased by contributions in Britain and grants of land from the proprietaries, to which the Assembly has since made considerable addition; and thus was established the present University of Philadelphia. I have been continued one of its trustees from the beginning, now near forty years, and have had the very great pleasure of seeing a number of the youth who have received their education in it, distinguished by their improved abilities, serviceable in public stations, and ornaments to their country.

When I disengaged myself, as above mentioned, from private business, I flattered myself that, by the sufficient tho' moderate fortune I had acquired, I had secured leisure during the rest of my life for philosophical studies and amusements. I purchased all Dr. Spence's apparatus, who had come from England to lecture here, and I proceeded in my electrical experiments with great alacrity; but the public, now considering me as a man of leisure, laid hold of me for their purposes, every part of our civil government, and almost at the same time, imposing some duty upon me. The governor put me into the commission of the peace; the corporation of the city chose me of the common council, and soon after an alderman; and the citizens at large chose me a burgess to represent them in Assembly. This latter station was the more agreeable to me, as I was at length tired with sitting there to hear debates, in which, as clerk, I could take no part, and which were often so unentertaining that I was induced to amuse myself with making magic squares or circles, or anything to avoid weariness; and I conceived my becoming a member would enlarge my power of doing good. I would not, however, insinuate that my ambition was not flattered by all these promotions; it certainly was; for, considering my low beginning, they were great things to me; and they were still more pleasing, as being so many spontaneous testimonies of the public good opinion, and by me entirely unsolicited.

The office of justice of the peace I tried a little, by attending a few courts, and sitting on the bench to hear causes; but finding that more knowledge of the common law than I possessed was necessary to act in that station with credit, I gradually withdrew from it, excusing myself by my being obliged to attend the higher duties of a legislator in the Assembly. My election to this trust was repeated every year for ten years, without my ever asking any elector for his vote, or signifying, either directly or indirectly, any desire of being chosen. On taking my seat in the House, my son was appointed their clerk.

The year following, a treaty being to be held with the Indians at Carlisle, the governor sent a message to the House, proposing that they should nominate some of their members, to be joined with some members of council, as commissioners for that purpose. The House named the speaker (Mr. Norris) and myself; and, being commissioned, we went to Carlisle, and met the Indians accordingly.

As those people are extremely apt to get drunk, and, when so, are very quarrelsome and disorderly, we strictly forbad the selling any liquor to them; and when they complained of this restriction, we told them that if they would continue sober during the treaty, we would give them plenty of rum when business was over. They promised this, and they kept their promise, because they could get no liquor, and the treaty was conducted very orderly, and concluded to mutual satisfaction. They then claimed and received the rum; this was in the afternoon: they were near one hundred men, women, and children, and were lodged in temporary cabins, built in the form of a square, just without the town. In the evening, hearing a great noise among them, the commissioners walked out to see what was the matter. We found they had made a great bonfire in the middle of the square; they were all drunk, men and women, quarreling and fighting. Their dark-colored bodies, half-naked, seen only by the gloomy light of the bonfire, running after and beating one another with firebrands, accompanied by their horrid yellings, formed a scene the most resembling our ideas of hell that could well be imagined; there was no appeasing the tumult, and we retired to our lodging. At midnight a number of them came thundering at our door, demanding more rum, of which we took no notice.

The next day, sensible they had misbehaved in giving us that disturbance, they sent three of their old counselors to make their apology. The orator acknowledged the fault, but laid it upon the rum; and then endeavored to excuse the rum by saying, "The Great Spirit, who made all things, made everything for some use, and whatever use he designed anything for, that use it should always be put to. Now, when he made rum, he said, 'Let this be for the Indians to get drunk with,' and it must be so." And, indeed, if it be the design of Providence to extirpate these savages in order to make room for cultivators of the earth, it seems not improbable that rum may be the appointed means. It has already annihilated all the tribes who formerly inhabited the sea-coast.

In 1751, Dr. Thomas Bond, a particular friend of mine, conceived the idea of establishing a hospital in Philadelphia (a very beneficent design, which has been ascribed to me, but was originally his), for the reception and cure of poor sick persons, whether inhabitants of the province or strangers. He was zealous and active in endeavoring to procure subscriptions for it, but the proposal being a novelty in America, and at first not well understood, he met but with small success.

At length he came to me with the compliment that he found there was no such thing as carrying a public-spirited project through without my being concerned in it. "For," says he, "I am often asked by those to whom I propose subscribing, Have you consulted Franklin upon this business? And what does he think of it? And when I tell them that I have not (supposing it rather out of your line), they do not subscribe, but say they will consider of it." I enquired into the nature and probable utility of his scheme, and receiving from him a very satisfactory explanation, I not only subscribed to it myself, but engaged heartily in the design of procuring subscriptions from others. Previously, however, to the solicitation, I endeavored to prepare the minds of the people by writing on the subject in the newspapers, which was my usual custom in such cases, but which he had omitted.

The subscriptions afterwards were more free and generous; but, beginning to flag, I saw they would be insufficient without some assistance from the Assembly, and therefore proposed to petition for it, which was done. The country members did not at first relish the project; they objected that it could only be serviceable to the city, and therefore the citizens alone should be at the expense of it; and they doubted whether the citizens themselves generally approved of it. My allegation on the contrary, that it met with such approbation as to leave no doubt of our being able to raise two thousand pounds by voluntary donations, they considered as a most extravagant supposition, and utterly impossible.

On this I formed my plan; and, asking leave to bring in a bill for incorporating the contributors according to the prayer of their petition, and granting them a blank sum of money, which leave was obtained chiefly on the consideration that the House could throw the bill out if they did not like it, I drew it so as to make the important clause a conditional one, viz., "And be it enacted, by the authority aforesaid, that when the said contributors shall have met and chosen their managers and treasurer, and shall have raised by their contributions a capital stock of——value (the yearly interest of which is to be applied to the accommodating of the sick poor in the said hospital, free of charge for diet, attendance, advice, and medicines), and shall make the same appear to the satisfaction of the speaker of the Assembly for the time being, that then it shall and may be lawful for the said speaker, and he is hereby required, to sign an order on the provincial treasurer for the payment of two thousand pounds, in two yearly payments, to the treasurer of the said hospital, to be applied to the founding, building, and finishing of the same."

This condition carried the bill through; for the members, who had opposed the grant, and now conceived they might have the credit of being charitable without the expense, agreed to its passage; and then, in soliciting subscriptions among the people, we urged the conditional promise of the law as an additional motive to give, since every man's donation would be doubled; thus the clause worked both ways. The subscriptions accordingly soon exceeded the requisite sum, and we claimed and received the public gift, which enabled us to carry the design into execution. A convenient and handsome building was soon erected; the institution has by constant experience been found useful, and flourishes to this day; and I do not remember any of my political manoeuvers, the success of which gave me at the time more pleasure, or wherein, after thinking of it, I more easily excused myself for having made some use of cunning.

It was about this time that another projector, the Rev. Gilbert Tennent, came to me with a request that I would assist him in procuring a subscription for erecting a new meeting-house. It was to be for the use of a congregation he had gathered among the Presbyterians, who were originally disciples of Mr. Whitefield. Unwilling to make myself disagreeable to my fellow-citizens by too frequently soliciting their contributions, I absolutely refused. He then desired I would furnish him with a list of the names of persons I knew by experience to be generous and public-spirited. I thought it would be unbecoming in me, after their kind compliance with my solicitations, to mark them out to be worried by other beggars, and therefore refused also to give such a list. He then desired I would at least give him my advice. "That I will readily do," said I; "and, in the first place, I advise you to apply to all those whom you know will give something; next, to those whom you are uncertain whether they will give anything or not, and show them the list of those who have given; and, lastly, do not neglect those who you are sure will give nothing, for in some of them you may be mistaken." He laughed and thanked me, and said he would take my advice. He did so, for he asked of everybody, and he obtained a much larger sum than he expected, with which he erected the capacious and very elegant meeting-house that stands in Arch-street.

Our city, tho' laid out with a beautiful regularity, the streets large, straight, and crossing each other at right angles, had the disgrace of suffering those streets to remain long unpaved, and in wet weather the wheels of heavy carriages ploughed them into a quagmire, so that it was difficult to cross them; and in dry weather the dust was offensive. I had lived near what was called the Jersey Market, and saw with pain the inhabitants wading in mud while purchasing their provisions. A strip of ground down the middle of that market was at length paved with brick, so that, being once in the market, they had firm footing, but were often over shoes in dirt to get there. By talking and writing on the subject, I was at length instrumental in getting the street paved with stone between the market and the bricked foot-pavement, that was on each side next the houses. This, for some time, gave an easy access to the market dry-shod; but, the rest of the street not being paved, whenever a carriage came out of the mud upon this pavement, it shook off and left its dirt upon it, and it was soon covered with mire, which was not removed, the city as yet having no scavengers.

After some inquiry, I found a poor, industrious man, who was willing to undertake keeping the pavement clean, by sweeping it twice a week, carrying off the dirt from before all the neighbors' doors, for the sum of sixpence per month, to be paid by each house. I then wrote and printed a paper setting forth the advantages to the neighborhood that might be obtained by this small expense; the greater ease in keeping our houses clean, so much dirt not being brought in by people's feet; the benefit to the shops by more custom, etc., etc., as buyers could more easily get at them; and by not having, in windy weather, the dust blown in upon their goods, etc., etc. I sent one of these papers to each house, and in a day or two went round to see who would subscribe an agreement to pay these sixpences; it was unanimously signed, and for a time well executed. All the inhabitants of the city were delighted with the cleanliness of the pavement that surrounded the market, it being a convenience to all, and this raised a general desire to have all the streets paved, and made the people more willing to submit to a tax for that purpose.

After some time I drew a bill for paving the city, and brought it into the Assembly. It was just before I went to England, in 1757, and did not pass till I was gone, and then with an alteration in the mode of assessment, which I thought not for the better, but with an additional provision for lighting as well as paving the streets, which was a great improvement. It was by a private person, the late Mr. John Clifton, his giving a sample of the utility of lamps, by placing one at his door, that the people were first impressed with the idea of enlighting all the city. The honor of this public benefit has also been ascribed to me, but it belongs truly to that gentleman. I did but follow his example, and have only some merit to claim respecting the form of our lamps, as differing from the globe lamps we were at first supplied with from London. Those we found inconvenient in these respects: they admitted no air below; the smoke, therefore, did not readily go out above, but circulated in the globe, lodged on its inside, and soon obstructed the light they were intended to afford; giving, besides, the daily trouble of wiping them clean; and an accidental stroke on one of them would demolish it, and render it totally useless. I therefore suggested the composing them of four flat panes, with a long funnel above to draw up the smoke, and crevices admitting air below, to facilitate the ascent of the smoke; by this means they were kept clean, and did not grow dark in a few hours, as the London lamps do, but continued bright till morning, and an accidental stroke would generally break but a single pane, easily repaired.

I have sometimes wondered that the Londoners did not, from the effect holes in the bottom of the globe lamps used at Vauxhall have in keeping them clean, learn to have such holes in their street lamps. But, these holes being made for another purpose, viz., to communicate flame more suddenly to the wick by a little flax hanging down through them, the other use, of letting in air, seems not to have been thought of; and therefore, after the lamps have been lit a few hours, the streets of London are very poorly illuminated.

The mention of these improvements puts me in mind of one I proposed, when in London, to Dr. Fothergill, who was among the best men I have known, and a great promoter of useful projects. I had observed that the streets, when dry, were never swept, and the light dust carried away; but it was suffered to accumulate till wet weather reduced it to mud, and then, after lying some days so deep on the pavement that there was no crossing but in paths kept clean by poor people with brooms, it was with great labour raked together and thrown up into carts open above, the sides of which suffered some of the slush at every jolt on the pavement to shake out and fall, sometimes to the annoyance of foot-passengers. The reason given for not sweeping the dusty streets was that the dust would fly into the windows of shops and houses.

An accidental occurrence had instructed me how much sweeping might be done in a little time. I found at my door in Craven-street, one morning, a poor woman sweeping my pavement with a birch broom; she appeared very pale and feeble, as just come out of a fit of sickness. I asked who employed her to sweep there; she said, "Nobody, but I am very poor and in distress, and I sweeps before gentle-folkses doors, and hopes they will give me something." I bid her sweep the whole street clean, and I would give her a shilling; this was at nine o'clock; at 12 she came for the shilling. From the slowness I saw at first in her working, I could scarce believe that the work was done so soon, and sent my servant to examine it, who reported that the whole street was swept perfectly clean, and all the dust placed in the gutter, which was in the middle; and the next rain washed it quite away, so that the pavement and even the kennel were perfectly clean.

I then judged that, if that feeble woman could sweep such a street in three hours, a strong, active man might have done it in half the time. And here let me remark the convenience of having but one gutter in such a narrow street, running down its middle, instead of two, one on each side, near the footway; for where all the rain that falls on a street runs from the sides and meets in the middle, it forms there a current strong enough to wash away all the mud it meets with; but when divided into two channels, it is often too weak to cleanse either, and only makes the mud it finds more fluid, so that the wheels of carriages and feet of horses throw and dash it upon the foot-pavement, which is thereby rendered foul and slippery, and sometimes splash it upon those who are walking. My proposal, communicated to the good doctor, was as follows:

"For the more effectual cleaning and keeping clean the streets of London and Westminster, it is proposed that the several watchmen be contracted with to have the dust swept up in dry seasons, and the mud raked up at other times, each in the several streets and lanes of his round; that they be furnished with brooms and other proper instruments for these purposes, to be kept at their respective stands, ready to furnish the poor people they may employ in the service.

"That in the dry summer months the dust be all swept up into heaps at proper distances, before the shops and windows of houses are usually opened, when the scavengers, with close-covered carts, shall also carry it all away.

"That the mud, when raked up, be not left in heaps to be spread abroad again by the wheels of carriages and trampling of horses, but that the scavengers be provided with bodies of carts, not placed high upon wheels, but low upon sliders, with lattice bottoms, which, being covered with straw, will retain the mud thrown into them, and permit the water to drain from it, whereby it will become much lighter, water making the greatest part of its weight; these bodies of carts to be placed at convenient distances, and the mud brought to them in wheelbarrows; they remaining where placed till the mud is drained, and then horses brought to draw them away."

I have since had doubts of the practicability of the latter part of this proposal, on account of the narrowness of some streets, and the difficulty of placing the draining-sleds so as not to encumber too much the passage; but I am still of opinion that the former, requiring the dust to be swept up and carried away before the shops are open, is very practicable in the summer, when the days are long; for, in walking through the Strand and Fleet-street one morning at seven o'clock, I observed there was not one shop open, tho' it had been daylight and the sun up above three hours; the inhabitants of London choosing voluntarily to live much by candle-light, and sleep by sunshine, and yet often complain, a little absurdly, of the duty on candles, and the high price of tallow.

Some may think these trifling matters not worth minding or relating; but when they consider that tho' dust blown into the eyes of a single person, or into a single shop on a windy day, is but of small importance, yet the great number of the instances in a populous city, and its frequent repetitions give it weight and consequence, perhaps they will not censure very severely those who bestow some attention to affairs of this seemingly low nature. Human felicity is produced not so much by great pieces of good fortune that seldom happen, as by little advantages that occur every day. Thus, if you teach a poor young man to shave himself, and keep his razor in order, you may contribute more to the happiness of his life than in giving him a thousand guineas. The money may be soon spent, the regret only remaining of having foolishly consumed it; but in the other case, he escapes the frequent vexation of waiting for barbers, and of their sometimes dirty fingers, offensive breaths, and dull razors; he shaves when most convenient to him, and enjoys daily the pleasure of its being done with a good instrument. With these sentiments I have hazarded the few preceding pages, hoping they may afford hints which some time or other may be useful to a city I love, having lived many years in it very happily, and perhaps to some of our towns in America.

Having been for some time employed by the postmaster-general of America as his comptroller in regulating several offices, and bringing the officers to account, I was, upon his death in 1753, appointed, jointly with Mr. William Hunter, to succeed him, by a commission from the postmaster-general in England. The American office never had hitherto paid anything to that of Britain. We were to have six hundred pounds a year between us, if we could make that sum out of the profits of the office. To do this, a variety of improvements were necessary; some of these were inevitably at first expensive, so that in the first four years the office became above nine hundred pounds in debt to us. But it soon after began to repay us; and before I was displaced by a freak of the ministers, of which I shall speak hereafter, we had brought it to yield three times as much clear revenue to the crown as the post-office of Ireland. Since that imprudent transaction, they have received from it—not one farthing!

The business of the post-office occasioned my taking a journey this year to New England, where the College of Cambridge, of their own motion, presented me with the degree of Master of Arts. Yale College, in Connecticut, had before made me a similar compliment. Thus, without studying in any college, I came to partake of their honors. They were conferred in consideration of my improvements and discoveries in the electric branch of natural philosophy.

XIV: Albany Plan of Union

IN 1754, war with France being again apprehended, a congress of commissioners from the different colonies was, by an order of the Lords of Trade, to be assembled at Albany, there to confer with the chiefs of the Six Nations concerning the means of defending both their country and ours. Governor Hamilton, having received this order, acquainted the House with it, requesting they would furnish proper presents for the Indians, to be given on this occasion; and naming the speaker (Mr. Norris) and myself to join Mr. Thomas Penn and Mr. Secretary Peters as commissioners to act for Pennsylvania. The House approved the nomination, and provided the goods for the present, and tho' they did not much like treating out of the provinces; and we met the other commissioners at Albany about the middle of June.

In our way thither, I projected and drew a plan for the union of all the colonies under one government, so far as might be necessary for defense, and other important general purposes. As we passed through New York, I had there shown my project to Mr. James Alexander and Mr. Kennedy, two gentlemen of great knowledge in public affairs, and, being fortified by their approbation, I ventured to lay it before the Congress. It then appeared that several of the commissioners had formed plans of the same kind. A previous question was first taken, whether a union should be established, which passed in the affirmative unanimously. A committee was then appointed, one member from each colony, to consider the several plans and report. Mine happened to be preferred, and, with a few amendments, was accordingly reported.

By this plan the general government was to be administered by a president-general, appointed and supported by the crown, and a grand council was to be chosen by the representatives of the people of the several colonies, met in their respective assemblies. The debates upon it in Congress went on daily, hand in hand with the Indian business. Many objections and difficulties were started, but at length they were all overcome, and the plan was unanimously agreed to, and copies ordered to be transmitted to the Board of Trade and to the assemblies of the several provinces. Its fate was singular; the assemblies did not adopt it, as they all thought there was too much prerogative in it, and in England it was judged to have too much of the democratic. The Board of Trade therefore did not approve of it, nor recommend it for the approbation of his majesty; but another scheme was formed, supposed to answer the same purpose better, whereby the governors of the provinces, with some members of their respective councils, were to meet and order the raising of troops, building of forts, etc., and to draw on the treasury of Great Britain for the expense, which was afterwards to be refunded by an act of Parliament laying a tax on America. My plan, with my reasons in support of it, is to be found among my political papers that are printed.

Being the winter following in Boston, I had much conversation with Governor Shirley upon both the plans. Part of what passed between us on the occasion may also be seen among those papers. The different and contrary reasons of dislike to my plan makes me suspect that it was really the true medium; and I am still of opinion it would have been happy for both sides the water if it had been adopted. The colonies, so united, would have been sufficiently strong to have defended themselves; there would then have been no need of troops from England; of course, the subsequent pretense for taxing America, and the bloody contest it occasioned, would have been avoided. But such mistakes are not new; history is full of the errors of states and princes.

"Look round the habitable world, how few
Know their own good, or, knowing it, pursue!"

Those who govern, having much business on their hands, do not generally like to take the trouble of considering and carrying into execution new projects. The best public measures are therefore seldom adopted from previous wisdom, but forced by the occasion.

The Governor of Pennsylvania, in sending it down to the Assembly, expressed his approbation of the plan, "as appearing to him to be drawn up with great clearness and strength of judgment, and therefore recommended it as well worthy of their closest and most serious attention." The House, however, by the management of a certain member, took it up when I happened to be absent, which I thought not very fair, and reprobated it without paying any attention to it at all, to my no small mortification.

XV: Quarrels With the Proprietary Governors

IN my journey to Boston this year, I met at New York with our new governor, Mr. Morris, just arrived there from England, with whom I had been before intimately acquainted. He brought a commission to supersede Mr. Hamilton, who, tired with the disputes his proprietary instructions subjected him to, had resigned. Mr. Morris asked me if I thought he must expect as uncomfortable an administration. I said, "No; you may, on the contrary, have a very comfortable one, if you will only take care not to enter into any dispute with the Assembly." "My dear friend," says he, pleasantly, "how can you advise my avoiding disputes? You know I love disputing; it is one of my greatest pleasures; however, to show the regard I have for your counsel, I promise you I will, if possible, avoid them." He had some reason for loving to dispute, being eloquent, an acute sophister, and, therefore, generally successful in argumentative conversation. He had been brought up to it from a boy, his father, as I have heard, accustoming his children to dispute with one another for his diversion, while sitting at table after dinner; but I think the practice was not wise; for, in the course of my observation, these disputing, contradicting, and confuting people are generally unfortunate in their affairs. They get victory sometimes, but they never get good will, which would be of more use to them. We parted, he going to Philadelphia, and I to Boston.

In returning, I met at New York with the votes of the Assembly, by which it appeared that, notwithstanding his promise to me, he and the House were already in high contention; and it was a continual battle between them as long as he retained the government. I had my share of it; for, as soon as I got back to my seat in the Assembly, I was put on every committee for answering his speeches and messages, and by the committees always desired to make the drafts. Our answers, as well as his messages, were often tart, and sometimes indecently abusive; and, as he knew I wrote for the Assembly, one might have imagined that, when we met, we could hardly avoid cutting throats; but he was so good-natured a man that no personal difference between him and me was occasioned by the contest, and we often din's together.

One afternoon, in the height of this public quarrel, we met in the street. "Franklin," says he, "you must go home with me and spend the evening; I am to have some company that you will like;" and, taking me by the arm, he led me to his house. In gay conversation over our wine, after supper, he told us, jokingly, that he much admired the idea of Sancho Panza, who, when it was proposed to give him a government, requested it might be a government of blacks, as then, if he could not agree with his people, he might sell them. One of his friends, who sat next to me, says, "Franklin, why do you continue to side with these damned Quakers? Had not you better sell them? The proprietor would give you a good price." "The governor," says I, "has not yet blacked them enough." He, indeed, had labored hard to blacken the Assembly in all his messages, but they wiped off his coloring as fast as he laid it on, and placed it, in return, thick upon his own face; so that, finding he was likely to be negrofied himself, he, as well as Mr. Hamilton, grew tired of the contest, and quitted the government.

These public quarrels were all at bottom owing to the proprietaries, our hereditary governors, who, when any expense was to be incurred for the defense of their province, with incredible meanness instructed their deputies to pass no act for levying the necessary taxes, unless their vast estates were in the same act expressly excused; and they had even taken bonds of these deputies to observe such instructions. The Assemblies for three years held out against this injustice, tho' constrained to bend at last. At length Captain Denny, who was Governor Morris's successor, ventured to disobey those instructions; how that was brought about I shall show hereafter.

But I am got forward too fast with my story: there are still some transactions to be mentioned that happened during the administration of Governor Morris.

War being in a manner commenced with France, the government of Massachusetts Bay projected an attack upon Crown Point, and sent Mr. Quincy to Pennsylvania, and Mr. Pownall, afterward Governor Pownall, to New York, to solicit assistance. As I was in the Assembly, knew its temper, and was Mr. Quincy's countryman, he applied to me for my influence and assistance. I dictated his address to them, which was well received. They voted an aid of ten thousand pounds, to be laid out in provisions. But the governor refusing his assent to their bill (which included this with other sums granted for the use of the crown), unless a clause were inserted exempting the proprietary estate from bearing any part of the tax that would be necessary, the Assembly, tho' very desirous of making their grant to New England effectual, were at a loss how to accomplish it. Mr. Quincy labored hard with the governor to obtain his assent, but he was obstinate.

I then suggested a method of doing the business without the governor, by orders on the trustees of the Loan office, which, by law, the Assembly had the right of drawing. There was, indeed, little or no money at that time in the office, and therefore I proposed that the orders should be payable in a year, and to bear an interest of five per cent. With these orders I supposed the provisions might easily be purchased. The Assembly, with very little hesitation, adopted the proposal. The orders were immediately printed, and I was one of the committee directed to sign and dispose of them. The fund for paying them was the interest of all the paper currency then extant in the province upon loan, together with the revenue arising from the excise, which being known to be more than sufficient, they obtained instant credit, and were not only received in payment for the provisions, but many moneyed people, who had cash lying by them, vested it in those orders, which they found advantageous, as they bore interest while upon hand, and might on any occasion be used as money; so that they were eagerly all bought up, and in a few weeks none of them were to be seen. Thus this important affair was by my means completed. Mr. Quincy returned thanks to the Assembly in a handsome memorial, went home highly pleased with this success of his embassy, and ever after bore for me the most cordial and affectionate friendship.

XVI: Braddock's Expedition

THE British government, not choosing to permit the union of the colonies as proposed at Albany, and to trust that union with their defense, lest they should thereby grow too military, and feel their own strength, suspicions and jealousies at this time being entertained of them, sent over General Braddock with two regiments of regular English troops for that purpose. He landed at Alexandria, in Virginia, and thence march's to Fredericktown, in Maryland, where he halted for carriages. Our Assembly apprehending, from some information, that he had conceived violent prejudices against them, as averse to the service, wished me to wait upon him, not as from them, but as postmaster-general, under the guise of proposing to settle with him the mode of conducting with most celerity and certainty the dispatches between him and the governors of the several provinces, with whom he must necessarily have continual correspondence, and of which they proposed to pay the expense. My son accompanied me on this journey.

We found the general at Fredericktown, waiting impatiently for the return of those he had sent through the back parts of Maryland and Virginia to collect wagons. I stayed with him several days, dined with him daily, and had full opportunity of removing all his prejudices, by the information of what the Assembly had before his arrival actually done, and were still willing to do, to facilitate his operations. When I was about to depart, the returns of wagons to be obtained were brought in, by which it appeared that they amounted only to twenty-five, and not all of those were in serviceable condition. The general and all the officers were surprised, declared the expedition was then at an end, being impossible, and exclaimed against the ministers for ignorantly landing them in a country destitute of the means of conveying their stores, baggage, etc., not less than one hundred and fifty wagons being necessary.

I happened to say I thought it was pity they had not been landed rather in Pennsylvania, as in that country almost every farmer had his wagon. The general eagerly laid hold of my words, and said, "Then you, sir, who are a man of interest there, can probably procure them for us; and I beg you will undertake it." I asked what terms were to be offered the owners of the wagons, and I was desired to put on paper the terms that appeared to me necessary. This I did, and they were agreed to, and a commission and instructions accordingly prepared immediately. What those terms were will appear in the advertisement I published as soon as I arrived at Lancaster, which being, from the great and sudden effect it produced, a piece of some curiosity, I shall insert it at length, as follows:

"Advertisement.

"Lancaster, April 26, 1755.

"Whereas, one hundred and fifty wagons, with four horses to each wagon, and fifteen hundred saddle or pack horses, are wanted for the service of his majesty's forces now about to rendezvous at Will's Creek, and his excellency General Braddock having been pleased to empower me to contract for the hire of the same, I hereby give notice that I shall attend for that purpose at Lancaster from this day to next Wednesday evening, and at York from next Thursday morning till Friday evening, where I shall be ready to agree for wagons and teams, or single horses, on the following terms, viz.: 1. That there shall be paid for each wagon, with four good horses and a driver, fifteen shillings per diem; and for each able horse with a pack-saddle, or other saddle and furniture, two shillings per diem; and for each able horse without a saddle, eighteen pence per diem. 2. That the pay commence from the time of their joining the forces at Will's Creek, which must be on or before the 20th of May ensuing, and that a reasonable allowance be paid over and above for the time necessary for their travelling to Will's Creek and home again after their discharge. 3. Each wagon and team, and every saddle or pack horse, is to be valued by indifferent persons chosen between me and the owner; and in case of the loss of any wagon, team, or other horse in the service, the price according to such valuation is to be allowed and paid. 4. Seven days' pay is to be advanced and paid in hand by me to the owner of each wagon and team, or horse, at the time of contracting, if required, and the remainder to be paid by General Braddock, or by the paymaster of the army, at the time of their discharge, or from time to time, as it shall be demanded. 5. No drivers of wagons, or persons taking care of the hired horses, are on any account to be called upon to do the duty of soldiers, or be otherwise employed than in conducting or taking care of their carriages or horses. 6. All oats, Indian corn, or other forage that wagons or horses bring to the camp, more than is necessary for the subsistence of the horses, is to be taken for the use of the army, and a reasonable price paid for the same.

"Note.—My son, William Franklin, is empowered to enter into like contracts with any person in Cumberland county.

"B. Franklin."

"To the inhabitants of the Counties of Lancaster, York, and Cumberland.

"Friends and Countrymen,

"Being occasionally at the camp at Frederic a few days since, I found the general and officers extremely exasperated on account of their not being supplied with horses and carriages, which had been expected from this province, as most able to furnish them; but, through the dissensions between our governor and Assembly, money had not been provided, nor any steps taken for that purpose.

"It was proposed to send an armed force immediately into these counties, to seize as many of the best carriages and horses as should be wanted, and compel as many persons into the service as would be necessary to drive and take care of them.

"I apprehended that the progress of British soldiers through these counties on such an occasion, especially considering the temper they are in, and their resentment against us, would be attended with many and great inconveniences to the inhabitants, and therefore more willingly took the trouble of trying first what might be done by fair and equitable means. The people of these back counties have lately complained to the Assembly that a sufficient currency was wanting; you have an opportunity of receiving and dividing among you a very considerable sum; for, if the service of this expedition should continue, as it is more than probable it will, for one hundred and twenty days, the hire of these wagons and horses will amount to upward of thirty thousand pounds, which will be paid you in silver and gold of the king's money.

"The service will be light and easy, for the army will scarce march above twelve miles per day, and the wagons and baggage-horses, as they carry those things that are absolutely necessary to the welfare of the army, must march with the army, and no faster; and are, for the army's sake, always placed where they can be most secure, whether in a march or in a camp.

"If you are really, as I believe you are, good and loyal subjects to his majesty, you may now do a most acceptable service, and make it easy to yourselves; for three or four of such as cannot separately spare from the business of their plantations a wagon and four horses and a driver, may do it together, one furnishing the wagon, another one or two horses, and another the driver, and divide the pay proportionately between you; but if you do not this service to your king and country voluntarily, when such good pay and reasonable terms are offered to you, your loyalty will be strongly suspected. The king's business must be done; so many brave troops, come so far for your defense, must not stand idle through your backwardness to do what may be reasonably expected from you; wagons and horses must be had; violent measures will probably be used, and you will be left to seek for a recompense where you can find it, and your case, perhaps, be little pitied or regarded.

"I have no particular interest in this affair, as, except the satisfaction of endeavoring to do good, I shall have only my labour for my pains. If this method of obtaining the wagons and horses is not likely to succeed, I am obliged to send word to the general in fourteen days; and I suppose Sir John St. Clair, the hussar, with a body of soldiers, will immediately enter the province for the purpose, which I shall be sorry to hear, because I am very sincerely and truly your friend and well-wisher,

"B. Franklin."

I received of the general about eight hundred pounds, to be disbursed in advance-money to the wagon owners, etc.; but that sum being insufficient, I advanced upward of two hundred pounds more, and in two weeks the one hundred and fifty wagons, with two hundred and fifty-nine carrying horses, were on their march for the camp. The advertisement promised payment according to the valuation, in case any wagon or horse should be lost. The owners, however, alleging they did not know General Braddock, or what dependence might be had on his promise, insisted on my bond for the performance, which I accordingly gave them.

While I was at the camp, supping one evening with the officers of Colonel Dunbar's regiment, he represented to me his concern for the subalterns, who, he said, were generally not in affluence, and could ill afford, in this dear country, to lay in the stores that might be necessary in so long a march, thro' a wilderness, where nothing was to be purchased. I commiserated their case, and resolved to endeavor procuring them some relief. I said nothing, however, to him of my intention, but wrote the next morning to the committee of the Assembly, who had the disposition of some public money, warmly recommending the case of these officers to their consideration, and proposing that a present should be sent them of necessaries and refreshments. My son, who had some experience of a camp life, and of its wants, drew up a list for me, which I enclosed in my letter. The committee approved, and used such diligence that, conducted by my son, the stores arrived at the camp as soon as the wagons. They consisted of twenty parcels, each containing

6 lbs. loaf sugar.
1 Gloucester cheese.
6 lbs. good Muscovado do.
1 keg containing 20 lbs. good butter.
1 lb. good green tea.
2 doz. old Madeira wine.
1 lb. good bohea do.
2 gallons Jamaica spirits.
6 lbs. good ground coffee.
1 bottle flour of mustard.
6 lbs. chocolate.
2 well-cured hams.
½ cwt. best white biscuit.
½ dozen dried tongues.
½ lb. pepper.
6 lbs. rice.
1 quart best white wine.
6 lbs. raisins.
1 quart best white wine vinegar.

These twenty parcels, well packed, were placed on as many horses, each parcel, with the horse, being intended as a present for one officer. They were very thankfully received, and the kindness acknowledged by letters to me from the colonels of both regiments, in the most grateful terms. The general, too, was highly satisfied with my conduct in procuring him the wagons, etc., and readily paid my account of disbursements, thanking me repeatedly, and requesting my farther assistance in sending provisions after him. I undertook this also, and was busily employed in it till we heard of his defeat, advancing for the service of my own money, upwards of one thousand pounds sterling, of which I sent him an account. It came to his hands, luckily for me, a few days before the battle, and he returned me immediately an order on the paymaster for the round sum of one thousand pounds, leaving the remainder to the next account. I consider this payment as good luck, having never been able to obtain that remainder, of which more hereafter.

This general was, I think, a brave man, and might probably have made a figure as a good officer in some European war. But he had too much self-confidence, too high an opinion of the validity of regular troops, and too mean a one of both Americans and Indians. George Croghan, our Indian interpreter, joined him on his march with one hundred of those people, who might have been of great use to his army as guides, scouts, etc., if he had treated them kindly; but he slighted and neglected them, and they gradually left him.

In conversation with him one day, he was giving me some account of his intended progress. "After taking Fort Duquesne," says he, "I am to proceed to Niagara; and, having taken that, to Frontenac, if the season will allow time; and I suppose it will, for Duquesne can hardly detain me above three or four days; and then I see nothing that can obstruct my march to Niagara." Having before revolved in my mind the long line his army must make in their march by a very narrow road, to be cut for them through the woods and bushes, and also what I had read of a former defeat of fifteen hundred French, who invaded the Iroquois country, I had conceived some doubts and some fears for the event of the campaign. But I ventured only to say, "To be sure, sir, if you arrive well before Duquesne, with these fine troops, so well provided with artillery, that place not yet completely fortified, and as we hear with no very strong garrison, can probably make but a short resistance. The only danger I apprehend of obstruction to your march is from ambuscades of Indians, who, by constant practice, are dexterous in laying and executing them; and the slender line, near four miles long, which your army must make, may expose it to be attacked by surprise in its flanks, and to be cut like a thread into several pieces, which, from their distance, cannot come up in time to support each other."

He smiled at my ignorance, and replied, "These savages may, indeed, be a formidable enemy to your raw American militia, but upon the king's regular and disciplined troops, sir, it is impossible they should make any impression." I was conscious of an impropriety in my disputing with a military man in matters of his profession, and said no more. The enemy, however, did not take the advantage of his army which I apprehended its long line of march exposed it to, but let it advance without interruption till within nine miles of the place; and then, when more in a body (for it had just passed a river, where the front had halted till all were come over), and in a more open part of the woods than any it had passed, attacked its advanced guard by heavy fire from behind trees and bushes, which was the first intelligence the general had of an enemy's being near him. This guard being disordered, the general hurried the troops up to their assistance, which was done in great confusion, thro' wagons, baggage, and cattle; and presently the fire came upon their flank: the officers, being on horseback, were more easily distinguished, picked out as marks, and fell very fast; and the soldiers were crowded together in a huddle, having or hearing no orders, and standing to be shot at till two-thirds of them were killed; and then, being seized with a panic, the whole fled with precipitation.

The waggoners took each a horse out of his team and scampered; their example was immediately followed by others; so that all the wagons, provisions, artillery, and stores were left to the enemy. The general, being wounded, was brought off with difficulty; his secretary, Mr. Shirley, was killed by his side; and out of eighty-six officers, sixty-three were killed or wounded, and seven hundred and fourteen men killed out of eleven hundred. These eleven hundred had been picked men from the whole army; the rest had been left behind with Colonel Dunbar, who was to follow with the heavier part of the stores, provisions, and baggage. The flyers, not being pursued, arrived at Dunbar's camp, and the panic they brought with them instantly seized him and all his people; and, tho' he had now above one thousand men, and the enemy who had beaten Braddock did not at most exceed four hundred Indians and French together, instead of proceeding, and endeavoring to recover some of the lost honor, he ordered all the stores, ammunition, etc., to be destroyed, that he might have more horses to assist his flight towards the settlements, and less lumber to remove. He was there met with requests from the governors of Virginia, Maryland, and Pennsylvania, that he would post his troops on the frontier, so as to afford some protection to the inhabitants; but he continued his hasty march through all the country, not thinking himself safe till he arrived at Philadelphia, where the inhabitants could protect him. This whole transaction gave us Americans the first suspicion that our exalted ideas of the prowess of British regulars had not been well founded.

In their first march, too, from their landing till they got beyond the settlements, they had plundered and stripped the inhabitants, totally ruining some poor families, besides insulting, abusing, and confining the people if they remonstrated. This was enough to put us out of conceit of such defenders, if we had really wanted any. How different was the conduct of our French friends in 1781, who, during a march through the most inhabited part of our country from Rhode Island to Virginia, near seven hundred miles, occasioned not the smallest complaint for the loss of a pig, a chicken, or even an apple.

Captain Orme, who was one of the general's aids-de-camp, and, being grievously wounded, was brought off with him, and continued with him to his death, which happened in a few days, told me that he was totally silent all the first day, and at night only said, "Who would have thought it?" That he was silent again the following day, saying only at last, "We shall better know how to deal with them another time"; and died in a few minutes after.

The secretary's papers, with all the general's orders, instructions, and correspondence, falling into the enemy's hands, they selected and translated into French a number of the articles, which they printed, to prove the hostile intentions of the British court before the declaration of war. Among these I saw some letters of the general to the ministry, speaking highly of the great service I had rendered the army, and recommending me to their notice. David Hume, too, who was some years after secretary to Lord Hertford, when minister in France, and afterward to General Conway, when secretary of state, told me he had seen among the papers in that office, letters from Braddock highly recommending me. But, the expedition having been unfortunate, my service, it seems, was not thought of much value, for those recommendations were never of any use to me.

As to rewards from himself, I asked only one, which was, that he would give orders to his officers not to enlist any more of our bought servants, and that he would discharge such as had been already enlisted. This he readily granted, and several were accordingly returned to their masters, on my application. Dunbar, when the command devolved on him, was not so generous. He being at Philadelphia, on his retreat, or rather flight, I applied to him for the discharge of the servants of three poor farmers of Lancaster county that he had enlisted, reminding him of the late general's orders on that head. He promised me that, if the masters would come to him at Trenton, where he should be in a few days on his march to New York, he would there deliver their men to them. They accordingly were at the expense and trouble of going to Trenton, and there he refused to perform his promise, to their great loss and disappointment.

As soon as the loss of the wagons and horses was generally known, all the owners came upon me for the valuation which I had given bond to pay. Their demands gave me a great deal of trouble, my acquainting them that the money was ready in the paymaster's hands, but that orders for paying it must first be obtained from General Shirley, and my assuring them that I had applied to that general by letter; but, he being at a distance, an answer could not soon be received, and they must have patience, all this was not sufficient to satisfy, and some began to sue me. General Shirley at length relieved me from this terrible situation by appointing commissioners to examine the claims, and ordering payment. They amounted to near twenty thousand pound, which to pay would have ruined me.

Before we had the news of this defeat, the two Doctors Bond came to me with a subscription paper for raising money to defray the expense of a grand firework, which it was intended to exhibit at a rejoicing on receipt of the news of our taking Fort Duquesne. I looked grave, and said it would, I thought, be time enough to prepare for the rejoicing when we knew we should have occasion to rejoice. They seemed surprised that I did not immediately comply with their proposal. "Why the d———l!" says one of them, "you surely don't suppose that the fort will not be taken?" "I don't know that it will not be taken, but I know that the events of war are subject to great uncertainty." I gave them the reasons of my doubting; the subscription was dropt, and the projectors thereby missed the mortification they would have undergone if the firework had been prepared. Dr. Bond, on some other occasion afterward, said that he did not like Franklin's forebodings.

Governor Morris, who had continually worried the Assembly with message after message before the defeat of Braddock, to beat them into the making of acts to raise money for the defense of the province, without taxing, among others, the proprietary estates, and had rejected all their bills for not having such an exempting clause, now redoubled his attacks with more hope of success, the danger and necessity being greater. The Assembly, however, continued firm, believing they had justice on their side, and that it would be giving up an essential right if they suffered the governor to amend their money-bills. In one of the last, indeed, which was for granting fifty thousand pounds, his proposed amendment was only of a single word. The bill expressed "that all estates, real and personal, were to be taxed, those of the proprietaries not excepted." His amendment was, for not read only: a small, but very material alteration. However, when the news of this disaster reached England, our friends there whom we had taken care to furnish with all the Assembly's answers to the governor's messages, raised a clamor against the proprietaries for their meanness and injustice in giving their governor such instructions; some going so far as to say that, by obstructing the defense of their province, they forfeited their right to it. They were intimidated by this, and sent orders to their receiver-general to add five thousand pounds of their money to whatever sum might be given by the Assembly for such purpose.

This, being notified to the House, was accepted in lieu of their share of a general tax, and a new bill was formed, with an exempting clause, which passed accordingly. By this act I was appointed one of the commissioners for disposing of the money, sixty thousand pounds. I had been active in modelling the bill and procuring its passage, and had, at the same time, drawn a bill for establishing and disciplining a voluntary militia, which I carried through the House without much difficulty, as care was taken in it to leave the Quakers at their liberty. To promote the association necessary to form the militia, I wrote a dialogue, stating and answering all the objections I could think of to such a militia, which was printed, and had, as I thought, great effect.

XVII: Franklin's Defense of the Frontier

WHILE the several companies in the city and country were forming, and learning their exercise, the governor prevailed with me to take charge of our North-western frontier, which was infested by the enemy, and provide for the defense of the inhabitants by raising troops and building a line of forts. I undertook this military business, tho' I did not conceive myself well qualified for it. He gave me a commission with full powers, and a parcel of blank commissions for officers, to be given to whom I thought fit. I had but little difficulty in raising men, having soon five hundred and sixty under my command. My son, who had in the preceding war been an officer in the army raised against Canada, was my aid-de-camp, and of great use to me. The Indians had burned Gnadenhut, a village settled by the Moravians, and massacred the inhabitants; but the place was thought a good situation for one of the forts.

In order to march thither, I assembled the companies at Bethlehem, the chief establishment of those people. I was surprised to find it in so good a posture of defense; the destruction of Gnadenhut had made them apprehend danger. The principal buildings were defended by a stockade; they had purchased a quantity of arms and ammunition from New York, and had even placed quantities of small paving stones between the windows of their high stone houses, for their women to throw down upon the heads of any Indians that should attempt to force into them. The armed brethren, too, kept watch, and relieved as methodically as in any garrison town. In conversation with the bishop, Spangenberg, I mentioned this my surprise; for, knowing they had obtained an act of Parliament exempting them from military duties in the colonies, I had supposed they were conscientiously scrupulous of bearing arms. He answered me that it was not one of their established principles, but that, at the time of their obtaining that act, it was thought to be a principle with many of their people. On this occasion, however, they, to their surprise, found it adopted by but a few. It seems they were either deceived in themselves, or deceived the Parliament; but common sense, aided by present danger, will sometimes be too strong for whimsical opinions.

It was the beginning of January when we set out upon this business of building forts. I sent one detachment toward the Minisink, with instructions to erect one for the security of that upper part of the country, and another to the lower part, with similar instructions; and I concluded to go myself with the rest of my force to Gnadenhut, where a fort was thought more immediately necessary. The Moravians procured me five wagons for our tools, stores, baggage, etc.

Just before we left Bethlehem, eleven farmers, who had been driven from their plantations by the Indians, came to me requesting a supply of firearms, that they might go back and fetch off their cattle. I gave them each a gun with suitable ammunition. We had not marched many miles before it began to rain, and it continued raining all day; there were no habitations on the road to shelter us, till we arrived near night at the house of a German, where, and in his barn, we were all huddled together, as wet as water could make us. It was well we were not attacked in our march, for our arms were of the most ordinary sort, and our men could not keep their gun locks dry. The Indians are dexterous in contrivances for that purpose, which we had not. They met that day the eleven poor farmers above mentioned, and killed ten of them. The one who escaped informed that his and his companions' guns would not go off, the priming being wet with the rain.

The next day being fair, we continued our march, and arrived at the desolated Gnadenhut. There was a saw-mill near, round which were left several piles of boards, with which we soon hutted ourselves; an operation the more necessary at that inclement season, as we had no tents. Our first work was to bury more effectually the dead we found there, who had been half interred by the country people.

The next morning our fort was planned and marked out, the circumference measuring four hundred and fifty-five feet, which would require as many palisades to be made of trees, one with another, of a foot diameter each. Our axes, of which we had seventy, were immediately set to work to cut down trees, and, our men being dexterous in the use of them, great dispatch was made. Seeing the trees fall so fast, I had the curiosity to look at my watch when two men began to cut at a pine; in six minutes they had it upon the ground, and I found it of fourteen inches diameter. Each pine made three palisades of eighteen feet long, pointed at one end. While these were preparing, our other men dug a trench all round, of three feet deep, in which the palisades were to be planted; and, our wagons, the bodies being taken off, and the fore and hind wheels separated by taking out the pin which united the two parts of the perch, we had ten carriages, with two horses each, to bring the palisades from the woods to the spot. When they were set up, our carpenters built a stage of boards all round within, about six feet high, for the men to stand on when to fire thro' the loopholes. We had one swivel gun, which we mounted on one of the angles, and fired it as soon as fixed, to let the Indians know, if any were within hearing, that we had such pieces; and thus our fort, if such a magnificent name may be given to so miserable a stockade, was finished in a week, though it rained so hard every other day that the men could not work.

This gave me occasion to observe, that, when men are employed, they are best contented; for on the days they worked they were good-natured and cheerful, and, with the consciousness of having done a good day's work, they spent the evening jollily; but on our idle days they were mutinous and quarrelsome, finding fault with their pork, the bread, etc., and in continual ill-humour, which put me in mind of a sea-captain, whose rule it was to keep his men constantly at work; and, when his mate once told him that they had done everything, and there was nothing further to employ them about, "Oh," says he, "make them scour the anchor."

This kind of fort, however contemptible, is a sufficient defense against Indians, who have no cannon. Finding ourselves now posted securely, and having a place to retreat to on occasion, we ventured out in parties to scour the adjacent country. We met with no Indians, but we found the places on the neighboring hills where they had lain to watch our proceedings. There was an art in their contrivance of those places that seems worth mention. It being winter, a fire was necessary for them; but a common fire on the surface of the ground would by its light have discovered their position at a distance. They had therefore dug holes in the ground about three feet diameter, and somewhat deeper; we saw where they had with their hatchets cut off the charcoal from the sides of burnt logs lying in the woods. With these coals they had made small fires in the bottom of the holes, and we observed among the weeds and grass the prints of their bodies, made by their laying all round, with their legs hanging down in the holes to keep their feet warm, which, with them, is an essential point. This kind of fire, so managed, could not discover them, either by its light, flame, sparks, or even smoke: it appeared that their number was not great, and it seems they saw we were too many to be attacked by them with prospect of advantage.

We had for our chaplain a zealous Presbyterian minister, Mr. Beatty, who complained to me that the men did not generally attend his prayers and exhortations. When they enlisted, they were promised, besides pay and provisions, a gill of rum a day, which was punctually served out to them, half in the morning, and the other half in the evening; and I observed they were as punctual in attending to receive it; upon which I said to Mr. Beatty, "It is, perhaps, below the dignity of your profession to act as steward of the rum, but if you were to deal it out and only just after prayers, you would have them all about you." He liked the thought, undertook the office, and, with the help of a few hands to measure out the liquor, executed it to satisfaction, and never were prayers more generally and more punctually attended; so that I thought this method preferable to the punishment inflicted by some military laws for non-attendance on divine service.

I had hardly finished this business, and got my fort well stored with provisions, when I received a letter from the governor, acquainting me that he had called the Assembly, and wished my attendance there, if the posture of affairs on the frontiers was such that my remaining there was no longer necessary. My friends, too, of the Assembly, pressing me by their letters to be, if possible, at the meeting, and my three intended forts being now completed, and the inhabitants contented to remain on their farms under that protection, I resolved to return; the more willingly, as a New England officer, Colonel Clapham, experienced in Indian war, being on a visit to our establishment, consented to accept the command. I gave him a commission, and, parading the garrison, had it read before them, and introduced him to them as an officer who, from his skill in military affairs, was much more fit to command them than myself; and, giving them a little exhortation, took my leave. I was escorted as far as Bethlehem, where I rested a few days to recover from the fatigue I had undergone. The first night, being in a good bed, I could hardly sleep, it was so different from my hard lodging on the floor of our hut at Gnaden wrapped only in a blanket or two.

While at Bethlehem, I inquired a little into the practice of the Moravians: some of them had accompanied me, and all were very kind to me. I found they worked for a common stock, ate at common tables, and slept in common dormitories, great numbers together. In the dormitories I observed loopholes, at certain distances all along just under the ceiling, which I thought judiciously placed for change of air. I was at their church, where I was entertained with good music, the organ being accompanied with violins, hautboys, flutes, clarinets, etc. I understood that their sermons were not usually preached to mixed congregations of men, women, and children, as is our common practice, but that they assembled sometimes the married men, at other times their wives, then the young men, the young women, and the little children, each division by itself. The sermon I heard was to the latter, who came in and were placed in rows on benches; the boys under the conduct of a young man, their tutor, and the girls conducted by a young woman. The discourse seemed well adapted to their capacities, and was delivered in a pleasing, familiar manner, coaxing them, as it were, to be good. They behaved very orderly, but looked pale and unhealthy, which made me suspect they were kept too much within doors, or not allowed sufficient exercise.

I inquired concerning the Moravian marriages, whether the report was true that they were by lot. I was told that lots were used only in particular cases; that generally, when a young man found himself disposed to marry, he informed the elders of his class, who consulted the elder ladies that governed the young women. As these elders of the different sexes were well acquainted with the tempers and dispositions of their respective pupils, they could best judge what matches were suitable, and their judgments were generally acquiesced in; but if, for example, it should happen that two or three young women were found to be equally proper for the young man, the lot was then recurred to. I objected, if the matches are not made by the mutual choice of the parties, some of them may chance to be very unhappy. "And so they may," answered my informer, "if you let the parties chuse for themselves;" which, indeed, I could not deny.

Being returned to Philadelphia, I found the association went on swimmingly, the inhabitants that were not Quakers having pretty generally come into it, formed themselves into companies, and chose their captains, lieutenants, and ensigns, according to the new law. Dr. B. visited me, and gave me an account of the pains he had taken to spread a general good liking to the law, and ascribed much to those endeavors. I had had the vanity to ascribe all to my Dialogue; however, not knowing but that he might be in the right, I let him enjoy his opinion, which I take to be generally the best way in such cases. The officers, meeting, chose me to be colonel of the regiment, which I this time accepted. I forget how many companies we had, but we paraded about twelve hundred well-looking men, with a company of artillery, who had been furnished with six brass field-pieces, which they had become so expert in the use of as to fire twelve times in a minute. The first time I reviewed my regiment they accompanied me to my house, and would salute me with some rounds fired before my door, which shook down and broke several glasses of my electrical apparatus. And my new honor proved not much less brittle; for all our commissions were soon after broken by a repeal of the law in England.

During this short time of my colonelship, being about to set out on a journey to Virginia, the officers of my regiment took it into their heads that it would be proper for them to escort me out of town, as far as the Lower Ferry. Just as I was getting on horseback they came to my door, between thirty and forty, mounted, and all in their uniforms. I had not been previously acquainted with the project, or I should have prevented it, being naturally averse to the assuming of state on any occasion; and I was a good deal chagrined at their appearance, as I could not avoid their accompanying me. What made it worse was, that, as soon as we began to move, they drew their swords and rode with them naked all the way. Somebody wrote an account of this to the proprietor, and it gave him great offense. No such honor had been paid him when in the province, nor to any of his governors; and he said it was only proper to princes of the blood royal, which may be true for aught I know, who was, and still am, ignorant of the etiquette in such cases.

This silly affair, however, greatly increased his rancor against me, which was before not a little, on account of my conduct in the Assembly respecting the exemption of his estate from taxation, which I had always opposed very warmly, and not without severe reflections on his meanness and injustice of contending for it. He accused me to the ministry as being the great obstacle to the King's service, preventing, by my influence in the House, the proper form of the bills for raising money, and he instanced this parade with my officers as a proof of my having an intention to take the government of the province out of his hands by force. He also applied to Sir Everard Fawkener, the postmaster-general, to deprive me of my office; but it had no other effect than to procure from Sir Everard a gentle admonition.

Notwithstanding the continual wrangle between the governor and the House, in which I, as a member, had so large a share, there still subsisted a civil intercourse between that gentleman and myself, and we never had any personal difference. I have sometimes since thought that his little or no resentment against me, for the answers it was known I drew up to his messages, might be the effect of professional habit, and that, being bred a lawyer, he might consider us both as merely advocates for contending clients in a suit, he for the proprietaries and I for the Assembly. He would, therefore, sometimes call in a friendly way to advise with me on difficult points, and sometimes, tho' not often, take my advice.

We acted in concert to supply Braddock's army with provisions; and, when the shocking news arrived of his defeat, the governor sent in haste for me, to consult with him on measures for preventing the desertion of the back counties. I forget now the advice I gave; but I think it was, that Dunbar should be written to, and prevailed with, if possible, to post his troops on the frontiers for their protection, till, by reinforcements from the colonies, he might be able to proceed on the expedition. And, after my return from the frontier, he would have had me undertake the conduct of such an expedition with provincial troops, for the reduction of Fort Duquesne, Dunbar and his men being otherwise employed; and he proposed to commission me as general. I had not so good an opinion of my military abilities as he professed to have, and I believe his professions must have exceeded his real sentiments; but probably he might think that my popularity would facilitate the raising of the men, and my influence in Assembly, the grant of money to pay them, and that, perhaps, without taxing the proprietary estate. Finding me not so forward to engage as he expected, the project was dropt, and he soon after left the government, being superseded by Captain Denny.

XVIII: Scientific Experiments

BEFORE I proceed in relating the part I had in public affairs under this new governor's administration, it may not be amiss here to give some account of the rise and progress of my philosophical reputation.

In 1746, being at Boston, I met there with a Dr. Spence, who was lately arrived from Scotland, and showed me some electric experiments. They were imperfectly performed, as he was not very expert; but, being on a subject quite new to me, they equally surprised and pleased me. Soon after my return to Philadelphia, our library company received from Mr. P. Collinson, Fellow of the Royal Society of London, a present of a glass tube, with some account of the use of it in making such experiments. I eagerly seized the opportunity of repeating what I had seen at Boston; and, by much practice, acquired great readiness in performing those, also, which we had an account of from England, adding a number of new ones. I say much practice, for my house was continually full, for some time, with people who came to see these new wonders.

To divide a little this encumbrance among my friends, I caused a number of similar tubes to be blown at our glass-house, with which they furnished themselves, so that we had at length several performers. Among these, the principal was Mr. Kinnersley, an ingenious neighbour, who, being out of business, I encouraged to undertake showing the experiments for money, and drew up for him two lectures, in which the experiments were ranged in such order, and accompanied with such explanations in such method, as that the foregoing should assist in comprehending the following. He procured an elegant apparatus for the purpose, in which all the little machines that I had roughly made for myself were nicely formed by instrument-makers. His lectures were well attended, and gave great satisfaction; and after some time he went through the colonies, exhibiting them in every capital town, and picked up some money. In the West India islands, indeed, it was with difficulty the experiments could be made, from the general moisture of the air.

Obliged as we were to Mr. Collinson for his present of the tube, etc., I thought it right he should be informed of our success in using it, and wrote him several letters containing accounts of our experiments. He got them read in the Royal Society, where they were not at first thought worth so much notice as to be printed in their Transactions. One paper, which I wrote for Mr. Kinnersley, on the sameness of lightning with electricity, I sent to Dr. Mitchel, an acquaintance of mine, and one of the members also of that society, who wrote me word that it had been read, but was laughed at by the connoisseurs. The papers, however, being shown to Dr. Fothergill, he thought them of too much value to be stifled, and advised the printing of them. Mr. Collinson then gave them to Cave for publication in his Gentleman's Magazine; but he chose to print them separately in a pamphlet, and Dr. Fothergill wrote the preface. Cave, it seems, judged rightly for his profit, for by the additions that arrived afterward, they swelled to a quarto volume, which has had five editions, and cost him nothing for copy-money.

It was, however, some time before those papers were much taken notice of in England. A copy of them happening to fall into the hands of the Count de Buffon, a philosopher deservedly of great reputation in France, and, indeed, all over Europe, he prevailed with M. Dalibard to translate them into French, and they were printed at Paris. The publication offended the Abbé Nollet, preceptor in Natural Philosophy to the royal family, and an able experimenter, who had formed and published a theory of electricity, which then had the general vogue. He could not at first believe that such a work came from America, and said it must have been fabricated by his enemies at Paris, to decry his system. Afterwards, having been assured that there really existed such a person as Franklin at Philadelphia, which he had doubted, he wrote and published a volume of Letters, chiefly addressed to me, defending his theory, and denying the verity of my experiments, and of the positions deduced from them.

I once purposed answering the abbé, and actually began the answer; but, on consideration that my writings contained a description of experiments which anyone might repeat and verify, and if not to be verified, could not be defended; or of observations offered as conjectures, and not delivered dogmatically, therefore not laying me under any obligation to defend them; and reflecting that a dispute between two persons, writing in different languages, might be lengthened greatly by mistranslations, and thence misconceptions of one another's meaning, much of one of the abbé's letters being founded on an error in the translation, I concluded to let my papers shift for themselves, believing it was better to spend what time I could spare from public business in making new experiments, than in disputing about those already made. I therefore never answered M. Nollet, and the event gave me no cause to repent my silence; for my friend M. le Roy, of the Royal Academy of Sciences, took up my cause and refuted him; my book was translated into the Italian, German, and Latin languages; and the doctrine it contained was by degrees universally adopted by the philosophers of Europe, in preference to that of the abbé; so that he lived to see himself the last of his sect, except Monsieur B——, of Paris, his élève and immediate disciple.

What gave my book the more sudden and general celebrity, was the success of one of its proposed experiments, made by Messrs. Dalibard and De Lor at Marly, for drawing lightning from the clouds. This engaged the public attention everywhere. M. de Lor, who had an apparatus for experimental philosophy, and lectured in that branch of science, undertook to repeat what he called the Philadelphia Experiments; and, after they were performed before the king and court, all the curious of Paris flocked to see them. I will not swell this narrative with an account of that capital experiment, nor of the infinite pleasure I received in the success of a similar one I made soon after with a kite at Philadelphia, as both are to be found in the histories of electricity.

Dr. Wright, an English physician, when at Paris, wrote to a friend, who was of the Royal Society, an account of the high esteem my experiments were in among the learned abroad, and of their wonder that my writings had been so little noticed in England. The society, on this, resumed the consideration of the letters that had been read to them; and the celebrated Dr. Watson drew up a summary account of them, and of all I had afterwards sent to England on the subject, which he accompanied with some praise of the writer. This summary was then printed in their Transactions; and some members of the society in London, particularly the very ingenious Mr. Canton, having verified the experiment of procuring lightning from the clouds by a pointed rod, and acquainting them with the success, they soon made me more than amends for the slight with which they had before treated me. Without my having made any application for that honor, they chose me a member, and voted that I should be excused the customary payments, which would have amounted to twenty-five guineas; and ever since have given me their Transactions gratis. They also presented me with the gold medal of Sir Godfrey Copley for the year 1753, the delivery of which was accompanied by a very handsome speech of the president, Lord Macclesfield, wherein I was highly honored.

XIX: Agent of Pennsylvania in London

OUR new governor, Captain Denny, brought over for me the before mentioned medal from the Royal Society, which he presented to me at an entertainment given him by the city. He accompanied it with very polite expressions of his esteem for me, having, as he said, been long acquainted with my character. After dinner, when the company, as was customary at that time, were engaged in drinking, he took me aside into another room, and acquainted me that he had been advised by his friends in England to cultivate a friendship with me, as one who was capable of giving him the best advice, and of contributing most effectually to the making his administration easy; that he therefore desired of all things to have a good understanding with me, and he begged me to be assured of his readiness on all occasions to render me every service that might be in his power. He said much to me, also, of the proprietor's good disposition towards the province, and of the advantage it might be to us all, and to me in particular, if the opposition that had been so long continued to his measures was dropt, and harmony restored between him and the people; in effecting which, it was thought no one could be more serviceable than myself; and I might depend on adequate acknowledgments and recompenses, etc., etc. The drinkers, finding we did not return immediately to the table, sent us a decanter of Madeira, which the governor made liberal use of, and in proportion became more profuse of his solicitations and promises.

My answers were to this purpose: that my circumstances, thanks to God, were such as to make proprietary favors unnecessary to me; and that, being a member of the Assembly, I could not possibly accept of any; that, however, I had no personal enmity to the proprietary, and that, whenever the public measures he proposed should appear to be for the good of the people, no one should espouse and forward them more zealously than myself; my past opposition having been founded on this, that the measures which had been urged were evidently intended to serve the proprietary interest, with great prejudice to that of the people; that I was much obliged to him (the governor) for his professions of regard to me, and that he might rely on everything in my power to make his administration as easy as possible, hoping at the same time that he had not brought with him the same unfortunate instruction his predecessor had been hampered with.

On this he did not then explain himself; but when he afterwards came to do business with the Assembly, they appeared again, the disputes were renewed, and I was as active as ever in the opposition, being the penman, first, of the request to have a communication of the instructions, and then of the remarks upon them, which may be found in the votes of the time, and in the Historical Review I afterward published. But between us personally no enmity arose; we were often together; he was a man of letters, had seen much of the world, and was very entertaining and pleasing in conversation. He gave me the first information that my old friend Jas. Ralph was still alive; that he was esteemed one of the best political writers in England; had been employed in the dispute between Prince Frederic and the king, and had obtained a pension of three hundred a year; that his reputation was indeed small as a poet, Pope having damned his poetry in the Dunciad, but his prose was thought as good as any man's.

The Assembly finally finding the proprietary obstinately persisted in manacling their deputies with instructions inconsistent not only with the privileges of the people, but with the service of the crown, resolved to petition the king against them, and appointed me their agent to go over to England, to present and support the petition. The House had sent up a bill to the governor, granting a sum of sixty thousand pounds for the king's use (ten thousand pounds of which was subjected to the orders of the then general, Lord Loudoun), which the governor absolutely refused to pass, in compliance with his instructions.

I had agreed with Captain Morris, of the packet at New York, for my passage, and my stores were put on board, when Lord Loudoun arrived at Philadelphia, expressly, as he told me, to endeavor an accommodation between the governor and Assembly, that his majesty's service might not be obstructed by their dissensions. Accordingly, he desired the governor and myself to meet him, that he might hear what was to be said on both sides. We met and discussed the business. In behalf of the Assembly, I urged all the various arguments that may be found in the public papers of that time, which were of my writing, and are printed with the minutes of the Assembly; and the governor pleaded his instructions, the bond he had given to observe them, and his ruin if he disobeyed, yet seemed not unwilling to hazard himself if Lord Loudoun would advise it. This his lordship did not chuse to do, though I once thought I had nearly prevailed with him to do it; but finally he rather chose to urge the compliance of the Assembly; and he entreated me to use my endeavors with them for that purpose, declaring that he would spare none of the king's troops for the defense of our frontiers, and that, if we did not continue to provide for that defense ourselves, they must remain exposed to the enemy.

I acquainted the House with what had passed, and, presenting them with a set of resolutions I had drawn up, declaring our rights, and that we did not relinquish our claim to those rights, but only suspended the exercise of them on this occasion thro' force, against which we protested, they at length agreed to drop that bill, and frame another conformable to the proprietary instructions. This of course the governor passed, and I was then at liberty to proceed on my voyage. But, in the meantime, the packet had sailed with my sea-stores, which was some loss to me, and my only recompense was his lordship's thanks for my service, all the credit of obtaining the accommodation falling to his share.

He set out for New York before me; and, as the time for dispatching the packet-boats was at his disposition, and there were two then remaining there, one of which, he said, was to sail very soon, I requested to know the precise time, that I might not miss her by any delay of mine. His answer was, "I have given out that she is to sail on Saturday next; but I may let you know, entre nous, that if you are there by Monday morning, you will be in time, but do not delay longer." By some accidental hindrance at a ferry, it was Monday noon before I arrived, and I was much afraid she might have sailed, as the wind was fair; but I was soon made easy by the information that she was still in the harbor, and would not move till the next day. One would imagine that I was now on the very point of departing for Europe. I thought so; but I was not then so well acquainted with his lordship's character, of which indecision was one of the strongest features. I shall give some instances. It was about the beginning of April that I came to New York, and I think it was near the end of June before we sailed. There were then two of the packet-boats, which had been long in port, but were detained for the general's letters, which were always to be ready tomorrow. Another packet arrived; she too was detained; and, before we sailed, a fourth was expected. Ours was the first to be dispatch's, as having been there longest. Passengers were engaged in all, and some extremely impatient to be gone, and the merchants uneasy about their letters, and the orders they had given for insurance (it being war time) for fall goods; but their anxiety avail's nothnothing; his lordship's letters were not ready; and yet whoever waited on him found him always at his desk, pen in hand, and concluded he must needs write abundantly.

Going myself one morning to pay my respects, I found in his antechamber one Innis, a messenger of Philadelphia, who had come from thence express with a packet from Governor Denny for the general. He delivered to me some letters from my friends there, which occasion's my inquiring when he was to return, and where he lodged, that I might send some letters by him. He told me he was ordered to call tomorrow at nine for the general's answer to the governor, and should set off immediately. I put my letters into his hands the same day. A fortnight after I met him again in the same place. "So, you are soon returned, Innis?" "Return's! no, I am not gone yet." "How so?" "I have called here by order every morning these two weeks past for his lordship's letter, and it is not yet ready." "Is it possible, when he is so great a writer? for I see him constantly at his escritoire." "Yes," says Innis, "but he is like St. George on the signs, always on horseback, and never rides on." This observation of the messenger was, it seems, well founded; for, when in England, I understood that Mr. Pitt gave it as one reason for removing this general, and sending Generals Amherst and Wolfe, that the minister never heard from him, and could not know what he was doing.

This daily expectation of sailing, and all the three packets going down to Sandy Hook, to join the fleet there, the passengers thought it best to be on board, lest by a sudden order the ships should sail, and they be left behind. There, if I remember right, we were about six weeks, consuming our sea-stores, and obliged to procure more. At length the fleet sailed, the general and all his army on board, bound to Louisburg, with the intent to besiege and take that fortress; all the packet-boats in company ordered to attend the general's ship, ready to receive his dispatches when they should be ready. We were out five days before we got a letter with leave to part, and then our ship quitted the fleet and steered for England. The other two packets he still detained, carried them with him to Halifax, where he stayed some time to exercise the men in sham attacks upon sham forts, then altered his mind as to besieging Louisburg, and returned to New York, with all his troops, together with the two packets above mentioned, and all their passengers! During his absence the French and savages had taken Fort George, on the frontier of that province, and the savages had massacred many of the garrison after capitulation.

I saw afterwards in London Captain Bonnell, who commanded one of those packets. He told me that, when he had been detained a month, he acquainted his lordship that his ship was grown foul, to a degree that must necessarily hinder her fast sailing, a point of consequence for a packet-boat, and requested an allowance of time to heave her down and clean her bottom. He was asked how long time that would require. He answered, three days. The general replied, "If you can do it in one day, I give leave; otherwise not; for you must certainly sail the day after tomorrow." So he never obtained leave, though detained afterwards from day to day during full three months.

I saw also in London one of Bonnell's passengers, who was so enraged against his lordship for deceiving and detaining him so long at New York, and then carrying him to Halifax and back again, that he swore he would sue him for damages. Whether he did or not, I never heard; but, as he represented the injury to his affairs, it was very considerable.

On the whole, I wondered much how such a man came to be entrusted with so important a business as the conduct of a great army; but, having since seen more of the great world, and the means of obtaining, and motives for giving places, my wonder is diminished. General Shirley, on whom the command of the army devolved upon the death of Braddock, would, in my opinion, if continued in place, have made a much better campaign than that of Loudoun in 1757, which was frivolous, expensive, and disgraceful to our nation beyond conception; for, tho' Shirley was not a bred soldier, he was sensible and sagacious in himself, and attentive to good advice from others, capable of forming judicious plans, and quick and active in carrying them into execution. Loudoun, instead of defending the colonies with his great army, left them totally exposed while he paraded idly at Halifax, by which means Fort George was lost, besides, he deranged all our mercantile operations, and distressed our trade, by a long embargo on the exportation of provisions, on pretense of keeping supplies from being obtained by the enemy, but in reality for beating down their price in favor of the contractors, in whose profits, it was said, perhaps from suspicion only, he had a share. And, when at length the embargo was taken off, by neglecting to send notice of it to Charlestown, the Carolina fleet was detained near three months longer, whereby their bottoms were so much damaged by the worm that a great part of them foundered in their passage home.

Shirley was, I believe, sincerely glad of being relieved from so burdensome a charge as the conduct of an army must be to a man unacquainted with military business. I was at the entertainment given by the city of New York to Lord Loudoun, on his taking upon him the command. Shirley, tho' thereby superseded, was present also. There was a great company of officers, citizens, and strangers, and, some chairs having been borrowed in the neighborhood, there was one among them very low, which fell to the lot of Mr. Shirley. Perceiving it as I sat by him, I said, "They have given you, sir, too low a seat." "No matter," says he, "Mr. Franklin, I find a low seat the easiest."

While I was, as afore mentioned, detained at New York, I received all the accounts of the provisions, etc., that I had furnished to Braddock, some of which accounts could not sooner be obtained from the different persons I had employed to assist in the business. I presented them to Lord Loudoun, desiring to be paid the balance. He caused them to be regularly examined by the proper officer, who, after comparing every article with its voucher, certified them to be right; and the balance due for which his lordship promised to give me an order on the paymaster. This was, however, put off from time to time; and tho' I called often for it by appointment, I did not get it. At length, just before my departure, he told me he had, on better consideration, concluded not to mix his accounts with those of his predecessors. "And you," says he, "when in England, have only to exhibit your accounts at the treasury, and you will be paid immediately."

I mentioned, but without effect, the great and unexpected expense I had been put to by being detained so long at New York, as a reason for my desiring to be presently paid; and on my observing that it was not right I should be put to any further trouble or delay in obtaining the money I had advanced, as I charged no commission for my service, "O, Sir," says he, "you must not think of persuading us that you are no gainer; we understand better those affairs, and know that everyone concerned in supplying the army finds means, in the doing it, to fill his own pockets." I assured him that was not my case, and that I had not pocketed a farthing; but he appeared clearly not to believe me; and, indeed, I have since learnt that immense fortunes are often made in such employments. As to my balance, I am not paid it to this day, of which more hereafter.

Our captain of the packet had boasted much, before we sailed, of the swiftness of his ship; unfortunately, when we came to sea, she proved the dullest of ninety-six sail, to his no small mortification. After many conjectures respecting the cause, when we were near another ship almost as dull as ours, which, however, gained upon us, the captain ordered all hands to come aft, and stand as near the ensign staff as possible. We were, passengers included, about forty persons. While we stood there, the ship mended her pace, and soon left her neighbour far behind, which proved clearly what our captain suspected, that she was loaded too much by the head. The casks of water, it seems, had been all placed forward; these he therefore ordered to be moved further aft, on which the ship recovered her character, and proved the best sailer in the fleet.

The captain said she had once gone at the rate of thirteen knots, which is accounted thirteen miles per hour. We had on board, as a passenger, Captain Kennedy, of the Navy, who contended that it was impossible, and that no ship ever sailed so fast, and that there must have been some error in the division of the log-line, or some mistake in heaving the log. A wager ensued between the two captains, to be decided when there should be sufficient wind. Kennedy thereupon examined rigorously the log-line, and, being satisfied with that, he determined to throw the log himself. Accordingly some days after, when the wind blew very fair and fresh, and the captain of the packet, Lutwidge, said he believed she then went at the rate of thirteen knots, Kennedy made the experiment, and owned his wager lost.

The above fact I give for the sake of the following observation. It has been remarked, as an imperfection in the art of ship-building, that it can never be known, till she is tried, whether a new ship will or will not be a good sailer; for that the model of a good-sailing ship has been exactly followed in a new one, which has proved, on the contrary, remarkably dull. I apprehend that this may partly be occasion's by the different opinions of seamen respecting the modes of lading, rigging, and sailing of a ship; each has his system; and the same vessel, laden by the judgment and orders of one captain, shall sail better or worse than when by the orders of another. Besides, it scarce ever happens that a ship is formed, fitted for the sea, and sailed by the same person. One man builds the hull, another rigs her, a third lades and sails her. No one of these has the advantage of knowing all the ideas and experience of the others, and, therefore, cannot draw just conclusions from a combination of the whole.

Even in the simple operation of sailing when at sea, I have often observed different judgments in the officers who commanded the successive watches, the wind being the same. One would have the sails trimmed sharper or flatter than another, so that they seemed to have no certain rule to govern by. Yet I think a set of experiments might be instituted; first, to determine the most proper form of the hull for swift sailing; next, the best dimensions and properest place for the masts; then the form and quantity of sails, and their position, as the wind may be; and, lastly, the disposition of the lading. This is an age of experiments, and I think a set accurately made and combined would be of great use. I am persuaded, therefore, that ere long some ingenious philosopher will undertake it, to whom I wish success.

We were several times chased in our passage, but out-sailed everything, and in thirty days had soundings. We had a good observation, and the captain judged himself so near our port, Falmouth, that, if we made a good run in the night, we might be off the mouth of that harbor in the morning, and by running in the night might escape the notice of the enemy's privateers, who often cruised near the entrance of the channel. Accordingly, all the sail was set that we could possibly make, and the wind being very fresh and fair, we went right before it, and made great way. The captain, after his observation, shaped his course, as he thought, so as to pass wide of the Scilly Isles; but it seems there is sometimes a strong indraught setting up St. George's Channel, which deceives seamen and caused the loss of Sir Cloudesley Shovel's squadron. This indraught was probably the cause of what happened to us.

We had a watchman placed in the bow, to whom they often called, "Look well out before there," and he as often answered, "Ay, ay"; but perhaps had his eyes shut, and was half asleep at the time, they sometimes answering, as is said, mechanically; for he did not see a light just before us, which had been hidden by the studding-sails from the man at the helm, and from the rest of the watch, but by an accidental yaw of the ship was discovered, and occasion's a great alarm, we being very near it, the light appearing to me as big as a cartwheel. It was midnight, and our captain fast asleep; but Captain Kennedy, jumping upon deck, and seeing the danger, ordered the ship to wear round, all sails standing; an operation dangerous to the masts, but it carried us clear, and we escaped shipwreck, for we were running right upon the rocks on which the lighthouse was erected. This deliverance impressed me strongly with the utility of lighthouses, and made me resolve to encourage the building more of them in America if I should live to return there.

In the morning it was found by the soundings, etc., that we were near our port, but a thick fog hid the land from our sight. About nine o'clock the fog began to rise, and seemed to be lifted up from the water like the curtain at a playhouse, discovering underneath, the town of Falmouth, the vessels in its harbor, and the fields that surrounded it. This was a most pleasing spectacle to those who had been so long without any other prospects than the uniform view of a vacant ocean, and it gave us the more pleasure as we were now free from the anxieties which the state of war occasioned.

I set out immediately, with my son, for London, and we only stopped a little by the way to view Stonehenge on Salisbury Plain, and Lord Pembroke's house and gardens, with his very curious antiquities at Wilton. We arrived in London the 27th of July, 1757.

As soon as I was settled in a lodging Mr. Charles had provided for me, I went to visit Dr. Fothergill, to whom I was strongly recommended, and whose counsel respecting my proceedings I was advised to obtain. He was against an immediate complaint to government, and thought the proprietaries should first be personally applied to, who might possibly be induced by the interposition and persuasion of some private friends, to accommodate matters amicably. I then waited on my old friend and correspondent, Mr. Peter Collinson, who told me that John Hanbury, the great Virginia merchant, had requested to be informed when I should arrive, that he might carry me to Lord Granville's, who was then President of the Council and wished to see me as soon as possible. I agreed to go with him the next morning. Accordingly Mr. Hanbury called for me and took me in his carriage to that nobleman's, who received me with great civility; and after some questions respecting the present state of affairs in America and discourse thereupon, he said to me: "You Americans have wrong ideas of the nature of your constitution; you contend that the king's instructions to his governors are not laws, and think yourselves at liberty to regard or disregard them at your own discretion. But those instructions are not like the pocket instructions given to a minister going abroad, for regulating his conduct in some trifling point of ceremony. They are first drawn up by judges learned in the laws; they are then considered, debated, and perhaps amended in Council, after which they are signed by the king. They are then, so far as they relate to you, the law of the land, for the king is the Legislator of the Colonies," I told his lordship this was new doctrine to me. I had always understood from our charters that our laws were to be made by our Assemblies, to be presented indeed to the king for his royal assent, but that being once given the king could not repeal or alter them. And as the Assemblies could not make permanent laws without his assent, so neither could he make a law for them without theirs. He assured me I was totally mistaken. I did not think so, however, and his lordship's conversation having a little alarmed me as to what might be the sentiments of the court concerning us, I wrote it down as soon as I returned to my lodgings. I recollected that about 20 years before, a clause in a bill brought into Parliament by the ministry had proposed to make the king's instructions laws in the colonies, but the clause was thrown out by the Commons, for which we adored them as our friends and friends of liberty, till by their conduct towards us in 1765 it seemed that they had refused that point of sovereignty to the king only that they might reserve it for themselves.

With his keen insight into human nature and his consequent knowledge of American character, he foresaw the inevitable result of such an attitude on the part of England. This conversation with Grenville makes these last pages of the Autobiography one of its most important parts.

After some days, Dr. Fothergill having spoken to the proprietaries, they agreed to a meeting with me at Mr. T. Penn's house in Spring Garden. The conversation at first consisted of mutual declarations of disposition to reasonable accommodations, but I suppose each party had its own ideas of what should be meant by reasonable. We then went into consideration of our several points of complaint, which I enumerated. The proprietaries justified their conduct as well as they could, and I the Assembly's. We now appeared very wide, and so far from each other in our opinions as to discourage all hope of agreement. However, it was concluded that I should give them the heads of our complaints in writing, and they promised then to consider them. I did so soon after, but they put the paper into the hands of their solicitor, Ferdinand John Paris, who managed for them all their law business in their great suit with the neighboring proprietary of Maryland, Lord Baltimore, which had subsisted 70 years, and wrote for them all their papers and messages in their dispute with the Assembly. He was a proud, angry man, and as I had occasionally in the answers of the Assembly treated his papers with some severity, they being really weak in point of argument and haughty in expression, he had conceived a mortal enmity to me, which discovering itself whenever we met, I declined the proprietary's proposal that he and I should discuss the heads of complaint between our two selves, and refused treating with anyone but them. They then by his advice put the paper into the hands of the Attorney and Solicitor-General for their opinion and counsel upon it, where it lay unanswered a year wanting eight days, during which time I made frequent demands of an answer from the proprietaries, but without obtaining any other than that they had not yet received the opinion of the Attorney and Solicitor-General. What it was when they did receive it I never learnt, for they did not communicate it to me, but sent a long message to the Assembly drawn and signed by Paris, reciting my paper, complaining of its want of formality, as a rudeness on my part, and giving a flimsy justification of their conduct, adding that they should be willing to accommodate matters if the As- Assembly would send out some person of candor to treat with them for that purpose, intimating thereby that I was not such.

The want of formality or rudeness was, probably, my not having addressed the paper to them with their assumed titles of True and Absolute Proprietaries of the Province of Pennsylvania, which I omitted as not thinking it necessary in a paper, the intention of which was only to reduce to a certainty by writing, what in conversation I had delivered viva voce.

But during this delay, the Assembly having prevailed with Gov'r Denny to pass an act taxing the proprietary estate in common with the estates of the people, which was the grand point in dispute, they omitted answering the message.

When this act however came over, the proprietaries, counselled by Paris, determined to oppose its receiving the royal assent. Accordingly they petitioned the king in Council, and a hearing was appointed in which two lawyers were employed by them against the act, and two by me in support of it. They alleged that the act was intended to load the proprietary estate in order to spare those of the people, and that if it were suffered to continue in force, and the proprietaries, who were in odium with the people, left to their mercy in proportioning the taxes, they would inevitably be ruined. We replied that the act had no such intention, and would have no such effect. That the assessors were honest and discreet men under an oath to assess fairly and equitably, and that any advantage each of them might expect in lessening his own tax by augmenting that of the proprietaries was too trifling to induce them to perjure themselves. This is the purport of what I remember as urged by both sides, except that we insisted strongly on the mischievous consequences that must attend a repeal, for that the money, £100,000, being printed and given to the king's use, expended in his service, and now spread among the people, the repeal would strike it dead in their hands to the ruin of many, and the total discouragement of future grants, and the selfishness of the proprietors in soliciting such a general catastrophe, merely from a groundless fear of their estate being taxed too highly, was insisted on in the strongest terms. On this, Lord Mansfield, one of the counsel, rose, and beckoning me took me into the clerk's chamber, while the lawyers were pleading, and asked me if I was really of opinion that no injury would be done the proprietary estate in the execution of the act. I said certainly. "Then," says he, "you can have little objection to enter into an engagement to assure that point." I answered, "None at all." He then called in Paris, and after some discourse, his lordship's proposition was accepted on both sides; a paper to the purpose was drawn up by the Clerk of the Council, which I signed with Mr. Charles, who was also an Agent of the Province for their ordinary affairs, when Lord Mansfield returned to the Council Chamber, where finally the law was allowed to pass. Some changes were however recommended and we also engaged they should be made by a subsequent law, but the Assembly did not think them necessary; for one year's tax having been levied by the act before the order of Council arrived, they appointed a committee to examine the proceedings of the assessors, and on this committee they put several particular friends of the proprietaries. After a full enquiry, they unanimously signed a report that they found the tax had been assessed with perfect equity.

The Assembly looked into my entering into the first part of the engagement, as an essential service to the Province, since it secured the credit of the paper money then spread over all the country. They gave me their thanks in form when I returned. But the proprietaries were enraged at Governor Denny for having passed the act, and turned him out with threats of suing him for breach of instructions which he had given bond to observe. He, however, having done it at the instance of the General, and for His Majesty's service, and having some powerful interest at court, despised the threats and they were never put in execution.... [unfinished]

Appendix

Electrical Kite

To Peter Collinson
[Philadelphia], Oct. 19, 1752.
Sir,

As frequent mention is made in public papers from Europe of the success of the Philadelphia experiment for drawing the electric fire from clouds by means of pointed rods of iron erected on high buildings, &c., it may be agreeable to the curious to be informed, that the same experiment has succeeded in Philadelphia, though made in a different and more easy manner, which is as follows:

Make a small cross of two light strips of cedar, the arms so long as to reach to the four corners of a large, thin silk handkerchief when extended; tie the corners of the handkerchief to the extremities of the cross, so you have the body of a kite; which being properly accommodated with a tail, loop, and string, will rise in the air, like those made of paper; but this being of silk, is fitter to bear the wet and wind of a thunder-gust without tearing. To the top of the upright stick of the cross is to be fixed a very sharp-pointed wire, rising a foot or more above the wood. To the end of the twine, next the hand, is to be tied a silk ribbon, and where the silk and twine join, a key may be fastened. This kite is to be raised when a thunder-gust appears to be coming on, and the person who holds the string must stand within a door or window, or under some cover, so that the silk ribbon may not be wet; and care must be taken that the twine does not touch the frame of the door or window. As soon as any of the thunder clouds come over the kite, the pointed wire will draw the electric fire from them, and the kite, with all the twine will be electrified, and the loose filaments of the twine will stand out every way and be attracted by an approaching finger. And when the rain has wet the kite and twine, so that it can conduct the electric fire freely, you will find it stream out plentifully from the key on the approach of your knuckle. At this key the phial may be charged; and from electric fire thus obtained, spirits may be kindled, and all the electric experiments be performed, which are usually done by the help of a rubbed glass globe or tube, and thereby the sameness of the electric matter with that of lightning completely demonstrated.

B. Franklin.

From "Father Abraham's Speech," 1760.

The Way to Wealth

(From "Father Abraham's Speech," forming the preface to *Poor Richard's Almanac* for 1758.)

It would be thought a hard Government that should tax its People one-tenth Part of their Time, to be employed in its Service. But Idleness taxes many of us much more, if we reckon all that is spent in absolute Sloth, or doing of nothing, with that which is spent in idle Employments or Amusements, that amount to nothing. Sloth, by bringing on Diseases, absolutely shortens Life. Sloth, like Rust, consumes faster than Labor wears; while the used key is always bright, as Poor Richard says. But dost thou love Life, then do not squander Time, for that's the stuff Life is made of, as Poor Richard says. How much more than is necessary do we spend in sleep, forgetting that The sleeping Fox catches no Poultry, and that There will be sleeping enough in the Grave, as Poor Richard says.

If Time be of all Things the most precious, wasting Time must be, as Poor Richard says, the greatest Prodigality; since, as he elsewhere tells us, Lost Time is never found again; and what we call Time enough, always proves little enough: Let us then up and be doing, and doing to the Purpose; so by Diligence shall we do more with less Perplexity. Sloth makes all Things difficult, but Industry all easy, as Poor Richard says; and He that riseth late must trot all Day, and shall scarce overtake his Business at Night; while Laziness travels so slowly, that Poverty soon overtakes him, as we read in Poor Richard, who adds, Drive thy Business, let not that drive thee; and Early to Bed, and early to rise, makes a Man healthy, wealthy, and wise.

Industry need not wish, and he that lives upon Hope will die fasting.

There are no Gains without Pains.

He that hath a Trade hath an Estate; and he that hath a Calling, hath an Office of Profit and Honor; but then the Trade must be worked at, and the Calling well followed, or neither the Estate nor the Office will enable us to pay our Taxes.

What though you have found no Treasure, nor has any rich Relation left you a Legacy, Diligence is the Mother of Good-luck, as Poor Richard says, and God gives all Things to Industry.

One Today is worth two Tomorrows, and farther, Have you somewhat to do Tomorrow, do it Today.

If you were a Servant, would you not be ashamed that a good Master should catch you idle? Are you then your own Master, be ashamed to catch yourself idle.

Stick to it steadily; and you will see great Effects, for Constant Dropping wears away Stones, and by Diligence and Patience the Mouse ate in two the Cable; and Little Strokes fell great Oaks.

Methinks I hear some of you say, Must a Man afford himself no Leisure? I will tell thee, my friend, what Poor Richard says, Employ thy Time well, if thou meanest to gain Leisure; and, since thou art not sure of a Minute, throw not away an Hour. Leisure, is Time for doing something useful; this Leisure the diligent Man will obtain, but the lazy Man never; so that, as Poor Richard says, A Life of Leisure and a Life of Laziness are two things.

Keep thy Shop, and thy Shop will keep thee; and again, If you would have your business done, go; if not, send.

If you would have a faithful Servant, and one that you like, serve yourself.

A little Neglect may breed great Mischief: adding, for want of a Nail the Shoe was lost; for want of a Shoe the Horse was lost; and for want of a Horse the Rider was lost, being overtaken and slain by the Enemy; all for the want of Care about a Horse-shoe Nail.

So much for Industry, my Friends, and Attention to one's own Business; but to these we must add Frugality.

What maintains one Vice, would bring up two Children. You may think perhaps, that a little Tea, or a little Punch now and then, Diet a little more costly, Clothes a little finer, and a little Entertainment now and then, can be no great Matter; but remember what Poor Richard says, Many a Little makes a Mickle.

Beware of little expenses; A small Leak will sink a great Ship; and again, Who Dainties love, shall Beggars prove; and moreover, Fools make Feasts, and wise Men eat them. Buy what thou hast no Need of, and ere long thou shalt sell thy Necessaries. If you would know the Value of Money, go and try to borrow some; for, he that goes a borrowing goes a sorrowing.

The second Vice is Lying, the first is running in Debt.

Lying rides upon Debt's Back.

Poverty often deprives a Man of all Spirit and Virtue: 'Tis hard for an empty Bag to stand upright.

And now to conclude, Experience keeps a dear School, but Fools will learn in no other, and scarce in that; for it is true, we may give Advice, but we cannot give Conduct, as Poor Richard says: However, remember this, They that won't be counseled, can't be helped, as Poor Richard says: and farther, That if you will not hear Reason, she'll surely rap your Knuckles.

The Whistle

To Madame Brillon
Passy, November 10, 1779.

I am charmed with your description of Paradise, and with your plan of living there; and I approve much of your conclusion, that, in the meantime, we should draw all the good we can from this world. In my opinion, we might all draw more good from it than we do, and suffer less evil, if we would take care not to give too much for whistles. For to me it seems, that most of the unhappy people we meet with, are become so by neglect of that caution. You ask what I mean? You love stories, and will excuse my telling one of myself.

When I was a child of seven year old, my friends, on a holiday, filled my pocket with coppers. I went directly to a shop where they sold toys for children; and being charmed with the sound of a whistle, that I met by the way in the hands of another boy, I voluntarily offered and gave all my money for one. I then came home, and went whistling all over the house, much pleased with my whistle, but disturbing all the family. My brothers, and sisters, and cousins, understanding the bargain I had made, told me I had given four times as much for it as it was worth; put me in mind what good things I might have bought with the rest of the money; and laughed at me so much for my folly, that I cried with vexation; and the reflection gave me more chagrin than the whistle gave me pleasure.

This, however, was afterwards of use to me, the impression continuing on my mind; so that often, when I was tempted to buy some unnecessary thing, I said to myself, Don't give too much for the whistle; and I saved my money.

As I grew up, came into the world, and observed the actions of men, I thought I met with many, very many, who gave too much for the whistle.

When I saw one too ambitious of court favor, sacrificing his time in attendance on levees, his repose, his liberty, his virtue, and perhaps his friends, to attain it, I have said to myself, This man gives too much for his whistle.

When I saw another fond of popularity, constantly employing himself in political bustles, neglecting his own affairs, and ruining them by neglect, He pays, indeed, said I, too much for his whistle.

If I knew a miser who gave up every kind of comfortable living, all the pleasure of doing good to others, all the esteem of his fellow citizens, and the joys of benevolent friendship, for the sake of accumulating wealth, Poor man, said I, you pay too much for your whistle.

When I met with a man of pleasure, sacrificing every laudable improvement of the mind, or of his fortune, to mere corporeal sensations, and ruining his health in their pursuit, Mistaken man, said I, you are providing pain for yourself, instead of pleasure; you give too much for your whistle.

If I see one fond of appearance, or fine clothes, fine houses, fine furniture, fine equipages, all above his fortune, for which he contracts debts, and ends his career in a prison, Alas! say I, he has paid dear, very dear, for his whistle.

When I see a beautiful, sweet-tempered girl married to an ill-natured brute of a husband, What a pity, say I, that she should pay so much for a whistle!

In short, I conceive that great part of the miseries of mankind are brought upon them by the false estimates they have made of the value of things, and by their giving too much for their whistles.

Yet I ought to have charity for these unhappy people, when I consider, that, with all this wisdom of which I am boasting, there are certain things in the world so tempting, for example, the apples of King John, which happily are not to be bought; for if they were put to sale by auction, I might very easily be led to ruin myself in the purchase, and find that I had once more given too much for the whistle. Adieu, my dear friend, and believe me ever yours very sincerely and with unalterable affection,

B. Franklin.

A Letter to Samuel Mather
Passy, May 12, 1784.
Revd. Sir,

It is now more than 60 years since I left Boston, but I remember well both your father and grandfather, having heard them both in the pulpit, and seen them in their houses. The last time I saw your father was in the beginning of 1724, when I visited him after my first trip to Pennsylvania. He received me in his library, and on my taking leave showed me a shorter way out of the house through a narrow passage, which was crossed by a beam overhead. We were still talking as I withdrew, he accompanying me behind, and I turning partly towards him, when he said hastily, "Stoop, stoop!" I did not understand him, till I felt my head hit against the beam. He was a man that never missed any occasion of giving instruction, and upon this he said to me, "You are young, and have the world before you; stoop as you go through it, and you will miss many hard thumps." This advice, thus beat into my head, has frequently been of use to me; and I often think of it, when I see pride mortified, and misfortunes brought upon people by their carrying their heads too high.

B. Franklin.

THE END

Autobiography of Thomas Jefferson by Thomas Jefferson

JANUARY 6, 1821

At the age of 77, I begin to make some memoranda, and state some recollections of dates and facts concerning myself, for my own more ready reference, and for the information of my family.

The tradition in my father's family was, that their ancestor came to this country from Wales, and from near the mountain of Snowdon, the highest in Great Britain. I noted once a case from Wales, in the law reports, where a person of our name was either plaintiff or defendant; and one of the same name was secretary to the Virginia Company. These are the only instances in which I have met with the name in that country. I have found it in our early records; but the first particular information I have of any ancestor was of my grandfather, who lived at the place in Chesterfield called Ozborne's, and owned the lands afterwards the glebe of the parish. He had three sons; Thomas who died young, Field who settled on the waters of Roanoke and left numerous descendants, and Peter, my father, who settled on the lands I still own, called Shadwell, adjoining my present residence. He was born February 29, 1707-8, and intermarried 1739, with Jane Randolph, of the age of 19, daughter of Isham Randolph, one of the seven sons of that name and family, settled at Dungeoness in Goochland. They trace their pedigree far back in England and Scotland, to which let everyone ascribe the faith and merit he chooses.

My father's education had been quite neglected; but being of a strong mind, sound judgment, and eager after information, he read much and improved himself, insomuch that he was chosen, with Joshua Fry, Professor of Mathematics in William and Mary college, to continue the boundary line between Virginia and North Carolina, which had been begun by Colonel Byrd; and was afterwards employed with the same Mr. Fry, to make the first map of Virginia which had ever been made, that of Captain Smith being merely a conjectural sketch. They possessed excellent materials for so much of the country as is below the Blue Ridge; little being then known beyond that ridge. He was the third or fourth settler, about the year 1737, of the part of the country in which I live. He died, August 17th, 1757, leaving my mother a widow, who lived till 1776, with six daughters and two sons, myself the elder. To my younger brother he left his estate on James River, called Snowdon, after the supposed birth-place of the family: to myself, the lands on which I was born and live.

He placed me at the English school at five years of age; and at the Latin at nine, where I continued until his death. My teacher, Mr. Douglas, a clergyman from Scotland, with the rudiments of the Latin and Greek languages, taught me the French; and on the death of my father, I went to the Reverend James Maury, a correct classical scholar, with whom I continued two years; and then, to wit, in the spring of 1760, went to William and Mary College, where I continued two years. It was my great good fortune, and what probably fixed the destinies of my life, that Dr. William Small of Scotland, was then Professor of Mathematics, a man profound in most of the useful branches of science, with a happy talent of communication, correct and gentlemanly manners, and an enlarged and liberal mind. He, most happily for me, became soon attached to me, and made me his daily companion when not engaged in the school; and from his conversation I got my first views of the expansion of science, and of the system of things in which we are placed.

Fortunately, the philosophical chair became vacant soon after my arrival at college, and he was appointed to fill it per interim: and he was the first whoever gave, in that college, regular lectures in Ethics, Rhetoric and Belles Letters. He returned to Europe in 1762, having previously filled up the measure of his goodness to me, by procuring for me, from his most intimate friend, George Wythe, a reception as a student of law, under his direction, and introduced me to the acquaintance and familiar table of Governor Fauquier, the ablest man who had ever filled that office. With him, and at his table, Dr. Small and Mr. Wythe, his amici omnium horarum, and myself, formed a partie quarrée, and to the habitual conversations on these occasions I owed much instruction. Mr. Wythe continued to be my faithful and beloved mentor in youth, and my most affectionate friend through life. In 1767, he led me into the practice of the law at the bar of the General court, at which I continued until the Revolution shut up the courts of justice.

In 1769, I became a member of the legislature by the choice of the county in which I live, and so continued until it was closed by the Revolution. I made one effort in that body for the permission of the emancipation of slaves, which was rejected: and indeed, during the regal government, nothing liberal could expect success. Our minds were circumscribed within narrow limits, by an habitual belief that it was our duty to be subordinate to the mother country in all matters of government, to direct all our labors in subservience to her interests, and even to observe a bigoted intolerance for all religions but hers. The difficulties with our representatives were of habit and despair, not of reflection and conviction. Experience soon proved that they could bring their minds to rights, on the first summons of their attention. But the King's Council, which acted as another house of legislature, held their places at will, and were in most humble obedience to that will: the Governor too, who had a negative on our laws, held by the same tenure, and with still greater devotedness to it: and, last of all, the Royal negative closed the last door to every hope of amelioration.

On the 1st of January, 1772, I was married to Martha Skelton, widow of Bathurst Skelton, and daughter of John Wayles, then twenty-three years old. Mr. Wayles was a lawyer of much practice, to which he was introduced more by his great industry, punctuality, and practical readiness, than by eminence in the science of his profession. He was a most agreeable companion, full of pleasantry and good humor, and welcomed in every society. He acquired a handsome fortune, and died in May, 1773, leaving three daughters: the portion which came on that event to Mrs. Jefferson, after the debts should be paid, which were very considerable, was about equal to my own patrimony, and consequently doubled the ease of our circumstances.

When the famous Resolutions of 1765, against the Stamp Act, were proposed, I was yet a student of law in Williamsburg. I attended the debate, however, at the door of the lobby of the House of Burgesses, and heard the splendid display of Mr. Patrick Henry's talents as a popular orator. They were great indeed; such as I have never heard from any other man. He appeared to me to speak as Homer wrote. Mr. Johnson, a lawyer, and member from the Northern Neck, seconded the resolutions, and by him the learning and the logic of the case were chiefly maintained. My recollections of these transactions may be seen page 60 of the life of Patrick Henry, by Wirt, to whom I furnished them.

In May, 1769, a meeting of the General Assembly was called by the Governor, Lord Botetourt. I had then become a member; and to that meeting became known the joint resolutions and address of the Lords and Commons, of 1768-9, on the proceedings in Massachusetts. Counter-resolutions, and an address to the King by the House of Burgesses, were agreed to with little opposition, and a spirit manifestly displayed itself of considering the cause of Massachusetts as a common one. The Governor dissolved us: but we met the next day in the Apollo of the Raleigh tavern, formed ourselves into a voluntary convention, drew up articles of association against the use of any merchandise imported from Great Britain, signed and recommended them to the people, repaired to our several counties, and were re-elected without any other exception than of the very few who had declined assent to our proceedings.

Nothing of particular excitement occurring for a considerable time, our countrymen seemed to fall into a state of insensibility to our situation; the duty on tea, not yet repealed, and the declaratory act of a right in the British Parliament to bind us by their laws in all cases whatsoever, still suspended over us. But a court of inquiry held in Rhode Island in 1762, with a power to send persons to England to be tried for offences committed here, was considered, at our session of the spring of 1773, as demanding attention. Not thinking our old and leading members up to the point of forwardness and zeal which the times required, Mr. Henry, Richard Henry Lee, Francis L. Lee, Mr. Carr and myself agreed to meet in the evening, in a private room of the Raleigh, to consult on the state of things. There may have been a member or two more whom I do not recollect. We were all sensible that the most urgent of all measures was that of coming to an understanding with all the other colonies, to consider the British claims as a common cause to all, and to produce a unity of action: and, for this purpose, that a committee of correspondence in each colony would be the best instrument for intercommunication : and that their first measure would probably be, to propose a meeting of deputies from every colony, at some central place, who should be charged with the direction of the measures which should be taken by all. We, therefore, drew up the resolutions which may be seen in Wirt, page 87. The consulting members proposed to me to move them, but I urged that it should be done by Mr. Dabney Carr, my friend and brother-in-law, then a new member, to whom I wished an opportunity should be given of making known to the house his great worth and talents. It was so agreed; he moved them, they were agreed to nem. con. and a committee of correspondence appointed, of whom Peyton Randolph, the speaker; was chairman. The Governor (then Lord Dunmore) dissolved us, but the committee met the next day, prepared a circular letter to the speakers of the other colonies, inclosing to each a copy of the resolutions, and left it in charge with their chairman to forward them by expresses.

The origination of these committees of correspondence between the colonies has been since claimed for Massachusetts, and Marshall has given into this error, although the very note of his appendix to which he refers, shows that their establishment was confined to their own towns. This matter will be seen clearly stated in a letter of Samuel Adams Wells to me of April 2nd, 1819, and my answer of May 12th. I was corrected by the letter of Mr. Wells in the information I had given Mr. Wirt, as stated in his note, page 87, that the messengers of Massachusetts and Virginia crossed each other on the way, bearing similar propositions; for Mr. Wells shows that Massachusetts did not adopt the measure, but on the receipt of our proposition, delivered at their next session. Their message, therefore, which passed ours, must have related to something else, for I well remember Peyton Randolph's informing me of the crossing of our messengers.

The next event which excited our sympathies for Massachusetts, was the Boston port bill, by which that port was to be shut up on the 1st of June, 1774. This arrived while we were in session in the spring of that year. The lead in the House, on these subjects, being no longer left to the old members, Mr. Henry, R. H. Lee, Fr. L. Lee, three or four other members, whom I do not recollect, and myself, agreeing that we must boldly take an unequivocal stand in the line with Massachusetts, determined to meet and consult on the proper measures, in the council-chamber, for the benefit of the library in that room. We were under conviction of the necessity of arousing our people from the lethargy into which they had fallen, as to passing events; and thought that the appointment of a day of general fasting and prayer would be most likely to call up and alarm their attention.

No example of such a solemnity had existed since the days of our distresses in the war of '55, since which a new generation had grown up. With the help, therefore, of Rushworth, whom we rummaged over for the revolutionary precedents and forms of the Puritans of that day, preserved by him, we cooked up a resolution, somewhat modernizing their phrases, for appointing the 1st day of June, on which the portbill was to commence, for a day of fasting, humiliation, and prayer, to implore Heaven to avert from us the evils of civil war, to inspire us with firmness in support of our rights, and to turn the hearts of the King and Parliament to moderation and justice.

To give greater emphasis to our proposition, we agreed to wait the next morning on Mr. Nicholas, whose grave and religious character was more in unison with the tone of our resolution, and to solicit him to move it. We accordingly went to him in the morning. He moved it the same day; the 1st of June was proposed; and it passed without opposition. The Governor dissolved us, as usual. We retired to the Apollo, as before, agreed to an association, and instructed the committee of correspondence to propose to the corresponding committees of the other colonies, to appoint deputies to meet in Congress at such place, annually, as should be convenient, to direct, from time to time, the measures required by the general interest: and we declared that an attack on any one colony, should be considered as an attack on the whole. This was in May. We further recommended to the several counties to elect deputies to meet at Williamsburg, the 1st of August ensuing, to consider the state of the colony, and particularly to appoint delegates to a general Congress, should that measure be acceded to by the committees of correspondence generally. It was acceded to; Philadelphia was appointed for the place, and the 5th of September for the time of meeting. We returned home, and in our several counties invited the clergy to meet assemblies of the people on the 1st of June, to perform the ceremonies of the day, and to address to them discourses suited to the occasion.

The people met generally, with anxiety and alarm in their countenances, and the effect of the day, through the whole colony, was like a shock of electricity, arousing every man, and placing him erect and solidly on his center. They chose, universally, delegates for the convention. Being elected one for my own county, I prepared a draught of instructions to be given to the delegates whom we should send to the Congress, which I meant to propose at our meeting. In this I took the ground that, from the beginning, I had thought the only one orthodox or tenable, which was, that the relation between Great Britain and these colonies was exactly the same as that of England and Scotland, after the accession of James, and until the union, and the same as her present relations with Hanover, having the same executive chief, but no other necessary political connection; and that our emigration from England to this country gave her no more rights over us, than the emigrations of the Danes and Saxons gave to the present authorities of the mother country, over England. In this doctrine, however, I had never been able to get anyone to agree with me but Mr. Withe. He concurred in it from the first dawn of the question, What was the political relation between us and England? Our other patriots, Randolph, the Lees, Nicholas, Pendleton, stopped at the half-way house of John Dickinson, who admitted that England had a right-to regulate our commerce, and to lay duties on it for the purposes of regulation, but not of raising revenue. But for this ground there was no foundation in compact, in any acknowledged principles of colonization, nor in reason: expatriation being a natural right, and acted on as such, by all nations, in all ages. I set out for Williamsburg some days before that appointed for our meeting, but was taken ill of a dysentery on the road, and was unable to proceed.

I sent on, therefore, to Williamsburg two copies of my draught, the one under cover to Peyton Randolph, who I knew would be in the chair of the convention, the other to Patrick Henry. Whether Mr. Henry disapproved the ground taken, or was too lazy to read it (for he was the laziest man in reading I ever knew) I never learned: but he communicated it to nobody. Peyton Randolph informed the convention he had received such a paper from a member, prevented by sickness from offering it in his place, and he laid it on the table for perusal.

It was read generally by the members approved by many, though thought too bold for the present state of things; but they printed it in pamphlet form, under the title of A Summary View of the Rights of British America. It found its way to England, was taken up by the opposition, interpolated a little by Mr. Burke so as to make it answer opposition purposes, and in that form ran rapidly through several editions. This information I had from Parson Hurt, who happened at the time to be in London, whither he had gone to receive clerical orders; and I was informed afterwards by Peyton Randolph, that it had procured me the honor of having my name inserted in a long list of proscriptions, enrolled in a bill of attainder commenced in one of the Houses of Parliament, but suppressed in embryo by the hasty step of events, which warned them to be a little cautious. Montague, agent of the House of Burgesses in England, made extracts from the bill, copied the names, and sent them to Peyton Randolph. The names, I think, were about twenty, which he repeated to me, but I recollect those only of Hancock, the two Adamses, Peyton Randolph himself, Patrick Henry, and myself. The convention met on the 1st of August, renewed their association, appointed delegates to the Congress, gave them instructions very temperately and properly expressed, both as to style and matter; and they repaired to Philadelphia at the time appointed. The splendid proceedings of that Congress, at their first session, belong to general history, are known to everyone, and need not therefore be noted here. They terminated their session on the 26th of October, to meet again on the 10th of May ensuing. The convention, at their ensuing session of March, approved of the proceedings of Congress, thanked their delegates, and reappointed the same persons to represent the colony at the meeting to be held in May: and foreseeing the probability that Peyton

Randolph, their president, and speaker also of the House of Burgesses, might be called off, they added me, in that event, to the delegation.

Mr. Randolph was, according to expectation, obliged to leave the chair of Congress, to attend the General Assembly summoned by Lord Dunmore, to meet on the 1st day of June, 1775. Lord North's conciliatory propositions, as they were called, had been received by the Governor, and furnished the subject for which this assembly was convened. Mr. Randolph accordingly attended, and the tenor of these propositions being generally known, as having been addressed to all the governors, he was anxious that the answer of our Assembly, likely to be the first, should harmonize with what he knew to be the sentiments and wishes of the body he had recently left. He feared that Mr. Nicholas, whose mind was not yet up to the mark of the times, would undertake the answer, and therefore pressed me to prepare it. I did so, and, with his aid, carried it through the House, with long and doubtful scruples from Mr. Nicholas and James Mercer, and a dash of cold water on it here and there, enfeebling it somewhat, but finally with unanimity, or a vote approaching it. This being passed, I repaired immediately to Philadelphia, and conveyed to Congress the first notice they had of it. It was entirely approved there. I took my seat with them on the 21st of June. On the 24th, a committee which had been appointed to prepare a declaration of the causes of taking up arms, brought in their report (drawn I believe by J. Rutledge) which, not being liked, the House recommitted it, on the 26th, and added Mr. Dickinson and myself to the committee.

On the rising of the House, the committee having not yet met, I happened to find myself near Governor W. Livingston, and proposed to him to draw the paper. He excused himself and proposed that. I should draw it. On my pressing him with urgency, we are as yet but new acquaintances, sir, said he, why are you so earnest for my doing it? Because, said I, I have been informed that you drew the Address to the people of Great Britain, a production, certainly, of the finest pen in America. On that, says he, perhaps, sir, you may not have been correctly informed. I had received the information in Virginia from Colonel Harrison on his return from that Congress. Lee, Livingston, and Jay had been the committee for that draught. The first, prepared by Lee, had been disapproved and recommitted. The second was drawn by Jay, but being presented by Governor Livingston, had led Colonel Harrison into the error. The next morning, walking in the hall of Congress, many members being assembled, but the House not yet formed, I observed Mr. Jay speaking to R. H. Lee, and leading him by the button of his coat to me. I understand, sir, said he to me, that this gentleman informed you, that Governor Livingston drew the Address to the people of Great Britain. I assured him, at once, that I had not received that information from Mr. Lee, and that not a word had ever passed on the subject between Mr. Lee and myself; and after some explanations the subject was dropped. These gentlemen had had some sparrings in debate before, and continued ever very hostile to each other.

I prepared a draught of the declaration committed to us. It was too strong for Mr. Dickinson. He still retained the hope of reconciliation with the mother country, and was unwilling it should be Lessened by offensive statements. He was so honest a man, and so able a one, that he was greatly indulged even by those who could not feel his scruples. We therefore requested him to take the paper, and put it into a form he could approve. He did so, preparing an entire new statement, and preserving of the former only the last four paragraphs and half of the preceding one. We approved and reported it to Congress, who accepted it. Congress gave a signal proof of their indulgence to Mr. Dickinson, and of their great desire not to go too fast for any respectable part of our body, in permitting him to draw their second petition to the King according to his own ideas, and passing it with scarcely any amendment. The disgust against this humility was general; and Mr. Dickinson's delight at its passage was the only circumstance which reconciled them to it. The vote being passed, although further observation on it was out of order, he could not refrain from rising and expressing his satisfaction, and concluded by saying, there is but one word, Mr. President, in the paper which I disapprove, and that is the word Congress; on which Ben Harrison rose and said, There is but one word in the paper, Mr. President, of which I approve, and that is the word Congress.

On the 22d of July, Dr. Franklin, Mr. Adams, R. H. Lee, and myself, were appointed a committee to consider and report on Lord North's conciliatory resolution. The answer of the Virginia Assembly on that subject having been approved, I was requested by the committee to prepare this report, which will account for the similarity of feature in the two instruments.

On the 15th of May, 1776, the convention of Virginia instructed their delegates in Congress, to propose to that body to declare the colonies independent of Great Britain, and appointed a committee to prepare a declaration of rights and plan of government.

In Congress, Friday, June 7, 1776. The delegates from Virginia moved, in obedience to instructions from their constituents, that the Congress should declare that these United colonies are, and of right ought to be, free and independent states, that they are absolved from all allegiance to the British crown, and that all political connection between them and the state of Great Britain is, and ought to be, totally dissolved; that measures should be immediately taken for procuring the assistance of foreign powers, and a Confederation be formed to bind the colonies more closely together.

The House being obliged to attend at that time to some other business, the proposition was referred to the next day, when the members were ordered to attend punctually at ten o'clock.

Saturday, June 8. They proceeded to take it into consideration, and referred it to a committee of the whole, into which they immediately resolved themselves, and passed that day and Monday, the 10th, in debating on the subject. It was argued by Wilson, Robert R. Livingston, E. Rutledge, Dickinson, and others that, though they were friends to the measures themselves, and saw the impossibility that we should ever again be united with Great Britain, yet they were against adopting them at this time:

That the conduct we had formerly observed was wise and proper now, of deferring to take any capital step till the voice of the people drove us into it:

That they were our power, and without them our declarations could not be carried into effect:

That the people of the middle colonies (Maryland, Delaware, Pennsylvania, the Jerseys and New York) were not yet ripe for bidding adieu to British connection, but that they were fast ripening, and, in a short time, would join in the general voice of America:

That the resolution, entered into by this House on the 15th of May, for suppressing the exercise of all powers derived from the crown, had shown, by the ferment into which it had thrown these middle colonies, that they had not yet accommodated their minds to a separation from the mother country:

That some of them had expressly forbidden their delegates to consent to such a declaration, and others had given no instructions, and consequently no powers to give such consent:

That if the delegates of any particular colony had no power to declare such colony independent, certain they were, the others could not declare it for them; the colonies being as yet perfectly independent of each other:

That the assembly of Pennsylvania was now sitting above stairs, their convention would sit within a few days, the convention of New York was now sitting, and those of the Jerseys and Delaware counties would meet on the Monday following, and it was probable these bodies would take up the question of Independence, and would declare to their delegates the voice of their state:

That if such a declaration should now be agreed to, these delegates must retire, and possibly their colonies might secede from the Union:

That such a secession would weaken us more than could be compensated by any foreign alliance:

That in the event of such a division, foreign powers would either refuse to join themselves to our fortunes, or, having us so much in their power as that desperate declaration would place us, they would insist on terms proportionally more hard and prejudicial

That we had little reason to expect an alliance with those to whom alone, as yet, we had cast our eyes:

That France and Spain had reason to be jealous of that rising power, which would one day certainly strip them of all their American possessions:

That it was more likely they should form a connection with the British court, who, if they should find themselves unable otherwise to extricate themselves from their difficulties, would agree to a partition of our territories, restoring Canada to France, and the Floridas to Spain, to accomplish for themselves a recovery of these colonies.

That it would not be long before we should receive certain information of the disposition of the French court, from the agent whom we had sent to Paris for that purpose:

That if this disposition should be favorable, by waiting the event of the present campaign, which we all hoped would be successful, we should have reason to expect an alliance on better terms:

That this would in fact work no delay of any effectual aid from such ally, as, from the advance of the season and distance of our situation, it was impossible we could receive any assistance during this campaign:

That it was prudent to fix among ourselves the terms on which we should form alliance, before we declared we would form one at all events:

And that if these were agreed on, and our Declaration of Independence ready by the time our Ambassador should be prepared to sail, it would be as well as to go into that Declaration at this day.

On the other side, it was urged by J. Adams, Lee, Withe, and others, that no gentleman had argued against the policy or the right of separation from Britain, nor had supposed it possible we should ever renew our connection; that they had only opposed its being now declared:

That the question was not whether, by a Declaration of Independence, we should make ourselves what we are not; but whether we should declare a fact which already exists:

That, as to the people or parliament of England, we had always been independent of them, their restraints on our trade deriving efficacy from our acquiescence only, and not from any rights they possessed of imposing them, and that so far, our connection had been federal only, and was now dissolved by the commencement of hostilities:

That, as to the King, we had been bound to him by allegiance, but that this bond was now dissolved by his assent to the last act of Parliament, by which he declares us out of his protection, and by his levying war on us, a fact which had long ago proved us out of his protection; it being a certain position in law, that allegiance and protection are reciprocal, the one ceasing when the other is withdrawn:

That James the Second never declared the people of England out of his protection, yet his actions proved it, and the Parliament declared it: No delegates then can be denied, or ever want, a power of declaring an existing truth: That the delegates from the Delaware counties having declared their constituents ready to join, there are only two colonies, Pennsylvania and Maryland, whose delegates are absolutely tied up, and that these had, by their instructions, only reserved a right of confirming or rejecting the measure:

That the instructions from Pennsylvania might be accounted for from the times in which they were drawn, near a twelvemonth ago, since which the face of affairs has totally changed:

That within that time, it had become apparent that Britain was determined to accept nothing less than a carte-blanche, and that the King's answer to the Lord Mayor, Aldermen and Common Council of London, which had come to hand four days ago, must have satisfied every one of this point:

That the people wait for us to lead the way:

That they are in favor of the measure, though the instructions given by some of their representatives are not:

That the voice of the representatives is not always consonant with the voice of the people, and that this is remarkably the case in these middle colonies:

That the effect of the resolution of the 15th of May has proved this, which, raising the murmurs of some in the colonies of Pennsylvania and Maryland, called forth the opposing voice of the freer part of the people, and proved them to be the majority even in these colonies:

That the backwardness of these two colonies might be ascribed, partly to the influence of proprietary power and connections, and partly, to their having not yet been attacked by the enemy:

That these causes were not likely to be soon removed, as there seemed no probability that the enemy would make either of these the seat of this summer's war:

That it would be vain to wait either weeks or months for perfect unanimity, since it was impossible that all men should ever become of one sentiment on any question:

That the conduct of some colonies, from the beginning of this contest, had given reason to suspect it was their settled policy to keep in the rear of the confederacy, that their particular prospect might be better, even in the worst event:

That, therefore, it was necessary for those colonies who had thrown themselves forward and hazarded all from the beginning, to come forward now also, and put all again to their own hazard:

That the history of the Dutch Revolution, of whom three states only confederated at first, proved that a secession of some colonies would not be so dangerous as some apprehended:

That a Declaration of Independence alone could render it consistent with European delicacy, for European powers to treat with us, or even to receive an Ambassador from us: That till this, they would not receive our vessels into their ports, nor acknowledge the adjudications of our courts of admiralty to be legitimate, in cases of capture of British vessels:

That though France and Spain may be jealous of our rising power, they must think it will be much more formidable with the addition of Great Britain; and will therefore see it their interest to prevent a coalition; but should they refuse, we shall be but where we are; whereas without trying, we shall never know whether they will aid us or not:

That the present campaign may be unsuccessful, and therefore we had better propose an alliance while our affairs wear a hopeful aspect:

That to wait the event of this campaign will certainly work delay, because, during the summer, France may assist us effectually, by cutting off those supplies of provisions from England and Ireland, on which the enemy's armies here are to depend; or by setting in motion the great power they have collected in the West Indies, and calling our enemy to the defense of the possessions they have there:

That it would be idle to lose time in settling the terms of alliance, till we had first determined we would enter into alliance:

That it is necessary to lose no time in opening a trade for our people, who will want clothes, and will want money too, for the payment of taxes:

And that the only misfortune is, that we did not enter into alliance with France six months sooner, as, besides opening her ports for the vent of our last year's produce, she might have marched an army into Germany, and prevented the petty princes there, from selling their unhappy subjects to subdue us.

It appearing in the course of these debates, that the colonies of New York, New Jersey, Pennsylvania, Delaware, Maryland, and South Carolina were not yet matured for falling from the parent stem, but that they were fast advancing to that state, it was thought most prudent to wait a while for them, and to postpone the final decision to July 1st; but, that this might occasion as little delay as possible, a committee was appointed to prepare a Declaration of Independence. The committee were John Adams, Dr. Franklin, Roger Sherman, Robert R. Livingston, and myself. Committees were also appointed, at the same time, to prepare a plan of confederation for the colonies, and to state the terms proper to be proposed for foreign alliance. The committee for drawing the Declaration of Independence, desired me to do it. It was accordingly done, and being approved by them, I reported it to the House on Friday, the 28th of June, when it was read, and ordered to lie on the table.

On Monday, the 1st of July, the House resolved itself into a committee of the whole, and resumed the consideration of the original motion made by the delegates of Virginia, which, being again debated through the day, was carried in the affirmative by the votes of New Hampshire, Connecticut, Massachusetts, Rhode Island, New Jersey, Maryland, Virginia, North Carolina and Georgia. South Carolina and Pennsylvania voted against it. Delaware had but two members present, and they were divided. The delegates from New York declared they were for it themselves, and were assured their constituents were for it; but that their instructions having been drawn near a twelve month before, when reconciliation was still the general object, they were enjoined by them to do nothing which should impede that object. They, therefore, thought themselves not justifiable in voting on either side, and asked leave to withdraw from the question; which was given them. The committee rose and reported their resolution to the House. Mr. Edward Rutledge, of South Carolina, then requested the determination might be put off to the next day, as he believed his colleagues, though they disapproved of the resolution, would then join in it for the sake of unanimity. The ultimate question, whether the House would agree to the resolution of the committee, was accordingly postponed to the next day, when it was again moved, and South Carolina concurred in voting for it. In the meantime, a third member had come post from the Delaware counties, and turned the vote of that colony in favor of the resolution. Members of a different sentiment attending that morning from Pennsylvania also, her vote was changed, so that the whole twelve colonies who were authorized to vote at all, gave their voices for it; and, within a few days, the convention of New York approved of it, and thus supplied the void occasioned by the withdrawing of her delegates from the vote.

Congress proceeded the same day to consider the Declaration of Independence, which had been reported and lain on the table the Friday preceding, and on Monday referred to a committee of the whole. The pusillanimous idea that we had friends in England worth keeping terms with, still haunted the minds of many. For this reason, those passages which conveyed censures on the people of England were struck out, lest they should give them offence. The clause too, reprobating the enslaving the inhabitants of Africa, was struck out in complaisance to South Carolina and Georgia, who had never attempted to restrain the importation of slaves, and who, on the contrary, still wished to continue it. Our northern brethren also, I believe, felt a little tender under those censures; for though their people had very few slaves themselves, yet they had been pretty considerable carriers of them to others. The debates, having taken up the greater parts of the 2d, 3d, and 4th days of July, were, on the evening of the last, closed; the Declaration was reported by the committee, agreed to by the House, and signed by every member present, except Mr. Dickinson. As the sentiments of men are known not only by what they receive, but what they reject also, I will state the form of the Declaration as originally reported. The parts struck out by Congress shall be distinguished by a black line drawn under them; and those inserted by them shall be placed in the margin, or in a concurrent column.

Alexander Hamilton by Charles A. Conant

I: Youth and Early Services

The life of Alexander Hamilton is an essential chapter in the story of the formation of the American Union. Hamilton's work was of that constructive sort which is vital for laying the foundations of new states. Whether the Union would have been formed under the Constitution and would have been consolidated into a powerful nation, instead of a loose confederation of sovereign states, without the great services of Hamilton, is one of those problems about which speculation is futile. It is certain that the conditions of the time presented a rare opportunity for such a man as Hamilton, and that without some directing and organizing genius like his, the consolidation of the Union must have been delayed, and have been accomplished with much travail.

The difference between the career of Hamilton in America and that of the two greatest organizing minds of other countries—Caesar and Napoleon—marks the difference between Anglo-Saxon political ideals and capacity for self-government and those of other races. Where the organization of a strong government degenerated in Rome and France into absolutism, it tended in America, under the directing genius of Hamilton, to place in the hands of the people a more powerful instrument for executing their own will. So powerful a weapon was thus created that Hamilton himself became alarmed when it was seized by the hands of Jefferson, Madison, and other democratic leaders as the instrument of democratic ideas, and those long strides were taken in the states and under the federal government which wiped out the distinctions between classes, abolished the relations of church and state, extended the suffrage, and made the government only the servant of the popular will.

The development of two principles marked the early history of the Republic,—one, the growth of sentiment for the Union under the inspiration of Hamilton and the Federalist party; the other, the growth of the power of the masses, typified by the leadership of Jefferson and the Democratic party. These two tendencies, seemingly hostile in many of their aspects, waxed in strength together until they became the united and guiding principles of a new political order,—a nation of giant strength whose power rests upon the will of all the people. It was the steady progress of these two principles in the heart of the American people which in "the fullness of time" made it possible for the Union to be preserved as a union of free men under a free constitution. To Hamilton, the creator of the machinery of the Union, and to John Marshall, the great Chief

Justice, who interpreted the Constitution as Hamilton would have had him do, in favor of the powers of the Union, this result was largely due.

If Caesar, fighting the battles of Rome on the frontier of Germany, and kept from party quarrels at home, and Napoleon, born outside of France and free by his campaign in Egypt from the compromising intrigues of Parisian politics, were preeminently fitted by these accidents to transmute the spirit of revolution from chaos into order, Hamilton stood in somewhat the same position in America. Born in the little island of Nevis in the West Indies (January 11, 1757), he came to the United States when his mind was already mature, in spite of his fifteen years. He came without the local prejudices or state pride which influenced so many of the Revolutionary leaders, and was therefore peculiarly qualified to fasten his eyes steadfastly upon the single end of the creation of a nation rather than the ascendency of any single state. He was so free from local attachments that he even hesitated at first on which side he should cast his lot,—whether with the imperial government of Great Britain, which appealed strongly to his love of system and organized power, or with the struggling revolutionists, with their poor and undisciplined army and uncertain future. The possibility of winning distinction in the service of Great Britain must have attracted him, but the justice of the colonial cause spoke more strongly to his sense of right and his well-ordered mind.

The great services of Hamilton were nearly all performed before he was forty years of age. His precocity was partly derived from his birth in the tropics and partly, perhaps, from the unfortunate conditions of his early life. A mystery hangs over his birth and parentage, which repeated inquiries have failed to clear away. He is believed to have been the son of James Hamilton, a Scottish merchant of Nevis, and a lady of French Hugenot descent, the divorced wife of a Dane named Lavine. But the history of his parents and their marriage is shrouded in much obscurity. The father, although reduced to poverty, lived nearly if not quite as long as his illustrious son, but the mother was reported to have died while Hamilton was only a child, leaving the memory of her beauty and charm in one of the chambers of his infant mind. Hamilton sought in his later years to establish regular communication with his father, and he had a brother in the West Indies with whom he corresponded; but the fact that all these relatives remained so much in the background gave some color to the slanders of his enemies concerning his birth.

To offset the disadvantages of birth, Hamilton had neither the fascinating manners which go straight to the hearts of men, nor the imposing personal presence which in the orator often invests trifling platitudes with sonorous dignity. He was possessed of a light and well-made frame, and was erect and dignified in bearing, but was much below the average height. His friends were wont to call him "the little lion," because of the vigor and dignity of his speech. He had the advantage of a head finely shaped, large and symmetrical. His complexion was fair, his cheeks were rosy, and in spite of a rather large nose his face was considered handsome. His dark, deep-set eyes were lighted in debate with a fire which controlled great audiences and cowed his enemies. But it was chiefly the power of pure intellect which gave him control over the minds of other men. There was nothing mean or low in his character, but he had not a high opinion of the average of humanity, and therefore lacked somewhat in that ready sympathy with the minds of others which is so useful to politicians and party leaders.

Hamilton was early thrown upon his own resources. His father became a bankrupt, and he was cared for by his mother's relatives. His education was aided by the Rev. Hugh Knox, a Presbyterian clergyman, with whom Hamilton kept up an affectionate correspondence in later years. The boy was only thirteen years of age when he was placed in the office of Nicholas Cruger, a West Indian merchant. Here his self-reliance and methodical habits made him master of the business and head of the establishment when his employer had occasion to be away. His remarkable capacity, and his occasional writings for the daily press, led to a determination by his relatives and friends to send him to a wider field. He was accordingly supplied with funds and sent to Boston, where he arrived in October, 1772, still less than sixteen years of age. He was fortunately provided with some strong letters of recommendation from Dr. Knox, and was soon at a grammar school at Elizabethtown, N.J., where he made rapid progress. He desired to enter Princeton, but his project of going through the courses as rapidly as he could, without regard to the regular classes, was in conflict with the rules. He therefore turned to King's College, New York, now Columbia University, where he was able, with the aid of a private tutor, to pursue his studies in the manner which he wished.

The decision of Hamilton to take the side of the colonies in the conflict with England was made early in 1774, partly as the result of a visit to Boston. Among the well-to-do classes of New York, the dominant feeling was in favor of Great Britain, and the control of the Assembly was in the hands of the friends of the Crown. Hamilton found Boston the hotbed of resistance to England, and listened attentively to the reasoning by which the "strong prejudices on the ministerial side," which he himself declares he had formed, gave way to "the superior force of the arguments in favor of the colonial claims." The opportunity soon came for him to make public proclamation of his position. A great meeting was held in the "Fields"[1] (July 6, 1774), to force the hand of the Tory Assembly in the matter of joining the other colonies in calling a Congress. Hamilton attended, and after listening to the speeches was so strongly impressed with what was left unsaid that he worked his way to the platform and began an impassioned argument for the colonial side. Below the normal stature and of slender form, he looked even younger than his seventeen years, but was recognized by the crowd as a collegian and received with great enthusiasm.

[1] The "Fields" of that day occupied what is now City Hall Park, then the upper limit of New York. King's College was in the immediate neighborhood, the name still lingering in College Place.

Hamilton was soon at the forefront of the fight for civil liberty, which was carried on by means of pamphlets and newspaper addresses. His papers, which appeared without signature, showed so much ability that they were attributed to the most eminent of the patriot leaders. After the die was cast at Lexington for armed conflict, Hamilton early in 1776 received the command of a company of artillery. Its thorough discipline attracted the favorable notice of Greene and other leaders. Greene introduced Hamilton to Washington, who had early occasion, in the disastrous battle of Long Island, when Hamilton protected the rear with great coolness and courage, to measure the mettle of his young artillery officer.

Washington on March 1, 1777, offered Hamilton the rank of Lieutenant-Colonel on his staff. In this position Hamilton found congenial occupation for his pen in the great mass of letters, reports, and proclamations which issued from headquarters. These communications, many of which still survive, while bearing the impress of Washington's clear, directing mind, bear also the mark of the skill and logic of the younger man. Hamilton rendered valuable service after the surrender of Burgoyne, in persuading Gates to detach a part of his forces to aid Washington. On this occasion, although he had in his pocket a positive order from Washington, he displayed a tact and diplomatic skill which were unusual in his dealings with men. It fell to the lot of Hamilton to meet André while a prisoner in the hands of the Americans, and his letters regarding the affair to Miss Schuyler, who afterwards became his wife, are among the most interesting contributions to this pathetic episode of Revolutionary history.

Hamilton's quarrel with Washington, about which much has been written, came after nearly four years' service over a trivial delay in obeying a call from the General. Washington rebuked his aide for disrespect, to which Hamilton hotly retorted, "I am not conscious of it, sir; but since you have thought it, we part." Washington endeavored to prevent the execution of his project, but Hamilton would not be reconciled and returned to service in the line. He led his men with great impetuosity upon one of the British redoubts at Yorktown, and carried the position in ten minutes, with much more promptness than the French, to whom the other redoubt had been assigned.

While the war was still in progress Hamilton was looking ahead with the constructive genius which afterwards found such wide opportunities in the cabinet of Washington. He addressed a letter in 1780 to Duane, a member of Congress, in which he made a remarkable analysis of the defects of the Articles of Confederation, urged that Congress should be clothed with complete sovereignty, and made suggestions regarding its powers which were afterwards embodied to a large extent in the Constitution. He addressed an anonymous letter to Robert Morris early in the same year, treating of the financial affairs of the confederacy. He discussed carefully the paper currency and the causes of its depreciation, and proposed to restore soundness to the finances by gradual contraction of the volume of paper, a tax in kind, and a foreign loan, which was to form the basis of a national bank. When the clumsiness and helplessness of the system of government by committees was finally appreciated by the Continental Congress in 1781, and several executive departments were established, Hamilton was suggested by John Sullivan to Washington for head of the Treasury Department. Washington replied that "few of his age have a more general knowledge, and no one is more firmly engaged in the cause, or exceeds him in probity and sterling virtue." Robert Morris was chosen for the Treasury, but Hamilton opened a correspondence with him regarding the work of the department, which established a firm friendship between the older and younger man.

Hamilton desired the unification of the debt and the creation of a national bank, for the combined objects of cementing the Union and putting the finances of the country upon a stable basis. "A national debt," he wrote, "if it is not excessive, will be a national blessing, a powerful cement of union, a necessity for keeping up taxation, and a spur to industry." Whether all these benefits fall within the economic effects of a debt may well be doubted, but the second advantage assigned was undoubtedly one of the chief motives of Hamilton in recommending its creation. The Bank of North America was established by Morris upon a much more modest scale than was proposed by Hamilton. The younger man, looking to the future needs of the country and to the example of European banks, recommended an institution with a capital of ten or fifteen millions, with authority to establish branches, and with the sole right to issue paper currency equal to the amount of its capital. He contemplated a close relation between the bank and the government, and the taking up, under contract with the United States, of all the paper issues of the Continental Congress.

Hamilton made a connection while still under twenty-four which fixed his status as a citizen of New York, and proved of value to him in many ways. While on his mission to Gates at Albany, he met Miss Elizabeth Schuyler, daughter of General Philip Schuyler, one of the social as well as political leaders of the best element in New York. The acquaintance with Miss Schuyler was renewed in the spring of 1780 and ripened into an engagement, followed by their marriage on December 14 of that year. With the conclusion of the war, Hamilton was left with nothing but his title to arrears of pay in the army, and with a wife and child to support. He refused generous offers of assistance from his father-in-law, applied himself for four months to the study of the law, and in the summer of 1782 was admitted to the bar at Albany. While waiting for clients he continued his studies on financial and political questions and his vigorous arguments through the public prints for a strong federal union. He declined several offers of public place, but finally accepted an appointment from Robert Morris (June, 1782) as continental receiver of taxes for New York. This afforded him an opportunity of meeting the New York legislature, which had been summoned in extra session at Poughkeepsie, in July, to receive a report from a committee of Congress.

Congress in May, 1782, had taken into consideration the desperate condition of the finances of the country, and divided among four of its members the duty of explaining the common danger of the states. It was at the request of the delegation which went north that Governor Clinton called an extra session, and a communication was submitted on the necessity of providing for a vigorous prosecution of the war. Hamilton went to Poughkeepsie to aid his father-in-law, General Schuyler, and it was upon the motion of the latter that the Senate resolved itself into a committee of the whole on the state of the nation. Two days of deliberation were sufficient to produce a series of resolutions, probably drafted by Hamilton, which were unanimously adopted by the Senate and concurred in by the House.

These resolutions set forth that recent experience afforded "the strongest reason to apprehend from a continuance of the present constitution of the continental government a subversion of public credit" and danger to the safety and independence of the states. Turning to practical remedies, it was pointed out that the source of the public embarrassments was the want of sufficient power in Congress, particularly the power of providing a revenue. The legislature of New York, therefore, invited Congress "to recommend and each state to adopt the measure of assembling a general convention of the states especially authorized to revise and amend the confederation, reserving a right to the respective legislatures to ratify their determinations." These resolutions the government was requested to transmit to Congress and to the executives of the other states. Hamilton appeared before the legislature and discussed the subject of revenue, and one of the results of his manifest interest in the subject and his knowledge of finance was his selection by the legislature as one of the members of Congress from New York.

The impress of the organizing mind and far-sighted purposes of Hamilton was felt during his brief service in Congress. He took his seat from New York in November, 1782, and resigned in August, 1783. He cast his influence from the beginning in favor of a strong executive organization, and did his best to strengthen the heads of the recently created departments of finance and foreign affairs. He was of great service to Robert Morris, and almost carried the project of a general duty on importations, which was finally defeated by the obstinacy of Rhode Island. Such a measure, if carried out, would have afforded the central government a permanent revenue. It would have greatly mitigated the evils of the time, but would perhaps by that very fact have postponed the more complete union of the states which was to come under the Constitution of 1789. This was only one of the many projects germinating in the fertile mind of Hamilton. In a letter to Washington (March 17, 1783) he wrote:—

"We have made considerable progress in a plan to be recommended to the several states for funding all the public debts, including those of the army, which is certainly the only way to restore public credit and enable us to continue the war by borrowing abroad, if it should be necessary to continue it."

That it might be necessary to continue the war Hamilton seriously feared, in spite of the fact that the provisional treaty of peace with Great Britain was then before Congress. A grave question had arisen whether faith had been kept with France in the negotiation of this treaty. Congress had resolved unanimously (October 4, 1782) that "they will not enter into any discussion of overtures of pacification but in confidence and in concert with His Most Christian Majesty," the King of France. Adams and Jay, against the advice of Franklin, negotiated secretly with Great Britain, and only the moderation of Vergennes, French Minister of Foreign Affairs, prevented serious friction between the allies.

Hamilton, though far from being a partisan of France, believed in acting towards her with the most scrupulous good faith. He advocated a middle course between subservience to Great Britain and implicit confidence in the disinterestedness of France. He declared (March 18, 1783), when the peace preliminaries were considered, that it was "not improbable that it had been the policy of France to procrastinate the definite acknowledgment of our independence on the part of Great Britain, in order to keep us more knit to herself, and until her own interests could be negotiated." Notwithstanding this caution regarding French purposes, he "disapproved highly of the conduct of our ministers in not showing the preliminary articles to our ally before they signed them, and still more so of their agreeing to the separate article." His own view was expressed in some resolutions which he offered, and which Congress adopted (May 2, 1783), asking a further loan from the French King, "and that His Majesty might be informed that Congress will consider his compliance in this instance as a new and valuable proof of his friendship, peculiarly interesting in the present conjuncture of the affairs of the United States."

II: The Fight for the Constitution

Hamilton was not a conspicuous national figure during the four years which elapsed between the termination of his term in Congress and his appearance in the Federal Convention of 1787. He was working none the less earnestly and persistently, however, in favor of a stronger union. Movements towards this union took form almost simultaneously in different parts of the country under the impulse of a common need. The wise and thoughtful words of Washington, in his circular letter to the governor of each state on surrendering the command of the army (June 8, 1783), sank into many hearts, and did much to soften local prejudices against giving more power to the central government. The State of Virginia in December, 1783, ceded her northwestern territory to Congress, and granted a general impost. Significance was given to the act by the policy of the governor in communicating it to the executive authority of the other states, with the suggestion that they do likewise.

Jefferson was as cordial a supporter as Madison at that time of the project of a federal union. As a member of Congress, he prepared a plan for intercourse with the powers of Europe and the Barbary States, in which he described "the United States as one nation upon the principles of the federal constitution." Only two states—Rhode Island and Connecticut—voted to substitute weaker words in describing the union. It was voted by eight states to two (March 26, 1784) that in treaties and in all cases arising under them, the United States formed "one nation." The need for uniform rules for the regulation of commerce on the Potomac and the creation of roads and canals led to a number of conferences during the next two years between Virginia and Maryland, in one of which Washington played the part of referee. The legislature of Maryland finally took a step which shot a bright ray of light through the darkness surrounding the prospects of a permanent union. In a letter to the legislature of Virginia (December, 1785), it proposed that commissioners from all the states should be invited to meet and regulate the restrictions on commerce for the whole. Madison in Virginia gave cordial welcome to the invitation. He had already gone beyond the sentiment of his state in his zeal for union, but at his instigation a meeting of delegates from the states was called by Virginia at Annapolis, Md., for September, 1786.

Hamilton snatched at the opportunity which this invitation presented. Several of his friends were elected to the legislature of New York, and made the appointment of delegates to Annapolis their paramount object. In spite of much hostility, they succeeded in wresting authority from the legislature for a commission of five. Hamilton and Benson were the only two of these delegates who appeared at Annapolis. They found only four other states represented there. It was determined that the best that could be done by the little gathering was to urge upon the states a general convention, to meet at Philadelphia on the second Monday of the next May, "to consider the situation of the United States, and devise such further provisions as should appear necessary to render the constitution of the federal government adequate to the exigencies of the Union." Hamilton was not a member of the committee appointed to prepare the report, but it was his draft which, with some modifications to meet the sensibilities of the Virginians, was accepted and adopted.

A path was now blazed in which those who favored a stronger union could walk in harmony. Hamilton returned to New York with the intention of exerting his whole strength in behalf of the convention. He secured an election to the legislature, and at once took the lead of the members opposed to the separatist policy of Governor Clinton. He assailed the governor on the question of granting an impost to Congress in a practicable form, but was beaten by the solid vote of the party in power. He succeeded better with his resolution for the appointment of five delegates to the convention at Philadelphia. The Senate cut down the number to three, and two of them—Chief Justice Robert Yates and John Lansing, Jr.—were resolute supporters of the governor; but Hamilton carried the vital point that New York should be represented in the Federal Convention, and he was himself one of the delegates. It was not until late in February, 1787, that this action was taken,—little more than three months before the meeting of the convention,—and it was a few days later when formal approval was given to the project by the Federal Congress.

Hamilton, although one of the three delegates from New York to the convention, was embarrassed throughout the proceedings by the open hostility of his associates to any vigorous steps towards a strong union. He had definite ideas and strong feelings, however, and could not restrain himself from setting forth his views of what the new government should be. When Dickinson proposed that the convention should seek union through a revision of the old Articles of Confederation, Hamilton took the floor (June 18, 1787) to show how inadequate such a measure would be, and to set forth his own long matured views. He spoke for six hours, reviewing the history of the colonies before the Revolution, during its progress, and afterwards, the steps which had been taken towards union, and the imperative necessity which had been disclosed for a government possessing complete powers within its fields of action. He urged that the convention "adopt a solid plan without regard to temporary opinions." He laid bare unsparingly the defects of the confederacy, and insisted that the Articles of Confederation could not be amended with benefit except in the most radical manner. He opposed strongly the creation of a general government through a single body like Congress, because it would be without checks. He continued:—

"The general government must not only have a strong soul, but strong organs by which that soul is to operate. I despair that a republican form of government can remove the difficulties; I would hold it, however, unwise to change it. The best form of government, not attainable by us, but the model to which we should approach as near as possible, is the British constitution, praised by Necker as 'the only government which unites public strength with individual security.' Its house of lords is a most noble institution. It forms a permanent barrier against every pernicious innovation, whether attempted on the part of the crown or of the commons."

Hamilton made little concealment of his belief that the new government should not be exclusively republican. He said on June 26, 1787:—

"I acknowledge I do not think favorably of republican government; but I address my remarks to those who do, in order to prevail on them to tone their government as high as possible. I profess myself as zealous an advocate for liberty as any man whatever; and trust I shall be as willing a martyr to it, though I differ as to the form in which it is most eligible. Real liberty is neither found in despotism nor in the extremes of democracy, but in moderate governments. Those who mean to form a solid republic ought to proceed to the confines of another government. If we incline too much to democracy, we shall soon shoot into a monarchy."

In pursuance of these views, Hamilton urged that all branches of the new government should originate in the action of the people rather than of the states. In this respect he came closer to democracy than some of his opponents, but he proposed to give strength and permanence to the government by providing that the Senators and the executive should hold office during good behavior. He contended that by making the chief executive subject to impeachment, the term monarchy would not be applicable to his office. Another step differing radically from the Constitution as adopted, and showing the unswerving purpose of Hamilton to give supremacy to the central government, was the proposal that the executive of each state should be appointed by the general government and have a negative on all state legislation.

Hamilton had no expectation that his plan would be adopted. What he sought was to key the temper of the delegates up to a pitch which would bring them as nearly to his ideal of what the new government should be as was possible under the circumstances of the times. His long speech was attentively listened to, and even Yates reported that it "was praised by everybody, but supported by none." Notwithstanding these criticisms, the Constitution, as it was finally adopted, embodied many of the features of the project which was outlined by Hamilton. A legislative body of two houses, the choice of the executive by electors, a veto for the executive over legislative acts, the grant of the treaty-making power to the executive and the Senate, the confirmation of appointments by the Senate, the creation of a federal judiciary, and the provision that state laws in conflict with the Constitution should be void; these and many other features of the existing Constitution were parts of the plan of Hamilton.

It was not the open preference which Hamilton expressed for the British form of government which caused distrust of his plan. This was neither startling nor offensive to the great majority of those who heard him. Representative government under a republican head had not then been tried upon a large scale in any part of the world. Such small republics as existed in ancient times and in Italy had been confined within narrow areas, and had in many cases presented examples of factional strife which were far from encouraging to the friends of liberty. The Americans, in revolting against Great Britain, revolted only against what they considered the false interpretation given by King George to the guarantees of the English constitution, wrested by their ancestors from King John and his successors and consecrated by the Revolution of 1688. It was far from the thoughts of the most extreme, with perhaps an occasional personal exception, to cut loose from the traditions of English liberty, tear down the ancient structure, and build from the ground up, as was done a few years later in France by the maddened victims of the oppression of the nobles.

The sentiment most strongly opposed to the views of Hamilton was not democratic sentiment, in the strictest sense of the word, but devotion to local self-government. Hamilton was democratic enough to insist, in the discussion of the manner of choosing members of the House of Representatives, "It is essential to the democratic rights of the community that the first branch be directly elected by the people." What he desired was strength at the center of authority, from whatever source that authority was derived. Coming from a little West Indian island where the traditions of parliamentary government had little footing, he attached no such importance as most of his associates to the reserved rights of the states. He was the man for the hour as the champion of a strong government, but it would not have been fortunate in some respects if his views had been adopted in their extreme form. There never was the slightest chance, as he doubtless knew, that they would be adopted by the descendants of English freemen who had founded self-governing states in accord with their own principles on the western shores of the Atlantic.

Having delivered a single strong speech, which pointed the way towards a strong union, Hamilton remained comparatively in the background during the remainder of the convention. It was inevitable, however, that he should make himself heard upon the proposal that the new government should have power "to emit bills on the credit of the United States." The power to issue unfunded paper had received his censure four years before, as one of the defects of the existing Articles of Confederation. He now opposed in the most emphatic manner the grant of authority to the new government to issue paper money in the form of its own notes, and to force them into circulation as a substitute for gold and silver coin. When Governor Morris moved to strike out the power to issue bills on the credit of the United States and was supported by Madison, it was supposed that, if the motion prevailed, the power to issue government paper money and make it a legal tender for debts was guarded against for all time. The power was stricken out of the Constitution by a vote of nine states against two. Madison decided the vote of Virginia, and declared that "the pretext for a paper currency, and particularly for making the bills a tender, either for public or private debts, was cut off." It is not surprising that Mr. Bancroft, the jealous friend of the Constitution, in spite of the opening of the door at a later period by the Supreme Court of the United States, declared:

"This is the interpretation of the clause, made at the time of its adoption alike by its authors and by its opponents, accepted by all the statesmen of that age, not open to dispute because too clear for argument, and never disputed so long as any one man who took part in framing the Constitution remained alive."

Hamilton spoke on a few other occasions on subsidiary points connected with the draft of the Constitution, but it was only at the close of the convention that he again came resolutely to the front to exert a strong influence over his associates. When the final draft of the new frame of government had been completed, several delegates showed symptoms of refusing to affix their signatures. The great weight of Franklin was thrown into the scale to urge that the delegates go back to the people presenting the semblance of harmony instead of divisions. "I consent to this Constitution," he declared, "because I expect no better, and because I am not sure that it is not the best." Washington sought also to secure unanimity, and Hamilton declared:—

"I am anxious that every member should sign. A few by refusing may do infinite mischief. No man's ideas are more remote from the plan than my own are known to be; but is it possible to deliberate between anarchy and convulsion on the one side, and the chance of good to be expected from the plan on the other?"

Such words had some weight, but not enough to secure unanimity. All the states voted for the Constitution, but several delegates went on record against it, and Hamilton's two associates from New York were absent. It was this alone which saved New York from being recorded against the Constitution. Hamilton did not shrink from putting down his signature as the representative of his state. It was he who, in a bold, plain hand, inscribed on the great sheet of parchment the name of each state, as the delegations came forward, one after another, in geographical order and affixed their signatures to the precious document which was to found the government of the United States.

Hamilton returned to New York determined to use his utmost powers to secure the ratification of the Constitution as the best attainable means of averting the dangers of disunion. Although cordially supported by John Jay and Edward Livingston, Hamilton, in the fight for ratification in New York, was the natural leader. He found arrayed against him the whole influence of Governor Clinton and the dominant party in New York politics. Clinton was not absolutely opposed to union, but he attached to it so many reservations that for practical purposes he was an opponent of the new Constitution. The battle over ratification began on the question of the choice of delegates to the state convention. It was in this field that Hamilton fought the great fight with his pen which has left to posterity the fine exposition of the Constitution known as "The Federalist." A society was formed in the city of New York to resist the adoption of the Constitution, and articles soon began to appear in the local press criticizing and opposing it.

Preparing a vigorous letter, while gliding down the Hudson, in reply to some of the first points of the opposition, Hamilton soon extended the project into a series of strong papers, which appeared twice a week for twenty weeks over the signature of "Publius." He secured the aid of Madison and Jay, who wrote some of the papers, but the project was Hamilton's, the majority of the papers were written by him, and to him has been justly given the credit of the well-knit and powerful arguments afterwards printed under the title of "The Federalist."

Taking up point by point the provisions of the new Constitution, Hamilton, by skillful argument, drawn from the closest abstract reasoning, the recent experience of the states, and the history of foreign countries, sought to show that the new Constitution was based upon sound principles of government, that it was well calculated to carry out these principles, and that its acceptance was practically the only course open to the American people to insure for themselves the benefits of liberty, prosperity, and peace. "The Federalist," although a purely political argument, has survived the occasion which called it forth, as one of the master documents of political writing. That it has a distinct place in literature is admitted by so severe a critic as Professor Barrett Wendell in his recent Literary History of America. It is worthwhile quoting his acute literary judgment of its merits:—

"As a series of formal essays, the 'Federalist' groups itself roughly with the Tatler, the Spectator, and those numerous descendants of theirs which fill the literary records of eighteenth century England. It differs, however, from all these, in both substance and purpose. The Tatler, the Spectator, and their successors dealt with superficial matters in a spirit of literary amenity: the 'Federalist' deals in an argumentative spirit as earnest as that of any Puritan divine with political principles paramount in our history; and it is so wisely thoughtful that one may almost declare it the permanent basis of sound thinking concerning American constitutional law. Like all the educated writing of the eighteenth century, too, it is phrased with a rhythmical balance and urbane polish which give it claim to literary distinction."

While the written arguments of Hamilton in "The Federalist" have survived for a hundred years and been consulted by foreign students in the formation of new constitutions, a more severe task was imposed upon him at the meeting of the state convention called to consider the report of the convention at Philadelphia. It was in some respects the hardest task ever set with any hope of success before a parliamentary leader. Indeed, to the superficial observer there would have seemed to be no hope of success, when in the elections to the state convention the supporters of Governor Clinton chose forty-six delegates and left on the side of Hamilton only nineteen of the sixty-five members. But this statement of the case gives a somewhat darker color to the situation than the real facts. There was a strong and growing body of public sentiment for the Constitution in New York city and the counties along the Hudson, which even led to the suggestion that they should join the Union in any event and leave the northern counties to shift for themselves. It was generally recognized, moreover, that however strong the objections were to the Constitution, the choice lay practically between this Constitution and none,—between the proposed government and anarchy.

So strong was the sentiment that the Constitution must be accepted in some form, that its opponents in the state convention did not venture upon immediate rejection. Fortunately, their course in fighting for delay only tended to make it clearer that New York would stand alone if she failed to ratify. While the dream of independent sovereignty, or the leadership in a federation which should dictate terms to the surrounding states, was not without its attractions to the more ambitious of the opposition leaders, there was a darker side to the proposition which was much less attractive. Independence for New York meant a heavy burden of taxation for a separate army and navy, for guarding long frontiers on the east, north, and south, for supporting an extensive customs service along the same frontiers, for maintaining ministers at foreign courts and consuls in the leading cities of the world, and for meeting all the other expenses of a sovereign nation.

It was fortunate for the state and the country that the leader of the opposition to the Constitution in the New York convention was a man of a high order of ability, whose mind was open in an unusual degree to the influence of logical reasoning. This man was Melancthon Smith, who is accorded by Chancellor Kent, the great authority on American law, the credit of being noted "for his love of reading, tenacious memory, powerful intellect, and for the metaphysical and logical discussions of which he was a master." It is as much to his credit as that of Hamilton that he finally admitted that he had been convinced by Hamilton, and that he should vote for the Constitution. This result was only reached, however, after a long and sometimes acrimonious struggle, in which Hamilton was on his feet day after day explaining and defending each separate clause of the Constitution,—not only in its real meaning, but against all the distorted constructions put upon it by the most acute and jealous of critics.

But events had been fighting with Hamilton. State after state had ratified the new document, and news of their action had reached New York. Nine states, the number necessary to put the Constitution in force, were made up by the ratification of New Hampshire (June 21, 1788). Still New York hesitated, and Hamilton wrote to Madison: "Our chance of success depends upon you. Symptoms of relaxation in some of the leaders authorize a gleam of hope if you do well, but certainly I think not otherwise." Virginia justified his hopes by a majority of 89 against 79 for ratification (June 25, 1788). The news reached New York on July 3. The opposition there, though showing signs of relenting, was still stubborn. Conditional ratification, with a long string of amendments, was first proposed. Jay firmly insisted that the word "conditional" must be erased. Finally, on July 11, he proposed unconditional ratification. Melancthon Smith then proposed ratification with the right to withdraw if the amendments should not be accepted. Hamilton exposed the folly of such a project in a brilliant speech, which led Smith to admit that conditional ratification was an absurdity. Other similar proposals were brought forward, but they were evidently equivalent to rejection by indirection, which would have left New York out of the new Union.

Finally, Samuel Jones, another broad-minded member of the opposition, proposed ratification without conditions, but "in full confidence" that Congress would adopt all needed amendments. With the support of Smith, this form of ratification was carried by the slender majority of three votes (July 26, 1788). By this narrow margin it was decided that New York should form a part of the Union, and that the great experiment in representative government should not begin with the two halves of the country separated by a hostile power, commanding the greatest seaport of the colonies.

Hamilton thus played an important part in winning the first great battle for the Constitution. Ratification was only one of many steps which remained to be taken before the new government was in working order. Hamilton hurried back to the Federal Congress, and carried an ordinance fixing the dates and the place for putting the new government in operation. When he returned to New York, he was beaten for reelection to Congress, and Governor Clinton and his party retained such a firm grip upon the legislature that a deadlock occurred between the Federalist House and the opposition Senate. New York was unrepresented in the first electoral college, and had no senators at the meeting of the First Congress. The state elections which followed resulted in defeat for the Federalists in the election of the governor, but they carried the legislature and elected two senators,—General Schuyler and Rufus King. King had recently come from Massachusetts, and Hamilton's insistence that he should be chosen caused a breach with the Livingstons, which contributed to the defeat of Schuyler two years later and the election of Aaron Burr. Hamilton's course in this matter was one of many cases in which he showed that he was not an astute politician, nor an adept at dealing with men. His highest qualities were those more distinctly intellectual, which led him to drive straight towards a desired object, with little patience for smaller men or the obstacles which stood in his way.

III: Establishing the Public Credit

The great work of Hamilton, which was to stamp his name forever upon American history and our frame of government, was yet before him. Washington was inaugurated in April, 1789, but it was not until September 2 that an act passed Congress establishing the Treasury Department. Hamilton was the selection of Washington for the new post. It was a selection so well approved by all who were familiar with Hamilton's great abilities as an organizer and financier that the nomination was confirmed on the day that it reached the Senate. The studies of many years, the program which had been outlined in letters to Morris and in the newspapers, were now to bear fruit under the directing genius of Hamilton. Only ten days passed after his appointment before Congress requested him to prepare a report upon the public credit. Then came calls for reports on the collection and management of the revenue; estimates of receipts and expenditures; the regulation of the currency; the navigation laws; the post-office, and the public lands. Money had to be found at once for the pressing needs of the new government before the more elaborate projects of the young minister of finance could be put in operation. But Hamilton did not delay long even for the more important and permanent work. When Congress met in January, he submitted his celebrated report "On Public Credit," which laid the corner-stone of American finance under the Constitution.

This report of Hamilton's on the public credit has long stood out as one of the master state papers of American history. Read today in the light of the economic progress of more than a century, its conclusions are not entirely novel, but are in the main clear and sound. To obtain a proper perspective regarding their value, the mind should be projected back to the beginning of 1790, when political economy as a science had barely been born, and the work of Adam Smith, although about fourteen years old, was probably known to but few in America. Many public men of today with the proper preliminary training might evolve as sound a report as that of Hamilton, but no ordinary man could have done it a hundred and ten years ago, and few men could do it today with the force of diction, precision and directness of statement, the grasp of principles, and the mastery of detail which marked the work of Hamilton.

He seemed to gather in his hands all the tangled threads of the disordered finances of the Continental Congress and of the states and show how they could be woven into a band of strength and symmetry, holding together by the motive of enlightened self-interest all the parts of the new Union. He proposed to plant the public credit upon a firm foundation, satisfy the public creditors, and put the nation on the high road to industrial and financial progress. The difficulties which Hamilton confronted were not merely a bankrupt Treasury and a loose system of finance under the federal government, but large expenditures by the states for carrying on the Revolutionary War, for which reimbursement was demanded by the states which had spent the most and was opposed by those which had spent the least. Hamilton endeavored to show that all would gain by the assumption of these debts by the federal government. Although a thinker rather than a tactician, he was shrewd enough to make an appeal early in his report to all men engaged in industry by pointing out the importance of public credit upon the volume and profits of private business. He endeavored first to make clear the benefit to any government of a sound fiscal system. He said upon this point:—

"As, on the one hand, the necessity for borrowing in particular emergencies cannot be doubted, so, on the other, it is equally evident that to be able to borrow upon good terms, it is essential that the credit of a nation should be well established. For, when the credit of a country is in any degree questionable, it never fails to give an extravagant premium, in one shape or another, upon all the loans it has occasion to make. Nor does the evil end here; the same disadvantage must be sustained upon whatever is to be bought on terms of future payment. From this constant necessity of borrowing and buying dear, it is easy to conceive how immensely the expenses of a nation, in the course of time, will be augmented by an unsound state of the public credit."

Taking up the demonstration how closely the public credit is linked with the fortune of the individual, Hamilton points out that public securities are a part of the medium of exchange, that sound credit will extend trade by preventing the export of money, and that agriculture and manufactures will be promoted because "more capital can be commanded to be employed in both," and that the interest of money will be lowered.

Hamilton took up and punctured in his report several fallacies regarding the treatment of the debt which had obtained lodgment in the public mind and threatened to influence the action of Congress. One of these was that a distinction should be made between those holders of the debt to whom it was originally issued and those who had acquired it by purchase. As the latter holders had bought the debt in some cases at a mere fraction of its face value and for speculative purposes, the specious argument was made that they were entitled in the settlement with the government only to what they had paid the original holders. Hamilton set himself to dissipate this prejudice by showing that the man who had been willing to purchase the public debt might be quite as patriotic as the man who had parted with it for a price. He suggested that if the debt was thus purchased in the confidence that it would rise to par, the act was a proof of the patriotism of the purchaser, and it would be a sorry return for this confidence to make it a reason for discrimination against him.

But much more important from the public point of view, he pointed out, was the sanctity of contracts guaranteed by the new Constitution, and absolutely required to give a stable character to the securities of the government. If the government were to discriminate between the original holders of the debt and other holders, he made it clear that a degree of discredit would be cast on all the obligations of the United States, no matter in whose hands they were found, which would tend to defeat the end and aim of all his measures,—the restoration of public credit. Upon this point he said:—

"The nature of the contract, in its origin, is, that the public will pay the sum expressed in the security, to the first holder or his assignee. The intent in making the security assignable is, that the proprietor may be able to make use of his property, by selling it for as much as it may be worth in the market, and that the buyer may be safe in the purchase.

"Every buyer, therefore, stands exactly in the place of the seller, has the same right with him to the identical sum expressed in the security, and having acquired that right, by fair purchase, and in conformity to the original agreement and intention of the government, his claim cannot be disputed without manifest injustice.

"The impolicy of a discrimination results from two considerations: one, that it proceeds upon a principle destructive of that quality of the public debt, or the stock of the nation, which is essential to its capacity for answering the purposes of money, that is, the security of transfer; the other, that, as well on this account as because it includes a breach of faith, it renders property in the funds less valuable, consequently induces lenders to demand a higher premium for what they lend, and produces every other inconvenience of a bad state of public credit."

One of the most serious obstacles which confronted Hamilton in carrying out his financial policy was the opposition to the assumption by the new federal government of the debts of the several states incurred in the prosecution of the war. The states which had been remiss in paying their quota for the general expenses and those which had not been called upon to pay much for local defense did not see why a burden should be imposed upon them, even in equitable proportion with the other states, for the purpose of relieving those states which had been prompt with their payments or had been compelled to spend freely for the protection of their own boundaries and people. This prejudice Hamilton faced with the same clear vision and resolute purpose as that against providing for the debt of the Union. He set forth at the outset that if these debts were to be paid at all, whether by the states or by the Union, "it will follow that no greater revenues will be required, whether that provision be made wholly by the United States, or partly by the states separately." He pointed out that the control of the entire matter by the federal government would secure uniformity of treatment for the public creditors, would prevent competition between the Union and the states for the sources of the revenue, which otherwise might cause collision and confusion, and would secure a distribution of taxation more just to industry in all the states. The assumption of the state debts, moreover, he insisted was vital to the credit of the Union. Upon this head, and upon the equity of charging to the Union of the states the debts which had been incurred for the benefit of all, Hamilton observed:—

"Should the state creditors stand upon a less eligible footing than the others, it is unnatural to expect they would see with pleasure a provision for them. The influence which their dissatisfaction might have could not but operate injuriously, both for the creditors and the credit of the United States. Hence it is even the interest of the creditors of the Union, that those of the individual states should be comprehended in a general provision. Any attempt to secure to the former either exclusive or peculiar advantages would materially hazard their interests. Neither would it be just that one class of the public creditors should be more favored than the other. The objects for which both descriptions of the debt were contracted are in the main the same. Indeed, a great part of the particular debts of the states has arisen from assumptions by them on account of the Union. And it is most equitable, that there should be the same measure of retribution for all.

"The general principle of it seems to be equitable, for it appears difficult to conceive a good reason why the expenses for the particular defense of a part, in a common war, should not be a common charge, as well as those incurred professedly for the general defense. The defense of each part is that of the whole, and unless all the expenditures are brought into a common mass, the tendency must be to add to the calamities suffered by being the most exposed to the ravages of war, an increase of burthens."

Hamilton found the public debt of the Union to be $54,124,464.56. This would not be a formidable debt today, even with full allowance for the difference in population, but it was formidable for that time because of the compara-comparative poverty of the country, and the scanty resources for paying it. The great increase in the productive power of man in our time, by means of machinery, improved means of communication, and other devices for saving labor and increasing its efficiency, makes it easy for prosperous nations to bear taxation without feeling the burden which would have paralyzed industry and arrested national progress a century ago. The United States in 1790 were not far beyond the primitive condition in which the entire sum of production is required for the necessaries of existence, and little is left for the luxuries of life and of state enterprise.

The total of the debt, as computed by Hamilton, was made up by adding the foreign debt, $10,070,307, with arrears of interest amounting to $1,640,071.62, to the principal of the domestic debt, $27,383,917.74, with arrears of interest amounting to $13,030,168.20, and estimating the unliquidated debt at $2,000,000. The amount of the state debts he was not able to ascertain with precision, but estimated at about $25,000,000. This made the total debt to be dealt with something more than $75,000,000. The annual interest required at the rates provided in the contract would amount to $542,599.66 on the foreign debt, and $4,044,845.15 on the domestic debt, including that of the states, making a total of $4,587,444.81. While urging the most conscientious fulfillment of obligations, Hamilton admitted that this demand would require the extension of taxation to a degree and to objects which the true interests of the public creditors themselves forbade. "It is therefore to be hoped," he said, "and even to be expected, that they will cheerfully concur in such modifications of their claims, on fair and equitable principles, as will facilitate to the government an arrangement substantial, durable, and satisfactory to the community."

This arrangement he did not propose to reach by repudiating any portion of the debt. He proposed to reduce the rate of interest, in course of time, in accordance with the decline in the rate for the rental of capital abroad, but to those holders of the debt who desired settlement in full at the old rates of interest, he made liberal offers. A number of optional plans for accepting funds at different rates of interest for different terms were presented, which it is not necessary to set forth in detail. The statement of the first two will give an idea of their general character:—

"First, That, for every hundred dollars subscribed, payable in the debt, (as well interest as principal,) the subscriber be entitled, at his option, either to have two-thirds funded at an annuity or yearly interest of six per cent., redeemable at the pleasure of the government, by payment of the principal, and to receive the other third in lands in the western territory, at the rate of twenty cents per acre.

Or, to have the whole sum funded at an annuity or yearly interest of four per cent, irredeemable by any payment exceeding five dollars per annum, on account both of principal and interest, and to receive, as a compensation for the reduction of interest, fifteen dollars and eighty cents, payable in lands, as in the preceding case."

Hamilton thus reserved the right to redeem the debt at the pleasure of the government, when new securities could be floated at reduced rates. This was in accordance with the enlightened policy of governments before and since in availing themselves of the increase of capital and the improved condition of the public credit. The holder of the public funds could find no fault if he received back his principal, while an attractive investment at current rates of return upon capital would be offered to new investors in the form of funds at a reduced rate of interest, if such new funds were not acceptable to the old holders of the debt.

The proposal for using the public lands in part settlement of the debt was a happy device for employing a resource of immense value to the country, and promoting early settlement of the great areas of uncultivated land which became the property of the Union. It was in pursuance of this comprehensive policy that Connecticut, Virginia, and other states had ceded to Congress, even before the adoption of the Constitution, their indefinite claims to the great stretches of country between the Allegheny Mountains and the Mississippi.

IV: Congress Sustains Hamilton

The plans of Hamilton having been formulated, it remained to be determined whether they should be adopted by the lawmaking power or should remain a splendid but abortive monument to the constructive skill of their author. Vigorous opposition was expected by Hamilton to the measures which he proposed. He had endeavored to meet and disarm such opposition as far as possible in the careful and illuminating language of his report, but it soon became evident that against nearly all parts of it a bitter and persistent battle would be waged. The owners of capital and the commercial element were represented in the Northern and Eastern States rather than in the South, and the representatives of the former states strongly supported from the first the entire policy of the Secretary of the Treasury. Rumors were already abroad that something was to be done to restore the national credit, but it was not until the reading of Hamilton's report in the House (January 14, 1790) that the full scope of his plans was made manifest.

The effect of the report was so favorable upon the public credit as to forge weapons for its enemies. This came about through the sudden rise in the public funds, and the promptness with which speculators bought them up from holders who were ignorant of their value. Funds which would have been gladly disposed of at three shillings to the pound, or fifteen per cent. of their face value, at any time within the previous three years, rose before noon the next day fifty per cent. of their quoted price. It was not yet certain that the project would be adopted by Congress, but shrewd men were willing to discount the future in much the same manner that brokers in Wall Street do at the present time. The absence of a well-organized stock market, with the ramifications of telegraphic quotations throughout the Union, put in the hands of the more daring of these speculators an opportunity to avail themselves of the ignorance of others to an extent which would not be possible today. Agents were soon scouring the country, buying up the certificates of the debt in all its varied forms, before the news of Hamilton's great report had reached the humble holders, some of whom were old soldiers or quiet farmers who had been compelled to furnish supplies for the army. Jefferson says in his Anas:—

"Couriers and relay horses by land, and swift-sailing pilot-boats by sea, were flying in all directions. Active partners and agents were associated and employed in every state, town, and county, and the paper bought up at five shillings, and even as low as two shillings in the pound, before the holder knew that Congress had already provided for its redemption at par."

This sudden and remarkable effect of Hamilton's recommendations put weapons in the hands of the enemies of the project, because it seemed to give force to their argument that a distinction should be made between those to whom the debt was originally issued at par and the new holders who had obtained it at a discount. Long and bitter were the debates in the House over this and other branches of Hamilton's project. But it was so obvious that a distinction between the holders of the debt would run directly counter to its character as negotiable paper, and would be almost impossible of just execution, that the friends of the funding project easily had the best of the argument. Madison, although inclined to oppose Hamilton, was forced to admit that the debt must be funded at par without discrimination. He brought forward a project to pay the original holders the difference between par and the price at which they had sold, and to pay to the present holders only what they had paid for the securities. This was shown to be so impracticable that only thirteen votes were given for it in a House of forty-nine members voting. The advocates of the entire funding project carried it in committee of the whole (March 9, 1790) by a vote of 31 to 26.

The debates had so strengthened the position of Hamilton that the wisdom of funding the debt of the Union at par was now generally admitted. His opponents and those who feared too great a concentration of power in the capitalist class and the central government made their stand on the proposal to assume the state debts. When the resolution reported by the committee of the whole was taken up in the House on March 29, several representatives from North Carolina appeared in the House and swelled the ranks of the opposition. North Carolina had been late in accepting the Constitution, and her members had not been present on previous votes. When, therefore, a motion to recommit the financial projects was made, it was carried by a vote of 29 to 27. The advocates of assumption were so indignant, and so convinced that one part of the project was as vital as the other, that they voted to recommit the original funding resolution. Further debate took place, but without shaking the firmness of the opposition to the assumption of the state debts. The project was rejected in committee (April 12) by a vote of 31 to 29.

The situation was a grave one. Hamilton felt that the future of the Union was at stake. If his projects were not adopted substantially as a whole, the new government would be without credit and the work of the Convention of 1789 would be in vain. The government at Washington would be as helpless as the Continental Congress and its committees had been. This opinion was shared by all those who favored a vigorous central government, and practically by all the members of the party in Congress which was forming in support of the measures of Hamilton and looking to him as their leader. While casting about for some means for meeting the emergency, Hamilton fell upon a plan which represents one of the few cases in which he had recourse to diplomacy in his public career. The question of the location of the national capital had been for some time pending in Congress. It had already become involved with the assumption of the state debts. A strong bid had been made by the opponents of assumption for the five votes of Pennsylvania by the offer to locate the capital for fifteen years at Philadelphia.

The importance of having Congress and its officials in a given city represented more at that time, in spite of the small size of the body and the relative insignificance of the interests before it, than would be the case today with either of the great commercial cities of New York, Boston, or Philadelphia. Local interests played the same part then as now in political maneuvering, and possession of the capital looked larger in the eyes of some members than the financial policy of the Union. In the sarcastic language of Professor McMaster, "The state debts might remain unpaid, the credit of the nation might fall, but come what might, the patronage of Congress must be drawn from New York and distributed among the grog-shops and taverns of Philadelphia."

Hamilton took advantage of this situation to save assumption and to fix the financial policy of the United States. The Senate had rejected the proposal to establish the capital at Philadelphia, and when the project came back to the House, Baltimore was substituted by a majority of two. The Pennsylvanians and their friends in the Senate retaliated by mutilating the funding bill and daring the assumptionists to reject it. The latter held to their position and rejected the bill, 35 to 23. It was while matters were in this acute stage, while threats were made on behalf of the North that the Union would be broken up if assumption were not carried, that Hamilton one day in front of the President's house met Thomas Jefferson. Jefferson had recently returned from France to assume the position of Secretary of State. What followed is best told in Jefferson's own words, because he afterwards claimed that he had been "duped" by Hamilton and acted without knowledge of the effect of what he was doing. Jefferson's account of the matter is as follows:—

"As I was going to the President's one day, I met him (Hamilton) in the street. He walked me backwards and forwards before the President's door for half an hour. He painted pathetically the temper into which the legislature had been wrought; the disgust of those who were called the creditor states: the danger of the secession of their members, and the separation of the states. He observed that the members of the administration ought to act in concert; that though this question was not of my department, yet a common duty should make it a common concern; that the President was the center on which all administrative questions ultimately rested, and that all of us should rally around him, and support, with joint efforts, measures approved by him; and that the question having been lost by a small majority only, it was probable that an appeal from me to the judgment and discretion of some of my friends might effect a change in the vote, and the machine of government, now suspended, might be again set into motion. I told him that I was really a stranger to the whole subject; that not having yet informed myself of the system of finance adopted, I knew not how far this was a necessary sequence; that undoubtedly, if its rejection endangered a dissolution of our Union at this incipient stage, I should deem that the most unfortunate of all consequences, to avert which all partial and temporary evils should be yielded. I proposed to him, however, to dine with me the next day, and I would invite another friend or two, bring them into conference together, and I thought it impossible that reasonable men, consulting together coolly, could fail, by some mutual sacrifices of opinion, to form a compromise which was to save the Union. The discussion took place. I could take no part in it but an exhortatory one, because I was a stranger to the circumstances which should govern it. But it was finally agreed, that whatever importance had been attached to the rejection of this proposition, the preservation of the Union and of concord among the states was more important, and that, therefore, it would be better that the vote of rejection should be rescinded, to effect which some members should change their votes. But it was observed that this pill would be peculiarly bitter to the Southern States, and that some concomitant measure should be adopted to sweeten it a little to them. There had been projects to fix the seat of government either at Philadelphia or at Georgetown on the Potomac; and it was thought that by giving it to Philadelphia for ten years, and to Georgetown permanently afterwards, this might, as an anodyne, calm in some degree the ferment which might be excited by the other measure alone. Some two of the Potomac members (White and Lee, but White with a revulsion of stomach almost convulsive) agreed to change their votes, and Hamilton undertook to carry the other point. In doing this, the influence he had established over the eastern members, with the agency of Robert Morris with those of the Middle States, effected his side of the engagement."

Hamilton had little of the state pride which influenced the men of Massachusetts, New York, Virginia, or of any other state who had grown up on the soil won by their English ancestors by their blood or the sweat of their brows. To him the question of the location of the capital seemed insignificant in comparison with the foundation of the Union upon the rock of a comprehensive financial policy. It is significant of the commanding influence which the young secretary had acquired, and the well-knit party which was gathering around him, that he had no difficulty in carrying his part of the program for seating the capital eventually on the banks of the Potomac. The bill to remove the capital was passed on July 9, 1790, by a majority of three, and the assumption of the state debts was carried soon after. The form of the assumption differed somewhat from the proposal of Hamilton, but it accomplished the result at which he aimed. A specific sum, $21,500,000, was assumed by the government and distributed among the states in set proportions. The project passed the Senate July 22, by a vote of 14 to 12, and the House on July 24, by a vote of 34 to 28. A great step was thus taken in the consolidation of the Union, and notice was given to the world that the United States proposed to pay their debts and fulfill with scrupulous honor their financial obligations.

V: Strengthening the Bonds of Union

The funding of the debt was only one of several parts of the policy of Hamilton for putting the new government upon a solvent and firm basis. The session of Congress which began in December, 1790, witnessed the presentation of his report in favor of a national bank. This report, like that on the debt, showed careful study of the subject in its theoretical as well as practical aspects. Hamilton referred in opening to the successful operation of public banks in Italy, Germany, Holland, England, and France. He then went on to point out some of their specific advantages in concentrating capital and permitting the easy transfer of credit. He declared that such a bank would afford "greater facility to the government, in obtaining pecuniary aid, especially in sudden emergencies." It would also facilitate the payment of taxes, by enabling tax-payers to borrow from the bank and by the aid which it would give in the transfer of funds. He did not shrink from declaring that the country would benefit if foreigners invested in the bank shares, since this would bring so much additional capital into the United States. Hamilton then pointed out the vital distinction between government paper issues and bank paper. He laid down thus the fundamental principle of a well-regulated bank-note currency:—

"Among other material differences between a paper currency, issued by the mere authority of government, and one issued by a bank, payable in coin, is this: That, in the first case, there is no standard to which an appeal can be made, as to the quantity which will only satisfy, or which will surcharge the circulation: in the last, that standard results from the demand. If more should be issued than is necessary, it will return upon the bank. Its emissions, as elsewhere intimated, must always be in a compound ratio to the fund and the demand: whence it is evident, that there is a limitation in the nature of the thing; while the discretion of the government is the only measure of the extent of the emissions, by its own authority."

The bank which Hamilton proposed was private in its ownership, but the United States were to pledge themselves not to authorize any similar institution during its continuance. The capital of the bank was not to exceed $10,000,000, for which the President of the United States might subscribe $2,000,000 on behalf of the government. It was further provided that three fourths of the amount of each share might be paid in the public debt instead of gold and silver.

It was the purpose of Hamilton not merely to create a useful financial institution, in which the government would be able to keep its deposits, but to weld the monetary system of the country into an harmonious whole. The result of this, which he foresaw and intended, was to bind the property-owning classes to the interests of the new government. The effect was much the same as the creation of the Bank of England by the loan of its capital to the government, which bound the moneyed classes firmly to King William, through the knowledge that the debt and the solvency of the bank depended on the perpetuation of his government and the exclusion of the Stuart Pretender. The tendency of Hamilton's project was clearly seen by Jefferson and other democratic leaders, and did not fail to arouse their hostility. It was not long before they promptly took sides against the national bank. Jefferson wrote regarding the meetings of the cabinet at this time that "Hamilton and myself were daily pitted in the cabinet like two cocks."

There was something deeper involved, from the standpoint of Jefferson, than the mere question of bringing the moneyed class to the side of the government. The latter object was sufficiently distasteful to him, but the extension of the powers granted by the Constitution beyond those which were directly enumerated in the document involved a question of public policy and constitutional law which afforded the basis for the creation of two great national parties. The Constitution did not anywhere grant in terms to the government the power to establish a national bank. Even Hamilton did not pretend to put his finger on the specific authority for his new project. He advanced a doctrine which was eagerly embraced by the party which was growing up around him, but which was as resolutely opposed by the other party. This was the doctrine of the implied powers granted to the new government by the Constitution. It is doubtful whether the Constitution would have been ratified by Virginia and other states if this doctrine had been set forth and defended in the state conventions by the friends of the Constitution. This by no means implies that the policy and doctrine of Hamilton were not wise and far-sighted. Hamilton had definite aims before him, and it was his legitimate mission to educate public sentiment up to the point of accepting those aims and of granting him the means for carrying them out.

The doctrine of the "implied powers" rested upon the theory that unless they were directly prohibited by the Constitution, all powers were granted to the government by implication which were found necessary and proper for carrying out the powers specifically granted. Jefferson came to believe, if he did not believe at the outset, that the government was one of delegated powers which were strictly limited to those enumerated in the Constitution. The doctrine of Hamilton, from this point of view, was revolutionary. It meant the conversion of a government holding limited delegations of power from the people and the states into a government having supreme power, capable of taking an infinite variety of measures whenever Congress, in the exercise of its discretion, believed that such measures would contribute to the well-being of the Union. The state governments, coming closer to the people than the federal government, were most directly threatened by this assumption of power, and it was as the champions of state rights as well as democratic ideas that Jefferson and his friends took their ground as the advocates of the strict construction of the Constitution.

It is not surprising, therefore, that the proposal to create the Bank of the United States called forth in Congress prolonged and heated debates. But the policy of Hamilton had been so far successful in restoring the public credit that he carried the project for the national bank through both houses, and it was laid before the President for his approval. Washington had watched with interest the struggle in the two houses, and was somewhat impressed by the weight of the argument against the constitutional power of Congress to establish the bank. The cabinet was divided. Jefferson and Randolph were against the constitutionality of the bill. Hamilton and Knox were in favor of it. Washington asked each of them to give him in writing the reasons for his opinion. He weighed them carefully and then affixed his signature to the bill (February 25, 1791). The new project realized all the benefits which Hamilton expected. Washington, in his tour of the Southern States in the spring of 1791, found the sentiment for union strengthening and the country recovering from the prostration of the era of bad money and political uncertainty which had followed the Revolution. He declared in a letter written after his return:

"Our public credit stands on that ground, which, three years ago, it would have been madness to have foretold. The astonishing rapidity with which the newly instituted bank was filled, gives an unexampled proof of the resources of our countrymen and their confidence in public measures. On the first day of opening the subscription, the whole number of shares (twenty thousand) were taken up in one hour, and application made for upwards of four thousand shares more than were granted by the institution, besides many others that were coming in from various quarters."

How much was likely to be done by a national bank to bind together the commercial interests of different sections of the country can hardly be appreciated today. At that time there were only four banks in the country; none of these was ten years old, and their combined capital was only $1,950,000. The Bank of the United States was authorized to establish offices of discount and deposit in all the states and to distribute parts of its capital among eight branches in the chief cities of the country. It was the drafts of these branches upon each other, and their means for reducing to a uniform and reasonable rate the cost of transferring funds, which contributed to knit all parts of the country together in commercial matters and so strengthened the bond of political union. The bank did not make regular reports to the Treasury Department, but its success is indicated by a special report communicated to Congress by Secretary Gallatin (January 24, 1811), which showed resources of $24,183,046. The average annual dividends paid upon the stock up to March, 1809, were over eight per cent.

So invaluable were the operations of the Bank of the United States to the public treasury that Jefferson himself when President came to its support. His support was perhaps never very hearty, and was due to Albert Gallatin, his Secretary of the Treasury, whose foresight and ability give him a rank next to Hamilton among the able men who have presided over the national finances. Gallatin made a strong report in 1809, recommending that the charter of the bank be renewed upon its expiration in 1811, with an increase of capital and wider powers. A new charter was voted in the House, but the bill was not acted on in the Senate, and before the next session the opposition of the state bankers had rallied sufficient strength to defeat the re-charter. The second United States Bank was authorized in 1816, under the administration of Madison and with his approval, but its career was terminated in 1836, as the result of the political hostility of President Jackson.

It was not until after the grant of this second charter that the question of the power of Congress to establish a bank came directly before the Supreme Court in 1819. At the head of this court sat John Marshall, who next to Hamilton, perhaps, did more than any other man to strengthen and extend the powers of the general government. The jealousy of the state banks had led the State of Maryland to impose a discriminating tax on the Bank of the United States. If the right to levy such a tax had been admitted, the Bank would have been completely at the mercy of the states, and one of the chief purposes of its creation would have been defeated. In order to sustain the right of the bank to exemption from taxation, it was necessary to prove that it was a constitutional instrument of federal power. Hence the question of the power of Congress to create such a corporation came directly before the court.

Hamilton found the power to create a bank partly in the preamble to the Constitution, which declares that the people of the United States have adopted it in order to "promote the general welfare," but more particularly in that concluding phrase of the clause defining the powers of Congress, which declares that that body shall have authority "to make all laws which shall be necessary and proper for carrying into execution the foregoing powers, and all other powers vested by this Constitution in the government of the United States or in any department or officer thereof." Marshall, in the series of great decisions by which he strengthened the power of the Union, often made use of these provisions to justify his reasoning. In one of the most famous of these decisions (McCulloch vs. Maryland), he sustained the constitutionality of the bank as an instrument of federal power and denied the right of the states to levy upon its property. He declared that the power to tax involved the power to destroy, and that if the federal government had not the power to withdraw its creations from discriminating legislation by the states, the latter might tax the mail or the mints, the papers of the custom-houses, or the forms of judicial process.

The view of Hamilton regarding the power of the federal government to create a bank was thus sustained in emphatic terms by the highest court in the land. It was partly his policy in providing for the bank and demonstrating its usefulness, with his other measures to develop the powers of the central government, which made possible the decisions of Marshall. If the question of the right to incorporate a bank could have been brought before the court at the beginning, before the institution had proved its value, and if men like Jefferson and Madison had been upon the bench, there is at least room for doubt whether a decision would have been rendered in favor of a power which is not granted directly to the government by the Constitution. But by the resolute executive policy of Hamilton and the broad judicial constructions of Marshall, the functions of the new government were extended to all those great objects necessary to create a vigorous and united nation.

The many other measures of Hamilton were directed by the same singleness of purpose to strengthen the hands of the government and consolidate the Union. The report on the mint followed the previous reports of Jefferson in recommending the adoption of the dollar as the unit of value. Hamilton observed that "upon the whole, it seems to be most advisable, as has been observed, not to attach the unit exclusively to either of the metals; because this cannot be done effectually, without destroying the office and character of one of them as money, and reducing it to the situation of a mere merchandise." He believed, however, that care should be taken to regulate the proportion between the metals with an eye to their average commercial value. He pointed out the danger of undervaluing either metal, and the inevitable result, in case of a difference of ratio in two countries, "if other things were equal, that the greatest part of the gold would be collected in one, and the greatest part of the silver in the other."

This discussion of the subject took place at a time when monetary principles were not very well fixed, when the standard and the state of the currency had hardly been settled on an orderly basis in any country, and when the means of transportation for the precious metals were much slower and less efficient than under modern conditions, and the cost was much greater. Hamilton endeavored to find the true commercial relation between gold and silver as a basis for the coinage values, in the hope that this would not change sufficiently to upset a bimetallic system founded upon such a basis. He was not a victim of the delusion that government can arbitrarily give value by law to money, but declared, "There can hardly be a better rule in any country for the legal, than the market proportion; if this can be supposed to have been produced by the free and steady course of commercial principles."

The report on manufactures and the bill providing for an excise were parts of the project of Hamilton for building up a vigorous and self-supporting nation. The report on manufactures was not presented to Congress until the beginning of the long session at the close of 1791, and was not carried out in legislation. It consisted chiefly of an argument for the encouragement of young industries in an undeveloped country. Hamilton strongly favored the diversification of the industries of the country between agriculture and various forms of manufacture, because he believed it would contribute to the solidity of the industrial system and to the financial independence of the United States. His conception of the best method for promoting American industries differed materially, however, from more recent developments of the protective system. He recommended bounties and premiums in many cases in preference to protectionist customs duties, in order to avoid the rise in the price of articles to the consumer which often results from such duties. The customs duties which he proposed, moreover, ranged only from seven and a half to fifteen per cent., and the latter rate was to be levied on only a few articles.

The country was not yet ripe for extensive industrial enterprises. The manufactures then existing were chiefly for supplying local needs, the factory system had not been introduced, and the capital had not been accumulated for the creation of large establishments. The country needed many foreign manufactured articles to put it upon the highroad to industrial development, and it was at a much later period that the manufacturing interests acquired the power which enabled them to increase the scale of duties. When this time came, they turned to the arsenal of Hamilton's report for weapons in support of the policy of diversifying industries; but they used these weapons in behalf of a scale of duties which was not recommended by him and they ignored his arguments for premiums and bounties for the protection of the consumer against excessive prices.

Whether Hamilton would have favored the policy of protection in its later developments, it is useless to inquire. It is idle to claim for any thinker of the past that he anticipated all future discoveries and reasoning in the fields of politics or economics. It is not necessary, in order to give a statesman a high place in history, to worship blindly all that he did or said or to make such deeds and words an authority for later generations. What can be said of Hamilton without reasonable ground of denial is that he did not recommend in any of his writings the high scale of duties advocated by some protectionists in recent years. On the contrary, he urged a scale of duties which would be treated by the protectionist of today as below even the level of a "tariff for revenue only." That his ideas were far from extreme is indicated by the project which he drew up in 1794 for a reciprocity treaty with Great Britain, which proposed to limit American import duties on the leading textiles and manufactured articles of metal to ten per cent. of their value. He even criticized Jefferson's message of 1801 for recommending the repeal of the internal revenue taxes, upon the ground that the duties on imports were high and that if any taxes were to be repealed, they should be those which weighed on commerce and navigation.

A measure which led to more immediate results than the report on manufactures was the report on the excise. Hamilton found it necessary, in order to obtain sufficient funds to meet the interest on the debt and other charges, to recommend an excise tax upon distilled liquors produced in the United States. The bill passed Congress in January, 1791, and was soon put in force. Violent resistance was made in western Pennsylvania, where the manufacture of whiskey was more extensively carried on than in any other part of the Union. The federal collector for Washington and Allegheny was tarred and feathered, and deputy marshals did not dare serve writs against those guilty of the outrage. Washington's journey through the South had a good effect in softening the opposition to the law, which first showed itself in Virginia and North Carolina; but in Pennsylvania conditions went from bad to worse, until it became necessary to give the federal government additional powers for collecting the tax and putting down insurrection. Masked mobs terrorized those who were inclined to obey the law, and forced them to publish the injury done to their stills. In order to protect themselves by embroiling the whole community, some of the insurgent leaders had the mail stopped, the militia called out on their side, and threatened to lay Pittsburg in ashes (July, 1794).

The opportunity had come for testing the question whether the Union was strong enough to put down rebellion by force. It was an opportunity which Hamilton did not shirk. At his earnest solicitation, an army was dispatched to the disturbed districts. Washington showed no hesitation in supporting the authority of the federal government. He obtained a certificate from a judge of the Supreme Court, setting forth that the laws of the United States were set at naught and that the courts were unable to enforce them. He then issued a proclamation commanding the insurgents to submit to the laws, and made a requisition for 12,950 militia from Pennsylvania, Maryland, Virginia, and New Jersey, to move on September 1, 1794, towards the disaffected districts.

The firmness of Washington put an end to the insurrection. Governor Mifflin of Pennsylvania, who had hesitated to put down the disturbances by the strong hand of the state, recovered his courage, and aided the federal government by proclamations and by his full quota of troops. Hamilton accompanied the army as it moved towards the West, and remained with it after Washington turned back to attend the opening of Congress. The strong display of force made by the government overawed the insurgents and finally compelled their submission. Albert Gallatin, although a citizen of the disaffected section and an opponent of the party in power, exerted his influence on behalf of order. Nego-Negotiations were set on foot between commissioners of the President, and a committee of citizens, of which Gallatin was a member. When this committee met to decide whether they would recommend compliance with the law, they were surrounded by riflemen who were ready to shoot if their leaders showed signs of yielding. But they adopted the clever device of a ballot upon which both yea and nay were written, with the option of destroying either word. A small majority voted to submit. Some of the obstinate spirits held out, but as the people fell away from them, they were arrested and put on trial, and the authority of the federal government was no longer disputed.

This suppression of the "Whiskey Rebellion," as it was called, was one of the most important steps in the consolidation of the Union. Many who had observed the aggressive and comprehensive projects of Hamilton, and seen them daily binding closer the bonds of union, did not believe that they would stand the test of armed conflict. They feared that the power of the government would wither and the people split into warring factions when men were called upon to march in arms against their fellow-citizens. The event proved that the new government had vindicated its right to exist, and that the sentiment of union was daily gaining a stronger hold upon the hearts of the people. That this new power had not only built up a cohesive financial system, but had shown its capacity to put down resistance to its lawful authority with a strong hand, was largely the work of Hamilton. It may be said that it was wholly his work, so far as any great national policy can be projected and carried out by a single man, independently of the support of his associates in the government and of the body of public opinion which make possible the execution of his plans.

The time had come when Hamilton felt that his constructive work was done. He withdrew from the cabinet (January 31, 1795), and Oliver Wolcott of Connecticut was appointed his successor. Hamilton chose the moment for retiring from office with a tact and judgment unusual with public men. He was moved partly by the desire to provide for his family upon a more liberal scale than his modest salary under the government permitted. He was too patriotic, however, to have abandoned his post until he felt that his constructive work was complete. It was with conscious satisfaction that in his report on the public credit at the beginning of 1795 he was able to marshal the measures already taken towards restoring order to the national finances and point out their results. The credit of the country had been raised from the lowest abyss of dishonor to that of the most enlightened nations of the old world; an adequate system of taxation had been provided for meeting the public obligations; the business interests had been knit together in support of the government by a national bank; a monetary system had been established; the Treasury had been organized in its various branches upon a basis which has survived to our day; and finally the strength of the fabric of the Union and of the financial system had been subjected to the test of a rebellion which, without serious bloodshed, but with a strong display of force, had been fully and firmly subdued.

VI: Foreign Affairs and Neutrality

The comprehensive measures of Hamilton for strengthening the Union gave a definite character and policy to the Federalist party. The foundations of this party had been laid by the struggle over the question whether the Constitution should be accepted by the states; but the measures of Hamilton were too strong for some of the friends of the Constitution, and many changes occurred in the temporary groupings of political leaders before a definite dividing line was established between the Federalism of Hamilton on the one side and the Democracy of Jefferson and Madison on the other. These two eminent Democratic leaders had, indeed, been among the most earnest supporters of the Constitution. Madison went farther than Jefferson in the direction of Federalism, and encountered the distrust of the states-rights element at home; but Jefferson, as has been already seen, made several reports in the Continental Congress in favor of declaring the United States a nation, and was the cordial promoter of those important steps towards union,—the transfer of the Western territory to Congress and the adoption of a common monetary system.

The plans of Hamilton in regard to the finances, however, and his resolute policy of neutrality between France and Great Britain, ran counter to the views of Jefferson. It is not surprising, therefore, that the latter found himself pitted against the great Federalist leader upon nearly every question of importance which came before the cabinet. The feeling that he had been duped in regard to the assumption of the state debts found vent in many complaints, which finally bore fruit in open attacks upon Hamilton, at first made indirectly through a clerk in the government service, and then directly in a long letter to Washington. Jefferson gave the post of translating clerk in the State Department to a Frenchman, Philip Freneau, who published a journal known as the "National Gazette." In this journal Freneau began a series of bitter and sometimes well-directed attacks upon the measures of the administration, and particularly those of Hamilton. A friend of Jefferson in Virginia, Colonel Mason, approached Washington in the summer of 1791, and made a long and severe criticism upon the Treasury measures and their effect upon the people.

Washington continued to stand above party, and sought to mitigate the friction between his cabinet officers. Where the judgments of Hamilton and Jefferson differed on constructive measures, however, Washington in nearly every case became convinced of the wisdom of the recommendations of Hamilton. He therefore had the appearance of leaning to his side, although he often mitigated the sharpness of the arguments of his vigorous young minister of finance and endeavored to temper his excess of zeal. After listening to Mason, Washington felt that the time had come to interpose in the growing hostility between his cabinet ministers. He submitted a brief summary to Hamilton of the criticisms which had been made upon his projects and asked him to submit a statement in reply. The charges were directed not only against the substance of the financial measures, but declared that they fostered speculation, corrupted Congress through the ownership of the public debt by members of that body, and that Hamilton was laboring secretly to introduce aristocracy and monarchy.

It was not difficult for Hamilton to brush away most of these criticisms. This he did in the cool, logical manner of which he was a master by numbering each objection to his policy and measures and showing that it was not founded upon solid reasoning or fact. Hamilton would have done well to have rested his case upon his letter to Washington, but he was now convinced that Jefferson was behind the attacks upon him, and he determined to strike back. He began a series of anonymous communications through the Federalist organ, *Fenno's Gazette*, which showed all his usual vigor and force of reasoning, but which only intensified the bitterness in the cabinet. President Washington was deeply disturbed by this open outbreak of hostilities, and remonstrated by letter with both Hamilton and Jefferson. Hamilton suspended his attacks, while Jefferson confined his hostility to less open methods.

When Congress met at the close of 1791, Giles of Virginia, a loud-spoken, hot-headed member of the House, called for accounts of the various foreign loans made by the government. An attempt was made to prove corruption in the management of the Treasury. Hamilton could not have found a better opportunity for defending himself, if he had sought it. He was no longer shut up to the unsatisfactory methods of unsigned communications through newspapers, but was in a position to speak openly and boldly in exposition and defense of his measures. Report after report was sent to Congress, setting forth the operations of the Treasury with a lucidity and power which silenced the opposition and almost overwhelmed Madison, who had been forced as a party leader to accept the responsibility for the attacks. The reports, to anyone who understood the subject, were absolutely convincing of the soundness and wisdom of Hamilton's measures.

Jefferson, perhaps, had some right to complain of the influence which Hamilton exerted over that department of the government which properly belonged under his exclusive jurisdiction. This was the management of foreign relations. Hamilton had such definite and well-considered views on foreign policy as well as finance that he could not forbear presenting them in the cabinet. His superiority in definiteness of aim and energy no doubt led him to believe that he was fitted for the functions of prime minister and that he was justified in exercising them as far as he could. The course of Washington encouraged him to the extent that the President often gave the preference to his views over those of Jefferson, but it was far from the purpose of the President to make any distinction in rank or in his confidence between his ministers. Hamilton, although an admirer of the British political system, permitted himself few prejudices in his theory of the foreign policy of the United States. Though often charged with British sympathies, he leaned much less towards Great Britain than Jefferson, through his admiration of the spirit of the French Revolution, leaned towards France.

The foreign relations of the country began to become acute with the outbreak of war between England and France in 1793. France had already abolished royalty, expelled the nobles, sent Louis XVI. to the scaffold, and was on the eve of the terrible massacres which did so much to revolt even her best friends outside the country. The news of war reached the United States early in April, 1793. News came also that a minister from the French Republic had landed at Charleston and would soon present his credentials at Philadelphia. Hamilton sent post haste for Washington, who was at Mount Vernon. The outbreak of war meant danger to American commerce on the ocean and the risk of trouble with both powers over the neutrality laws. The serious question confronting the American government was whether they should maintain strict neutrality between the belligerents or should side with France, to whom they were bound by the treaties made with her when she came to the rescue of the colonies. When Washington reached Philadelphia, he found both Jefferson and Hamilton ready with suggestions for meeting the crisis, but these suggestions differed widely. Jefferson, although not an advocate of war against England, believed that Congress should be called together in extra session to deal with the emergency.

A stronger program was urged upon the President by Hamilton. He regarded the question of neutrality and the reception of the French envoy as one for the executive rather than for Congress. He believed also that these subjects would be safer in the hands of Washington than midst the passions of a legislative body. He drew up a statement, embodying a series of questions regarding the policy of the United States, which was laid by Washington before the cabinet. The first question was whether a declaration of neutrality should be issued. This was decided in the affirmative, and the proclamation was soon issued by Washington. It was decided that the French minister, Genet, should be received, but that early occasion should be taken to explain to him that the United States did not consider themselves bound by the treaties to plunge into war in behalf of France. While it was admitted by Hamilton that it would not be the province of the United States under ordinary circumstances to cavil over the character of the government in France, but would be their duty to accept the government which existed, nevertheless, the extraordinary events which had taken place at Paris justified a certain reserve towards the revolutionary powers.

Entirely apart from the changes in the character of the French government, it was felt by Hamilton that the time had come to give an interpretation to the early treaties in harmony with a more unchallenged independence for the United States, and a more complete separation from the intrigues of European politics.

The radical character of the Revolution in France, and the action of the French government itself, gave an excuse for an interpretation of the treaties which otherwise might not have been found without blushing. The treaties provided for a defensive alliance with France, and it was promptly decided by the cabinet that the war of France against Great Britain was not defensive. Hamilton proposed not only to revise the treaties, but to resist by the utmost efforts of the federal government the enlistment of men and the fitting out of privateers in America in aid of the French. He did not propose, as some of the friends of France would have desired, that the proclamation of neutrality should be only a mask for underhanded aid to that country.

The situation was made as difficult as possible for the government by the hot temper and indiscretions of the new French minister. These qualities in him were encouraged by the reception which he received on the way from Charleston to Philadelphia. He was everywhere welcomed with such enthusiastic demonstrations of sympathy for France as tended to make him believe that he was something more than the diplomatic representative of a foreign country, and could safely interfere in the politics of the United States. As he approached Philadelphia (May 16, 1793) he found Captain Bompard of the French frigate *L'Ambuscade* ready to fire a salute of three guns, and men on swift horses posted along the road to give notice to the citizens of his coming.

Genet had no sooner landed at Charleston than he began to fit out privateers to prey upon British commerce. The *Ambuscade* herself, which brought Genet to Charleston, seized several English merchant vessels on her way to Philadelphia, and crowned her insolence to the United States by seizing an English vessel, the *Grange*, within the Delaware capes, in the jurisdiction of the United States. The *Grange* was restored to her owners, but her seizure was only one of many flagrant violations of international law which were systematically carried out by the French, and which were defended and often planned by Genet. When the Polly was stopped from leaving New York fitted out for a French privateer, Hauterive, the French consul, addressed a note to Governor Clinton, telling him it was not in a land where Frenchmen had spilled their blood that they were to be thus harassed. When the *Little Sarah* was fitted out as a privateer in Philadelphia, Hamilton and Knox urged that a battery be placed on one of the islands and that the vessel be fired upon if she attempted to leave the harbor. Jefferson was hoodwinked by assurances from Genet that the vessel would not sail, and himself indulged in some glittering talk against the United States joining in "the combination of kings against France." The vessel at once put to sea, and Washington was so indignant that Jefferson was almost driven to resignation.

Hamilton had a more direct interest officially in the demands of Genet for money which was owed to France. Genet not only asked for the anticipation of payments soon to mature, but insisted that he should receive the whole amount of the debt. He threw a bait to American sentiment by the suggestion that the money would be spent in the United States for provisions and supplies. Hamilton treated his rude demands just as he would those of any other creditor. He was willing to anticipate certain payments when the Treasury resources justified it, but absolutely refused to do more. Genet then threatened to pay for what he bought with drafts upon the Treasury. Hamilton coolly retorted that the drafts would not be honored. The Frenchman was compelled to consume his wrath, not exactly in silence, but without result upon the government.

Genet, encouraged by some of the enemies of the administration, succeeded in working up a strong pro-French sentiment in various parts of the country. At a dinner in Philadelphia, following his arrival, songs were sung to France and America, and the red cap of liberty, which had been forced upon the reluctant head of Louis XVI. in the great demonstration of the preceding August at the Tuileries, was passed around the table and successively worn by each of the American guests. Hamilton, who never had much confidence in pure democracy, went close to the other extreme in his alarm over these signs of public opinion. He felt compelled in the summer of 1793 to publish a series of essays signed "Pacificus," defending the policy of the administration. These papers, in the language of Mr. Lodge, "served their purpose of awakening the better part of the community to the gravity of the situation, and began the work of rallying the friends of the government to its active support." Genet addressed such offensive letters to the Department of State, and his conduct became so intolerable, that the cabinet agreed to send the correspondence to Paris and ask for his recall. Genet himself published a letter which revealed his insolence to the public, and caused a revulsion of sentiment which brought the more sober men of all parties to the side of Washington. Genet's course was run, and in February, 1794, his successor came out from France.

Hamilton soon had opportunities for proving that his policy of neutrality was directed as much against English as against French aggression. When Great Britain issued the first Orders in Council, directing the seizure of all vessels loaded with French produce, Hamilton declared the British order an outrage, and urged the fortification of the seaports and the raising of troops. He exerted himself, however, to restrain popular passion and preserve peace. He suggested to Washington that a special mission be sent to London to treat with the British government. The idea was cordially accepted by Washington. He desired to send Hamilton, but the Virginia party, headed by Madison and Monroe, strongly opposed the appointment. They were embittered by recent party conflicts, and regarded Hamilton as too friendly to British interests. Chief Justice John Jay of New York was then recommended by Hamilton for the mission. Opposition was made even to Jay, but the nomination was confirmed (April 19, 1794), and Hamilton himself drew the outline of the instructions with which Jay sailed from New York.

The conflict over the treaty which Jay brought back in the following winter was one of the most bitter ever waged in American politics. The contracting parties to the treaty—the United States and Great Britain—looked at the situation from widely different points of view. Jay secured the promise of the withdrawal of the British troops from the frontier posts and an agreement to compensate Americans for losses through British privateering. The last was an important concession, because it covertly admitted the British position in regard to privateering to be in conflict with international law. Some important commercial concessions were also made by Great Britain, which were regarded at London as purely gratuitous. But the treaty failed to secure any compensation for the claims of American citizens for negroes and other property carried away by the British troops, and American vessels were forbidden carrying to Europe from English ports or even from the United States coffee and the other chief colonial products. Among the latter was named cotton, which was then just becoming a large element in the production of the South.

Hamilton himself is said to have characterized the treaty as "an old woman's treaty," when he first read it, but it soon became evident that it must be accepted substantially as presented, if war was to be avoided. Washington called the Senate in extra session in June, 1795, and after two weeks' debate in secret session the treaty was ratified by exactly the necessary two thirds vote,—twenty to ten. It was not until the adjournment of the Senate that the contents of the document reached the public through Senator Mason of Virginia. The news was followed by town meetings all over the country demanding that President Washington refuse to exchange ratifications. So intense was the feeling that a vessel suspected of being a British privateer was seized and burned at Boston, a great meeting in Faneuil Hall ordered a committee to take a protest to Philadelphia, and Hamilton himself was stoned and refused a hearing at a meeting in New York. But Washington remained calm. Hamilton, as the responsible leader of the party, took up the cudgels for ratification. He submitted an elaborate argument to the cabinet (July 9, 1795), and with an amendment which the Senate recommended and Great Britain accepted, the treaty went into operation.

VII: Hamilton as a Party Leader

The ratification of the Jay treaty did much to shake the power of the Federalists, and for a moment seemed to threaten their ruin. It was divisions in their own ranks, however, which contributed as much to this event as any real blunders in public policy. Hamilton was not at his best in conciliating those who differed from him, and he did not encounter a more yielding or tactful associate in John Adams. Hamilton had gone out of his way with little reason at the first presidential election, in 1788, to secure votes against Adams. His avowed object was to insure the election of Washington by preventing a tie vote between Washington and Adams. The original Constitution authorized each elector to vote for two persons for President and Vice-President, without designating the office for which either was voted for. This led to complications which were corrected by an amendment after the election of 1800. In the case of the first election, however, few sane men doubted that Washington would have the majority of the votes, and the only effect of the intrigue of Hamilton was to reduce the vote for Adams to a point which almost caused his defeat. Hamilton supported Adams in the second election, in 1792, and the relations between the two men were reasonably cordial.

When Washington retired from the presidency, in 1797, the commanding men in the Federalist party were Hamilton, John Jay, Thomas Pinckney, and John Adams. Hamilton was the controlling mind in the consultations of the leaders rather than the sort of man who appealed to the people. He was not seriously thought of by himself or others as a candidate for President. Jay was barred by the odium attaching to the treaty with Great Britain. The choice was therefore reduced to Pinckney and Adams. Most of the leaders were for Adams, who was superior to Pinckney in Revolutionary services and ability. It was determined that the Federalist electors should vote for both Adams and Pinckney, with the purpose of choosing the former for President and the latter for Vice-President. Hamilton on this occasion urged that all the Federalist electors should vote for both Adams and Pinckney. If each had received an equal number of votes, the choice would have been thrown into the House and Adams would probably have been elected. Hamilton erred in letting it be known that he was indifferent whether the outcome was favorable to Adams or Pinckney, especially when there was a strong suspicion that he was really for Pinckney. Party discipline had not then reached its modern development, and votes were thrown away by Federalist electors,—in the North to prevent a majority for Pinckney over Adams and in the South to prevent the same chance in favor of Adams.

The result of these jealousies was that Adams barely escaped defeat. He was chosen by a plurality of three, but Pinckney was beaten, and Jefferson, having the next highest vote, was elected Vice-President. Adams became firmly convinced that Hamilton was his personal enemy and would stop at nothing to injure him. That Hamilton was recognized by all the party leaders as the master mind and the guiding spirit of the party made no difference to a man of the hot temper and resolute spirit of John Adams. Tact and conciliation were as far removed from his nature as from that of any American public man. The indifference of Hamilton whether he was beaten by Pinckney, in connection with Hamilton's intrigue in 1788, had convinced Adams that Hamilton did not feel proper respect for him, and that he was seeking to dictate the policy of the administration and to thwart and degrade him. Adams resented any sort of suggestion or consultation, and took delight in disregarding the suggestions of Hamilton, while the latter struck back through several members of the cabinet, who were more in sympathy with him than with the President.

The country having escaped the danger of immediate war with England by the Jay treaty, was soon threatened with war with France. Monroe had been recalled as American Minister at Paris and Charles Pinckney, who was sent in his place, had been refused a reception. Some of the Federalists were so incensed against France that they were eager for war. Hamilton was opposed to war if it could be avoided, but was in favor of a resolute policy. Adams, although as far as possible from sympathy with France, believed every reasonable effort should be made to preserve peace. It was decided, with the approval of both Adams and Hamilton, to send a commission of three to Paris, to negotiate. Over the appointment of this commission new differences broke out between Hamilton and the President. Hamilton favored the appointment of a Northern and a Southern Federalist and of a Democrat of the highest standing, like Madison or even Jefferson. Adams was at first disposed to make these appointments, but finally took both the Federalists from the South,—Pinckney of South Carolina and John Marshall of Virginia,—and selected as the third member a Democrat of comparatively minor standing, Gerry of Massachusetts.

The commissioners accomplished little good at Paris. They were insulted and browbeaten and told that only bribery would secure what they desired. When their treatment became known in the United States, in the spring of 1798, there was a popular outburst which restored the Federalists to power in Congress in the following autumn, with a larger majority than ever before since party divisions became fixed. Enthusiastic addresses poured in upon President Adams, war vessels were fitted out by private subscription, and bills were carried at once for a provisional army, for fortifications, and for the increase of the navy. Even under this stress of excitement, however, Hamilton opposed alliance with Great Britain, and persuaded Pickering, the Secretary of State, to abandon the advocacy of it.

It was over the organization of the new army that the hostility of Adams to Hamilton became open and bitter. Washington was selected as commander-in-chief, but only consented to serve upon the condition that he should have the choice of the officers who were to rank next him, and should not be called upon to take an active part until the army took the field. He recommended to the President that rank in the Revolutionary army be disregarded and that the three major-generals to be appointed should be Hamilton, Charles Pinckney, and Knox. This gave the practical command and the work of the organization to Hamilton. Adams sent the names to the Senate, in the order suggested by Washington, and they were promptly confirmed. When he came to signing the commissions, however, he took the ground that Knox was the senior officer on account of his rank during the Revolution. Hamilton would not consent to this arrangement, and all the Federalist leaders, including members of the cabinet, remonstrated with the President against it. One of the saddest results of the quarrel was the alienation from Hamilton of Knox, who had been a friend of many years and when Secretary of War in Washington's first cabinet had stood loyally by Hamilton against Jefferson in the controversy over the financial projects.

Adams at first seemed to grow more stubborn with the protests which were made against his action. The leaders finally turned to Washington. The latter informed the President that if the original agreement as to the rank of the officers was not kept, he should resign. Adams, with all his stubbornness and brav-bravery, did not dare defy the country by forcing Washington from the service. He gave way, and appointed Hamilton to the first place, but the good feeling which might have been promoted if he had done so at first was replaced on both sides by bitterness which was never softened.

Hamilton, as the practical head of the army, showed the same abounding energy and capacity for organization which he had shown at the head of the Treasury. He drafted a plan for the fortification of New York harbor, made an apportionment of officers and men among the states, and drew up projects for the organization of the new army, dealing with the questions of pay, uniforms, rations, promotions, police in garrisons and camps, and the many other branches of the service. All these projects received the cordial approval of Washington. When Congress met, Hamilton was ready with a bill putting the army upon a basis which would permit its increase or diminution in future without changing the form of the organization. In the spring of 1799 he was providing for the defense of the frontiers and planning the invasion of Louisiana and the Floridas.

The projects of these invasions of Spanish territory justify a reference to the continental policy of Hamilton. He was among the first to maintain that the United States should have complete control of the valley of the Mississippi, and even during his short term in the Congress of the Confederation the last resolution which he presented declared the "navigation of the Mississippi to be a clear and essential right and to be supported as such." It was left for Jefferson, Hamilton's great opponent, to carry out his conception of the acquisition of the Mississippi valley by the purchase of Louisiana. The admirers of Hamilton credit him with a still wider vision of the future power of the United States, which was eventually to bear fruit in the Monroe doctrine and in the celebrated declaration of Secretary Olney in 1895, that "today the United States is practically sovereign on this continent, and its fiat is law upon the subjects to which it confines its interposition." Hamilton wrote in "The Federalist," before the adoption of the Constitution, that "our situation invites and our situation prompts us to aim at an ascendant in American affairs."

The firm attitude of the United States towards France had its effect at Paris. Talleyrand sent an intimation indirectly to President Adams that the French government would be glad to receive an American envoy. Again the impetuosity of Adams divided his party and intensified his quarrel with the leaders who stood around Hamilton. The name of Vans Murray was sent to the Senate by the President for Minister to France, without even consulting the cabinet. Many doubted the wisdom of snapping up so promptly the offer made by Talleyrand, and more were incensed at the President's method of doing it. There was at first a strong disposition among the Federalist leaders to defeat the nomination in the

Senate. Hamilton, however, checked the indignation of his friends and suggested a way out of the difficulty by appointing a strong commission.

The downfall of the Federal party and the retirement of Hamilton from the active control of national policy were at hand. The passage of the alien and sedition laws, arrogating to the federal government intolerable powers of interference with the rights of the press and of free speech, was one of the causes contributing to the revulsion of feeling in favor of the party of Jefferson. Hamilton opposed the first drafts of these laws as cruel, violent, and tyrannical, but he did not disapprove their final form. The Federalists carried the congressional elections of 1798, under the impulse of the feeling against France, but began to lose ground soon after. As the presidential election of 1800 approached, a desperate struggle was made to hold New York for Federalism as the only hope of defeating Jefferson and reelecting Adams. The New York election went against the administration, and Hamilton pleaded in vain with Governor Jay to defeat the will of the people by calling the old legislature together and giving the choice of presidential electors to the congressional districts. It was perhaps the most discreditable proposal which ever came from Hamilton, and was promptly rejected by Jay.

Hamilton's motive was a sincere fear that the country would go to ruin and the Constitution be endangered by the triumph of the political school of Jefferson. This might have been the case if it had been the first election under the Constitution, but Hamilton himself had built better than he knew. The financial projects, the national bank, the suppression of the "Whiskey Insurrection," and the other measures taken under Washington and Adams had built up a Federal Union, whose strength could not be seriously shaken by the transfer of power from one party to another.

With the shadow of defeat hanging over them, the course of the Federalist leaders seemed to justify the maxim, "Whom the gods destroy they first make mad." With the utmost need for harmony and unity, quarrels broke out which would have wrecked the party even if there had been otherwise some prospect of its success. Adams drove McHenry and Pickering from his cabinet because they had betrayed his secrets to Hamilton, and denounced Hamilton and his friends as a British faction. Hamilton asked in writing for a denial or explanation of the charge, but was treated with contemptuous silence. As the presidential election approached, Hamilton scarcely concealed his preference for Pinckney, who was again to be voted for by the electors along with Adams. Hamilton had been so badly treated by the President that he announced his purpose to prepare a pamphlet, exposing the failings of Adams and vindicating his own position.

His best friends stood aghast at the project and labored with him to abandon it. Hamilton persevered, however, in the preparation of the pamphlet. He denounced Adams as a man of disgusting egotism, intense jealousy, and ungovernable temper, and reviewed in a scathing manner his entire public career, and especially the recent dismissal of the secretaries who were friendly to Hamilton. After all this criticism, Hamilton wound up with the lame conclusion that the electors should vote equally for Adams and Pinckney, in order to preserve Federal ascendency. He yielded to the protests of his friends so far as to keep the circulation of the pamphlet within a small circle, but it was hardly off the press before a copy was in the hands of Aaron Burr, the Democratic leader in New York, and was used with effect against the Federalist President.

The downfall of Federalism came with the presidential election of 1800. Jefferson and Burr were the Democratic candidates for President and Vice-President. Each was voted for by all the Democratic electors, giving them an equal number of votes and a majority of the electoral college. This threw the election into the House of Representatives, which was Federalist but was compelled by the provisions of the Constitution to decide between the two leading candidates, Jefferson and Burr. Some of the Federalists were ready to stoop to any means for striking at Jefferson, the great representative of Democratic ideals. If the Federalists in Congress could have effected a combination with the Democrats from states where Burr was influential, they might have been able to elect Burr President instead of Jefferson. But the Democrats, even from New York, voted for Jefferson, and it was evident that he must be chosen or there would be no election. Feeling in the country ran high, and there were threats of violence if the election of Jefferson should be defeated by intrigue.

Hamilton behaved on this occasion with the high sense of public duty which marked most of his acts. Familiar as he was with the unscrupulous methods and doubtful character of Burr in New York politics, he felt that it would be criminal to put him in office. He had little reason to love Jefferson, who had filled the ears of Washington with slurs against himself, but he felt that the election belonged to Jefferson and that his defeat by a political intrigue would be a greater menace than his election to the system established by the Constitution. With Bayard of Delaware, the Federalist leader in the House, Hamilton threw himself strongly into the contest against Burr. His advice was not at first followed. The House balloted from the eleventh to the sixteenth of February without reaching a choice. A caucus of the Federalists was then held; it appeared that Jefferson had given some assurances of a conservative policy in office, the views of Hamilton and Bayard prevailed, and on February 17, 1801, the Federalist members from several states withheld their votes, and Jefferson was elected.

The retirement of the Federalists from power substantially ended the public services of Hamilton. He continued to watch public events with interest during the remaining five years of his life, and to be regarded as the leader of the Federalist party, but the party had shrunk to a corporal's guard in Congress and the long reign of the Democratic party had begun, which was to be interrupted during only two presidential terms until the election of Lincoln in 1860. Hamilton, therefore, at the age of forty-three, had completed his constructive work and ceased to influence public affairs except by his writings and speeches. It might almost be said that this work was done with the close of the administration of Washington in 1797, and that his great fame would have shone with brighter luster if he had not lived to take part in the later differences and quarrels of the Adams administration. His life was not without service, however, under Adams, since his influence over members of the cabinet several times restrained rash policies, and between the conflicting passions of the champions of France and of the friends of Great Britain, kept the ship of state steady upon a safe course.

VIII: Hamilton's Death and Character

The death of Hamilton was in a peculiar sense a part of his public career. He had never hesitated to denounce in strong terms the public career and some of the private acts of Aaron Burr. The latter, after losing the presidency, sought the governorship of New York, and entered into correspondence with the Federalist leaders in New England with a view to the formation of a Northern confederacy. Hamilton succeeded in dividing the Federalist vote in New York so as to give the election to Lewis, Burr's democratic rival. Burr then determined to force a personal quarrel upon Hamilton in order to obtain revenge upon the man who had so often thwarted him. Hamilton had no desire to fight, but he did not feel able to repudiate the code of the duelist as it was then accepted among gentlemen.

It was on June 17, 1804, that Colonel Burr, through his intimate friend Judge Van Ness, demanded an apology for a criticism by Hamilton which had reached Burr's ears. Several letters were exchanged before it became plain that Burr was bound to force a quarrel or to humiliate Hamilton to a point which he knew would not be endured. When Burr's true purpose became plain to Hamilton, he requested a short time to close up several important cases for his clients, which were then pending in the circuit court. The circuit having terminated, Colonel Burr was informed (Friday, July 6, 1804) that Hamilton would be ready to meet him at any time after the following Sunday. Both men realized that the meeting might be fatal, and prepared for it in a characteristic way. Burr, who because of his fascinating manners was a great favorite with women, destroyed the compromising letters which he had received and devoted his spare hours to pistol practice. Hamilton had fewer such letters to destroy, and was determined not to kill Burr if it could be avoided. He drew up his will, and prepared a statement of his reasons for fighting. This statement set forth that he was opposed to the practice of dueling and had done all that was practicable, even beyond the demands of a punctilious delicacy, to secure an accommodation. He then said:—

"I have resolved, if our interview is conducted in the usual manner, and it pleases God to give me the opportunity, to reserve and throw away my first fire;

and I have thought even of reserving my second, and thus giving a double opportunity to Colonel Burr to pause and repent."

The arrangements for the duel were made on Monday, and on the following Wednesday (July 11) the meeting took place at seven o'clock in the morning at Weehawken, three miles above Hoboken, on the west shore of the Hudson. Burr and Hamilton exchanged salutations, the seconds measured the distance, which was ten paces, and the parties took their respective stations. At the first word, Burr fired. Hamilton's weapon was discharged in the air, and he almost instantly fell, mortally wounded. The ball struck the second or third false rib, fractured it about the middle, passed through the liver and diaphragm, and lodged in the first or second lumbar vertebra. Hamilton was at first thought to be dead, but he revived when put on board the boat which was in waiting, and was able to utter a few words as he was borne towards his home. He died on the day after the meeting at two o'clock in the afternoon. Even in his death he rendered a parting service to his countrymen, by the revulsion of feeling which was everywhere aroused against the practice of dueling. The news of his premature taking off caused a wave of grief and indignation to spread over the country, differing from the chastened sorrow felt over the death of Washington, because Washington had met his end full of years and honors, and in the natural order of nature.

The concluding statement made by Hamilton in the paper which he left regarding his meeting with Burr gives some clue to his reasons for fighting. This paragraph ran as follows:—

"To those who, with me, abhorring the practice of dueling, may think that I ought on no account to have added to the number of bad examples, I answer that my relative situation, as well in public as private, enforcing all the considerations which constitute what men of the world denominate honor, imposed on me (as I thought) a peculiar necessity not to decline the call. The ability to be in future useful, whether in resisting mischief or effecting good, in those crises of our public affairs which seem likely to happen would probably be inseparable from a conformity with public prejudice in this particular."

This statement has been construed to mean that Hamilton looked forward to the time when the Constitution would be assailed by extremists and he would be called by events to put himself at the head of a movement for a stronger government, and perhaps even to lead an army. Several passages in his writings, especially after the downfall of the Federalists, gave color to the view that he feared an outbreak of Jacobin violence in America, and the failure of the Constitution in such an event to resist the strain which would be put upon it. In a letter to Gouverneur Morris (February 27, 1802), he drops into the following gloomy forebodings:—

"Mine is an odd destiny. Perhaps no man in the United States has sacrificed or done more for the present Constitution than myself; and, contrary to all my anticipations of its fate, as you know, from the very beginning, I am still laboring to prop the frail and worthless fabric. Yet I have the murmurs of its friends no less than the curses of its foes for my reward. What can I do better than withdraw from the scene? Every day proves to me more and more that this American world was not made for me."

This mood of despondency was not the usual mood of Hamilton. Much as he abhorred the sympathy with France shown by the Democrats and the tendency towards French ideas, his habitual temper was for combination and action rather than surrender. During the three years which followed the inauguration of Jefferson, he continued, though busy with his law practice, to keep up in private life an active correspondence with Federalist leaders throughout the country, and to advise earnest efforts to defeat Democratic policies. Only the day before the duel, in a letter to Sedgwick of Massachusetts, he indirectly condemned a project which was on foot for a combination of the Northern States into a separate confederacy. He said that "dismemberment of our empire will be a clear sacrifice of great positive advantages without any counterbalancing good, administering no relief to our real disease, which is Democracy."

Hamilton had fears for the future of the Union under the Constitution which were much exaggerated by his leanings towards a strong, self-centered government like that of Great Britain. It is not unreasonable to believe that he felt that he might again be called upon to play a great part in politics as the leader of his party, and that under the prejudices then prevailing he would weaken his personal influence if he refused a challenge. The public man of that day who could be charged with cowardice or lack of regard for his personal honor would suffer much with the masses, if not with the party leaders, who understood his character and abilities. Hamilton hardly needed to prove his personal courage to any reasonable man after his services in the Revolution, including his reckless charge upon the redoubt at Yorktown, but political foes might forget these evidences of his character if he should tamely submit to insult from a political opponent. It is doubtful whether his purpose in meeting Burr went beyond this submission to the general prejudice in favor of dueling and the belief on his part that his position as a gentleman and a political leader required him to accept the challenge.

The high abilities and great services of Hamilton to the new Union have been sufficiently set forth in these pages to make unnecessary any elaborate estimate of his character and attainments. His essential merit was that of a constructive and organizing mind, which saw the opportunity for action and was equal to the opportunity. Hamilton was governed to a large extent by his intellect, but having reasoned out a proposition to be sound and wise, he rode resolutely to its accomplishment, taking little account of the obstacles in the way. He was not a closet philosopher, pursuing abstract propositions to their sources, and searching, through the discordant threads of human destiny, the ultimate principles of all things; but his mind was keen and alert in seizing upon reasoning which seemed obviously sound, laboring in behalf of his convictions, and presenting them with force and simplicity to others. He found the career for which he was preeminently fitted in the organization of the financial system and the consolidation of the Union, under the first administration of Washington. He was less fitted for the career of a politician in times less strenuous, or when tact and finesse were more useful in securing results than clear reasoning and strong argument.

Hamilton was cut off when he had only recently resumed his professional career, but was making a distinguished record at the bar. Always a great lawyer, he would soon have accumulated a fortune if he had lived amid the tempting opportunities of today. As it was, his legal fees were modest and his sudden death left large debts. He bequeathed the request to his sons that they should assume these debts if his estate was insufficient, but the gratitude of some of the wealthy Federalists relieved them of this filial obligation. Hamilton had six sons, but most of them were already approaching a self-supporting age when he died. His oldest son had fallen a victim to the barbarous practice of dueling in a petty quarrel at a theatre three years before the father's death. The fourth son, Mr. John C. Hamilton, gave much time to the study of his father's career, and prepared the Life of Hamilton which has been the source of the later work of historians. Hamilton's widow, the daughter of General Schuyler, survived until 1854, when she died at the age of ninety-seven years and three months.

As a man in private life, Hamilton was loved and respected by those who came closest to him, but it was as much by the qualities of his mind as by the special fascinations of his manner. He commanded the respect and support of most of the leaders of his party, because they were great enough to grasp and appreciate his reasoning, but he was never the idol of the people to the same extent as many other leaders. He would probably have made a great career in whatever direction he might have turned his high abilities, but he was fortunate in finding an opportunity for their exercise in a crisis which enabled him to render greater services to the country than have been rendered by almost any man in her history, with the exception of Washington and Lincoln.

John Jay by Elbert Hubbard

Calm repose and the sweets of undisturbed retirement appear more distant than a peace with Britain.

It gives me pleasure, however, to reflect that the period is approaching when we shall be citizens of a better ordered State, and the spending of a few troublesome years of our eternity in doing good to this and future generations is not to be avoided nor regretted. Things will come right, and these States will yet be great and flourishing.

—Letter to Washington.

America should feel especially charitable towards Louis the Great, called by Carlyle, Louis the Little, for banishing the Huguenots from France. What France lost America gained. Tyranny and intolerance always drive from their homes the best: those who have ability to think, courage to act, and a pride that cannot be coerced.

The merits possessed by the Huguenots are exactly those which every man and nation needs. And these are simple virtues, too, whose cultivation stands within the reach of all. These are the virtues of the farmers and peasants and plain people who do the work of the world, and give good government its bone and sinew. To a great degree, so-called society is made up of parasites who fasten and feed upon the industrious and methodical.

If you have read history you know that the men who go quietly about their business have been cajoled, threatened, driven, and often, when they have been guilty of doing a little independent thinking on their own account, banished. And further than this, when you read the story of nations dead and gone you will see that their decline began when the parasites got too numerous and flauntingly asserted their supposed power. That contempt for the farmer, and indifference to the rights of the man with tin pail and overalls, which one often sees in America, are portents that mark disintegrating social bacilli. If the Republic of the United States ever becomes but a memory, like Carthage, Athens and Rome, drifting off into senile decay like Italy and Spain or France, where a man may yet be tried and sentenced without the right of counsel or defense, it will be because we forgot—we forgot!

In moral fiber and general characteristics the Huguenots and the Puritans were one. The Huguenots had, however, the added virtue of a dash of the Frenchman's love of beauty. By their excellent habits and loyalty to truth, as they saw it, they added a vast share to the prosperity and culture of the United States.

Of seven men who acted as presiding officer over the deliberations of Congress during the Revolutionary Period, three were of Huguenot parentage: Laurens, Boudinot and Jay. John Jay was a typical Huguenot, just as Samuel Adams was a typical Puritan. In his life there was no glamour of romance. Stern, studious and inflexibly honest, he made his way straight to the highest positions of trust and honor. Good men who are capable are always needed. The world wants them now more than ever. We have an over-plus of clever individuals; but for the faithful men who are loyal to a trust there is a crying demand.

The life of Jay quite disproves the oft-found myth that a dash of Mephisto in a young man is a valuable adjunct. John Jay was neither precocious nor bad. It is further a refreshing fact to find that he was no prig, simply a good, healthy youngster who took to his books kindly and gained ground—made head upon the whole by grubbing.

His father was a hard-headed, prosperous merchant, who did business in New York, and moved his big family up to the little village of Rye because life in the country was simple and cheap. Thus did Peter Jay prove his commonsense.

Peter Jay copied every letter he wrote, and we now have these copy-books, revealing what sort of man he was. Religious he was, and scrupulously exact in all things. We see that he ordered Bibles from England, "and also six groce of Church Wardens," which I am told is a long clay pipe, "that hath a goodly flavor and doth not bite the tongue." He also at one time ordered a chest of tea, and then countermanded the order, having taken the resolve to "use no tea in my family while that rascally Tax is on—having a spring of good, pure water near my house." Which shows that a man can be very much in earnest and still joke.

John was the baby, scarcely a year old, when the Jay family moved up to Rye. He was the eighth child, and as he grew up he was taught by the older ones. He took part in all the fun and hardships of farm life—going to school in Winter, working in Summer, and on Sundays hearing long sermons at church.

We find by Peter Jay's letter-book that: "Johnny is about our brightest child. We have great hopes of him, and believe it will be wise to educate him for a preacher." In order to educate boys then, they were sent to live in the family of some man of learning. And so we find "Johnny" at twelve years of age installed in the parsonage at New Rochelle, the Huguenot settlement. The pastor was a Huguenot, and as only French was spoken in the household, the boy acquired the language, which afterwards stood him in good stead.

The pastor reported favorably, and when fifteen, young Jay was sent to King's College, which is now Columbia University, kings not being popular in America.

Doctor Samuel Johnson, who nowise resembled Ursa Major, was the president of the College at that time. He was also the faculty, for there were just thirty students and he did all the teaching himself. Doctor Johnson, true to his name, dearly loved a good book, and when teaching mathematics would often forget the topic and recite Ossian by the page, instead. Jay caught it, for the book craze is contagious and not sporadic. We take it by being exposed.

And thus it was while under the tutelage of Doctor Johnson that Jay began to acquire the ability to turn a terse sentence; and this gained him admittance into the world of New York letters, whose special guardians were Dickinson and William Livingston.

Livingston invited the boy to his house, and very soon we find the young man calling without special invitation, for Livingston had a beautiful daughter about John's age, who was fond of Ossian, too, or said she was.

And as this is not a serial love-story, there is no need of keeping the gentle reader in suspense, so I will explain that some years later John married the girl, and the mating was a very happy one.

After John had been to King's College two years we find in the faded and yellow old letter-book an item written by the father to the effect that: "Our Johnny is doing well at College. He seems sedate and intent on gaining knowledge; but rather inclines to Law instead of the Ministry."

Doctor Johnson was succeeded by Doctor Myles Cooper, a Fellow of Oxford, who used to wear his mortarboard cap and scholar's gown up Broadway. In young Jay's veins there was not a drop of British blood. Of his eight great-grandparents, five were French and three Dutch, a fact he once intimated in the Oxonian's presence. And then it was explained to the youth that if such were the truth it would be as well to conceal it.

Alexander Hamilton got along very well with Doctor Cooper, but John Jay found himself rusticated shortly before graduation. Some years after this Doctor Cooper hastily climbed the back fence, leaving a sample of his gown on a picket, while Alexander Hamilton held the Whig mob at bay at the front door.

Cooper sailed very soon for England, anathematizing "the blarsted country" in classic Latin as the ship passed out of the Narrows.

"England is a good place for him," said the laconic John Jay.

So John Jay was to be a lawyer. And the only way to be a lawyer in those days was to work in a lawyer's office. A goodly source of income to all established lawyers was the sums they derived for taking embryo Blackstones into their keeping. The greater a man's reputation as a lawyer, the higher he placed his fee for taking a boy in.

In those days there were no printed blanks, and a simple lease was often a day's work to write out; so it was not difficult to keep the boys busy. Besides that, they took care of the great man's horse, blacked his boots, swept the office, and ran errands. During the third year of apprenticeship, if all went well, the young man was duly admitted to the Bar. A stiff examination kept out the rank outsiders, but the nomination by a reputable attorney was equivalent to admittance, for all members knew that if you opposed an attorney today, tomorrow he might oppose you.

To such an extent was this system of taking students carried that, in Seventeen Hundred Sixty-eight, we find New York lawyers alarmed "by the awful influx of young Barristers upon this Province." So steps were taken to make all attorneys agree not to have more than two apprentices in their office at one time. About the same time the Boston newspaper, called the Centinel, shows there was a similar state of overproduction in Boston. Only the trouble there was principally with the doctors, for doctors were then turned loose in the same way, carrying a diploma from the old physician with whom they had matriculated and duly graduated.

Law schools and medical colleges, be it known, are comparatively modern institutions—not quite so new, however, as business colleges, but pretty nearly so. And now in Chicago there is a "Barbers' University," which issues diplomas to men who can manipulate a razor and shears, whereas, until yesterday, boys learned to be barbers by working in a barber's shop. The good old way was to pass a profession along from man to man.

And it is so yet in a degree, for no man is allowed to practice either medicine or law until he has spent some time in the office of a practitioner in good standing.

In the Catholic Church, and also in the Episcopal, the novitiate is expected to serve for a time under an older clergyman; but all the other denominations have broken away, and now spring the fledgling on the world straight from the factory.

Several other of his children having sorely disappointed him, Peter Jay seemed to center his ambitions on his boy John. So we find him paying Benjamin Kissam, the eminent lawyer, two hundred pounds in good coin of the Colony to take John Jay as a 'prentice for five years. John went at it and began copying those endless, wordy documents in which the old-time attorney used to delight. John sat at one end of a table, and at the other was seated one Lindley Murray, at the mention of whose name terror used to seize my soul.

Murray has written some good, presentable English to the effect that young Jay, even at that time, had the inclination and ability to focus his mind upon the subject in hand. "He used to work just as steadily when his employer was away as when he was in the office," a fact which the grammarian seemed to regard as rather strange.

In a year we find that when Mr. Kissam went away he left the keys of the safe in John Jay's hands, with orders what to do in case of emergencies. Thus does responsibility gravitate to him who can shoulder it, and trust to the man who deserves it.

It was in Kissam's office that Jay acquired that habit of reticence and serene poise which, becoming fixed in character, made his words carry such weight in later years. He never gave snapshot opinions, or talked at random, or voiced any sentiment for which he could not give a reason.

His companions were usually men much older than he. At the "Moot Club" he took part with James Duane, who was to be New York's first continental mayor; Gouverneur Morris, who had not at that time acquired the wooden leg which he once snatched off and brandished with happy effect before a Paris mob; and Samuel Jones, who was to take as 'prentice and drill that strong man, De Witt Clinton.

Before his years of apprenticeship were over, John Jay, the quiet, the modest, the reticent, was known as a safe and competent lawyer—Kissam having pushed him forward as associate counsel in various difficult cases.

Meantime, certain chests of tea had been dumped into Boston Harbor, and the example had been followed by the "Mohawks" in New York. British oppression had made many Tories lukewarm, and then English rapacity had transformed these Tories into Whigs. Jay was one of these; and in newspapers and pamphlets, and from the platform, he had pleaded the cause of the Colonies. Opposition crystallized his reasons, and threats only served to make him reaffirm the truths he had stated.

So prominent had his utterances made his name, that one fine day he was nominated to attend the first Congress of the Colonies to be held in Philadelphia.

In August, Seventeen Hundred Seventy-four, we find him leaving his office in New York in charge of a clerk, and riding horseback over to the town of Elizabeth, there joining his father-in-law, and the two starting for Philadelphia. On the road they fell in with John Adams, who kept a diary. That night at the tavern where they stopped, the sharp-eyed Yankee recorded the fact of meeting these new friends and added, "Mr. Jay is a young gentleman of the law ... and Mr. Scott says a hard student and a very good speaker."

And so they journeyed on across the State to Trenton and down the Delaware River to Philadelphia, visiting, and cautiously discussing great issues as they went. Samuel Adams, too, was in the party, as reticent as Jay. Jay was twenty-nine and Samuel Adams fifty-two years old, but they became good friends, and Samuel once quietly said to John Adams, "That man Jay is young in years, but he has an old head."

Jay was the youngest man of the Convention, save one.

When the Second Congress met, Jay was again a delegate. He served on several important committees, and drew up a statement that was addressed to the people of England; but he was recalled to New York before the supreme issue was reached, and thus, through accident, the Declaration of Independence does not contain the signature of John Jay.

In Seventeen Hundred Seventy-eight, Jay was chosen president of the Continental Congress to succeed that other patriotic Huguenot, Laurens. The following year he was selected as the man to go to Spain, to secure from that country certain friendly favors.

His reception there was exceedingly frosty, and the mention of his two years on the ragged edge of court life at Madrid, in later years brought to his face a grim smile.

Spain's diplomatic policy was smooth hypocrisy and rank untruth, and all her promises, it seems, were made but to be broken. Jay's negotiations were only partially successful, but he came to know the language, the country and the people in a way that made his knowledge very valuable to America.

By Seventeen Hundred Eighty-one, England had begun to see that to compel the absolute submission of the Colonies was more of a job than she had anticipated. News of victories was duly sent to the "mother country" at regular intervals, but with these glad tidings were requests for more troops, and requisitions for ships and arms.

The American army was a very hard thing to find. It would fight one day, to retreat the next, and had a way of making midnight attacks and flank movements that, to say the least, were very confusing. Then it would separate, to come together—Lord knows where! This made Lord Cornwallis once write to the Home Secretary: "I could easily defeat the enemy, if I could find him and engage him in a fair fight." He seemed to think it was "no fair," forgetting the old proverb which has something to say about love and war.

Finally, Cornwallis got the thing his soul desired—a fair fight. He was then acting on the defensive. The fight was short and sharp; and Colonel Alexander Hamilton, who led the charge, in ten minutes planted the Stars and Stripes on his ramparts.

That night Cornwallis was the "guest" of Washington, and the next day a dinner was given in his honor.

He was then obliged to write to the Home Secretary, "We have met the enemy, and we are theirs"—but of course he did not express it just exactly that way. Then it was that King George, for the first time, showed a disposition to negotiate for peace.

As peace commissioners, America named Franklin, John Adams, Laurens, Jay and Jefferson.

Jefferson refused to leave his wife, who was in delicate health. Adams was at The Hague, just closing up a very necessary loan. Laurens had been sent to Holland on a diplomatic mission, and his ship having been overhauled by a British man-of-war, he was safely in that historic spot, the Tower of London.

So Jay and Franklin alone met the English commissioners, and Jay stated to them the conditions of peace.

In a few weeks Adams arrived, still keeping a diary. In that diary is found this item: "The French call me 'Le Washington de la Negociation': a very flattering compliment indeed, to which I have no right, but sincerely think it belongs to Mr. Jay."

Jay quitted Paris in May, Seventeen Hundred Eighty-four, having been gone from his native land eight years. When he reached New York there was a great demonstration in his honor. Triumphal arches were erected across Broadway, houses and stores were decorated with bunting, cannons boomed, and bells rang. The freedom of the city was presented to him in a gold box, with an exceedingly complimentary address, engrossed on parchment, and signed by one hundred of the leading citizens.

Jay spent just one day in New York, and then rode on horseback up to the old farm at Rye, Westchester County, to see his father. That evening there was a service of thanksgiving at the village church, after which the citizens repaired to the Jay mansion, one story high and eighty feet long, where a barrel of cider was tapped, and "a groce of Church Wardens" passed around, with free tobacco for all.

John Jay stood on the front porch and made a modest speech just five minutes long, among other things saying he had come home to be a neighbor to them, having quit public life for good. But he refused to talk about his own experiences in Europe. His reticence, however, was made up for by good old Peter Jay, who assured the people that John Jay was America's foremost citizen; and in this statement he was backed up by the village preacher, with not a dissenting voice from the assembled citizens.

It is rather curious (or it isn't, I'm not sure which) how most statesmen have quit public life several times during their careers, like the prima donnas who make farewell tours. The ingratitude of republics is proverbial, but to limit ingratitude to republics shows a lack of experience. The progeny of the men who tired of hearing Aristides called The Just are very numerous. Of course it is easy to say that he who expects gratitude does not deserve it; but the fact remains that the men who know it are yet stung by calumny when it comes their way.

That fine demonstration in Jay's honor was in great part to overwhelm and stamp out the undertone of growl and snarl that filled the air. Many said that peace had been gained at awful cost, that Jay had deferred to royalty and trifled with the wishes of the people in making terms.

And now Jay had got home, back to his family and farm, back to quiet and rest. The long, hard fight had been won and America was free. For eight years had he toiled and striven and planned: much had been accomplished—not all he hoped, but much.

He had done his best for his country, his own affairs were in bad shape, Congress had paid him meagerly, and now he would turn public life over to others and live his own life.

All through life men reach these places where they say, "Here will we build three tabernacles"; but out of the silence comes the imperative Voice, "Arise, and get thee hence, for this is not thy rest."

And now the war was over, peace was concluded; but war leaves a country in chaos. The long, slow work of reconstruction and of binding up a nation's wounds must follow. America was independent, but she had yet to win from the civilized world the recognition that she must have in order to endure.

Jay was importuned by Washington to take the position of Secretary of Foreign Affairs, one of the most important offices to be filled.

He accepted, and discharged the exacting duties of the place for five years.

Then came the adoption of the Federal Constitution, and the election of Washington as President of the United States.

Washington wrote to Jay: "There must be a Court, perpetual and Supreme, to which all questions of internal dispute between States or people be referred. This Court must be greater than the Executive, greater than any individual State, separated and apart from any political party. You must be the first official head of the Executive."

And Jay, as every schoolboy knows, was the first Chief Justice of the Supreme Court of the United States. By his sagacity, his dignity, his knowledge of men, and love of order and uprightness, he gave it that high place which it yet holds, and which it must hold; for when the decisions of the Supreme Court are questioned by a State or people, the fabric of our government is but a spider's web through which anarchy and unreason will stalk.

In Seventeen Hundred Ninety-four, came serious complications with Great Britain, growing out of the construction of terms of peace made in Paris eleven years before.

Some one must go to Great Britain and make a new treaty in order to preserve our honor and save us from another war.

Franklin was dead; Adams as Vice-President could not be spared; Hamilton's fiery temper was dangerous—no one could accomplish the delicate mission so well as Jay.

Jay, self-centered and calm, said little; but in compliance with Washington's wish resigned his office, and set sail with full powers to use his own judgment in everything, and the assurance that any treaty he made would be ratified.

Arriving in England, he at once opened negotiations with Lord Grenville, and in five months the new treaty was signed.

It provided for the payment to American citizens for losses of private shipping during the war; and over ten million dollars were paid to citizens of the United States under this agreement.

It fixed the boundary-line between the State of Maine and Canada; provided for the surrender of British posts in the Far West; that neither nation was to allow enlistments within its territory by a third nation at war with another; arranged for the surrender of fugitives charged with murder or forgery; and made definite terms as to various minor, but none the less important, questions.

A storm of opposition greeted the treaty when its terms were made known in America. Jay was accused of bartering away the rights of America, and indignation meetings were held, because Jay had not insisted on apologies, and set sums of indemnity on this, that and the other.

Nevertheless, Washington ratified the treaty; and when Jay arrived in America there was a greeting fully as cordial and generous as that on the occasion of his other homecoming.

In fact, while he was absent, his friends had put him in nomination as Governor of New York. His election to that office occurred just two days before he arrived, and when he landed his senses were mystified by hearing loud hurrahs for "Governor Jay."

When his term of office expired he was re-elected, so he served as Governor, in all, six years. The most important measure carried out during that time was the abolition of slavery in the State of New York, an act he had strenuously insisted on for twenty years, but which was not made possible until he had the power of Governor, and crowded the measure upon the Legislature.

Over a quarter of a century had passed since John Adams and John Jay had met on horseback out there on the New Jersey turnpike. Their intimacy had been continuous and their labors as important as ever engrossed the minds of men, but in it all there was neither jealousy nor bickering. They were friends.

At the close of Jay's gubernatorial term, President Adams nominated him for the office of Chief Justice, made vacant by the resignation of Oliver Ellsworth. The Senate unanimously confirmed the nomination, but Jay refused to accept the place.

For twenty-eight years he had served his country—served it in its most trying hours. He was not an old man in years, but the severity and anxiety of his labors had told on his health, and the elasticity of youth had gone from his brain forever. He knew this, and feared the danger of continued exertion. "My best work is done," he said; "if I continue I may undo the good I have accomplished. I have earned a rest."

He retired to the ancestral farm at Bedford, Westchester County, to enjoy his vacation. In a year his wife died, and the shock told on his already shattered nerves.

"The habit of reticence grew upon him," says one writer, "until he could not be tricked into giving an opinion even about the weather."

And so he lived out his days as a partial recluse, deep in problems of "raising watermelons, and sheep that would not jump fences." He worked with his hands, wore blue jeans, voted at every town election, but to a great degree lived only in the past. The problems of church and village politics and farm life filled his declining days.

To a great degree his physical health came back, but the problems of statecraft he left to other heads and hands.

His religious nature manifested itself in various philanthropic schemes, and the Bible Society he founded endures even unto this day. These things afforded a healthful exercise for that tireless brain which refused to run down.

His daughters made his home ideal, their love and gentleness soothing his declining years.

Death to him was kindly, gathering him as Autumn, the messenger of Winter, reaps the leaves.

No one has ever made the claim that Jay possessed genius. He had something which is better, though, for most of the affairs of life, and that is commonsense. In his intellect there was not the flash of Hamilton, nor the creative quality possessed by Jefferson, nor the large all-roundness of Franklin.

He was the average man who has trained and educated and made the best use of every faculty and every opportunity. He was genuine; he was honest; and if he never surprised his friends by his brilliancy, he surely never disappointed them through duplicity.

He made no promises that he could not keep; he held out no vain hopes.

As a diplomat he seems nearly the ideal. We have been taught that the line of demarcation between diplomacy and untruth is very shadowy. But truth is very good policy and in the main answers the purpose much better than the other thing. I am quite willing to leave the matter to those who have tried both.

We cannot say that Jay was "magnetic," for magnetic men win the rabble; but Jay did better: he won the confidence and admiration of the strong and discerning. His manner was gentle and pleasing; his words few, and as a listener he set a pace that all novitiates in the school of diplomacy would do well to follow.

To talk well is a talent, but to listen is a fine art. If I really wished to win the love of a man I'd practice the art of listening. Even dull people often talk well when there is some one near who cultivates the receptive mood; and to please a man you must give him an opportunity to be both wise and witty. Men are pleased with their friends when they are pleased with themselves, and no man is ever so pleased with himself as when he has expressed himself well.

The sympathetic listener at a lecture or sermon is the only one who gets his money's worth. If you would get good, lend your sympathy to a speaker, and if, accidentally, you imbibe heresy, you can easily throw it overboard when you get home.

John Jay was quiet and undemonstrative in speech, cultivating a fine reserve. In debate he never fired all his guns, and his best battles were won with the powder that was never exploded. "You had always better keep a small balance to your credit," he once advised a young attorney.

When the first Congress met, Jay was not in favor of complete independence from England. He asked only for simple justice, and said, "The middle course is best." He listened to John Adams and Patrick Henry and quietly discussed the matter with Samuel Adams; but it was some time before he saw that the density of King George was hopeless, and that the work of complete separation was being forced upon the Colonies by the blindness and stupidity of the British Parliament.

He then accepted the issue.

During those first days of the Revolution, New York did not stand firm, as did Boston, for the cause of independence. "The foes at home are the only ones I really fear," once wrote Hamilton.

First to pacify and placate, then to win and hold those worse than neutrals, was the work of John Jay. While Washington was in the field, Jay, with tireless pen, upheld the cause, and by his speech and presence kept anarchy at bay.

As president of the Committee of Safety he showed he could do something more than talk and write. When Tories refused to take the oath of allegiance he quietly wrote the order to imprison or banish; and with friend, foe or kinsman there was neither dalliance nor turning aside. His heart was in the cause—his property, his life. The time for argument had passed.

In the gloom that followed the defeat of Washington at Brooklyn, Jay issued an address to the people that is a classic in its fine, stern spirit of hope and strength. Congress had the address reprinted and sent broadcast, and also translated and printed in German.

His work divides itself by a strange coincidence into three equal parts. Twenty-eight years were passed in youth and education; twenty-eight years in continuous public work; and twenty-eight years in retirement and rest.

As one of that immortal ten, mentioned by a great English statesman, who gave order, dignity, stability and direction to the cause of American Independence, the name of John Jay is secure.

Made in the USA
Coppell, TX
25 April 2022